Judicial Deviation in Talmudic Law

Jewish Law in Context

A series edited by Neil S. Hecht

Volume 1
Judicial Deviation in Talmudic Law
Governed by Men, Not by Rules
by Hanina Ben-Menahem

The Institute of Jewish Law
Boston University School of Law
765 Commonwealth Avenue
Boston, MA 02215
Publication No. 11

This book is part of a series. Harwood Academic Publishers will accept continuation orders which may be cancelled at any time and which provide for automatic billing and shipping of each title in the series upon publication. Please write for details.

Judicial Deviation in Talmudic Law
Governed by Men, Not by Rules

by

Hanina Ben-Menahem
Faculty of Law
The Hebrew University of Jerusalem

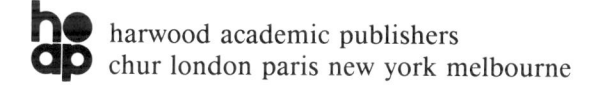

harwood academic publishers
chur london paris new york melbourne

Copyright © 1991 by Trustees of Boston University.
All rights reserved.

Published by Harwood Academic Publishers GmbH

Poststrasse 22
7000 Chur
Switzerland

Post Office Box 197
London WC2E 9PX
United Kingdom

58, rue Lhomond
75005 Paris
France

Post Office Box 786
Cooper Station
New York, New York 10276
United States of America

Private Bag 8
Camberwell, Victoria 3124
Australia

Library of Congress Cataloging-in-Publication Data
Ben-Menahem, Hanina.
   Judicial deviation in Talmudic law/by Hanina Ben-Menahem.
     p. cm. – (Jewish law in context; v. 1)
   Includes bibliographical references.
   ISBN 3-7186-0509-0
   1. Judicial discretion (Jewish law) 2. Talmud–Criticism, interpretation, etc.
   I. Title. II. Series
LAW <GENERAL Ben-M 199|l|>   89-48309
296.1'8–dc20   CIP

No part of this book may be reproduced or utilized in any form or by any means, electronic or mechanical, including photocopying and recording, or by any information storage or retrieval system, without permission in writing from the publisher. Printed in the United States of America.

We express our appreciation to David Lewis Feld through whose generosity this volume has been published in memory of his parents, Emmanuel and Bertha Feld

Contents

List of Abbreviations	ix
Acknowledgements	xiii
Foreword	1

CHAPTER 1   INTRODUCTION
1.1 Judicial Deviation from the Law	5
1.2 A Jurisprudential Analysis Rather Than a Historical Reconstruction	7
1.3 Judges' Self-Awareness of the Judicial Process	8
1.4 Extra-Legal Considerations in Judicial Decisions	14
1.5 Social and Individual Extra-Legal Considerations	16

CHAPTER 2   CASE REPORTS IN TALMUDIC LAW
2.1 Introduction	19
2.2 Absence of a Requirement for a Written Decision	20
2.3 Absence of a Requirement to State Reasons for a Decision	23
2.4 What Should be Viewed as a Judicial Case?	33

CHAPTER 3   TWO PROTOTYPE CASES OF EXTRA-LEGAL CONSIDERATIONS
3.1 The Case of the Kidnapper	41
3.2 The Case of the Fictitious Transaction	50

CHAPTER 4   TWO CONCEPTS OF JUDICIAL POWER: YERUSHALMI VERSUS BAVLI
4.1 Introduction	55
A. The Case of Pishon	56
B. The Case of the Needy Father	61
C. The Case of the Sons of Rokhel	66
D. The Case of Maintenance of Orphans	70
E. The Case of the Negligent Porters	74
4.2 Power-Conferring Rules	80
A. Samuel's Rule: *Shuda Dedaynee* (Discretion of the Judges)	80

CONTENTS

    B. The Rule of Rabbi Eliezer ben Jacob: Beth Din May
         Pronounce Sentences even where Not Warranted
         by the Halakhah   82
    C. The Invalidity of Erroneous Rulings   84
4.3 Yerushalmi versus Bavli Reconsidered   86

CHAPTER 5   OPPOSITION TO EXTRA-LEGAL
                  CONSIDERATIONS
5.1 Criticism of Judicial Decisions Which Were Allegedly
     Based on Extra-Legal Considerations   99
    A. The Case of the False Witness   100
    B. The Case of the Rebellious Wife   107
    C. The Case of the Notorious Robber   112
    D. The Case of the Informer   113
5.2 Principles and Statements Which Imply Opposition to
     Extra-Legal Considerations   118
    A. The Midreshei Halakhah   118
    B. Let the Law Cut through the Mountain   124
    C. No Pity is to be Shown in a Matter of Law   128
    D. Mistakes in the Law and Extra-Legal Considerations   131

CHAPTER 6   POWER-CONFERRING RULES ALLOWING
                  JUDGES TO DEPART FROM THE
                  GENERALLY ACCEPTED RULES
6.1 General Considerations   141
6.2 The Rule of Rabbi Eliezer ben Jacob: Beth Din May
     Pronounce Sentences Even Where Not Warranted by Law   142
    A. Limits of the Maxim   148
6.3 *Shuda Dedaynee*   150
6.4 Judges May Deviate from the Halakhah on the Basis of a
     Minority View   158
6.5 Absolute Obligation to Obey the Law   165
6.6 *Horat Sha'a*   173

CHAPTER 7   CONCLUSION

Appendix of Hebrew Sources   183
Index of Sources   199
Index of Authorities   211
Index of Names   213
Subject Index   217

Abbreviations

In Rabbinic citations, the prefixed m, t, b and y refer to the Mishnah, Tosefta, Babylonian Talmud (Bavli) and Palestinian Talmud (Yerushalmi).

Arabic figures appearing in the margin of the pages refer to the Hebrew sources in the Appendix of Hebrew Sources.

AJCL	*American Journal of Comparative Law*
Arakh.	*Arakhin*
Aruch	*Aruch Completum, Lexicon*
Av.	*Avot*
A.Z.	*Avodah Zarah*
B.B.	*Baba Bathra*
B.K.	*Baba Kamma*
B.M.	*Baba Metzia*
B.T.	*Babylonian Talmud*
Bartenura	*R. Obadiah Bertinoro*
Bekh.	*Bekhorot*
Ber.	*Berakhot*
Bez.	*Betza*
C.L.J.	*Cambridge Law Journal*
Deut.	*Deuteronomy*
Dik.Sof.	*Dikduke Soferim*
Ed.	*Eduyot*
Elon, Jewish Law.	*Elon Jewish Law, History, Sources, Principles*
Erub.	*Erubin*
ET; E.T.	*Encyclopedia Talmudit*
Ex.	*Exodus*
Gen.	*Genesis*
Git.	*Gittin*
G.L.R.	*Georgia Law Review*
Hag.	*Hagigah*
Hor.	*Horayot*
HUCA	*Hebrew Union College Annual*
Hul.	*Hullin*

ABBREVIATIONS

Isr.L.R.	*Israel Law Review*
Jev.	*Jevamot*
JJS	*Journal of Jewish Studies*
JQR	*Jewish Quarterly Review*
JSJ	*Journal for the Study of Judaism*
Judaica	*Encyclopaedia Judaica*
Ker.	*Keritot*
Ket.	*Ketubot*
Kid.	*Kiddushin*
Kil.	*Kilayim*
Lev.	*Leviticus*
Maharik	*Joseph b. Solomon Colon*
Maharsha	*Samuel Eliezer b. Judah Halevi*
Mak.	*Makkot*
Malbim	*Meir Loeb b. Jehiel Michael*
Meg.	*Megilah*
Men.	*Menahot*
MGWJ	*Monatsschrift für Geschichte und Wissenschaft Des Judentums*
Mik.	*Mikvaot*
M.K.	*Moed Katan*
M.T.	*Megilat Ta'anit*
Naz.	*Nazir*
Ned.	*Nedarim*
Nid.	*Nidah*
Num.	*Numbers*
Ob.	*Obadiah*
Or.	*Orlah*
Pes.	*Pesahim*
Prov.	*Proverbs*
Ps.	*Psalms*
R.H.	*Rosh Hashanah*
Ramban	*Nahmanides, Moses b. Nahman*
Ran	*Nissim b. Reuben Gerondi*
Rashai	*Solomon b. Jehiel Luria*
Rashba	*Solomon b. Abraham Adret*
Rashbam	*Samuel b. Meir*

ABBREVIATIONS

Rashi	*Solomon b. Isaac of Troyes*
Ravad	*Abraham b. David of Posquieres*
REJ	*Revue des Etudes Juives*
Rema	*Moses b. Israel Isserles*
Rif	*Isaac b. Jacob haCohen Alfasi*
Ritba	*Yom Tov b. Abraham Ishbili*
Rosh	*Asher b. Jehiel*
S.A.L.J.	*South Africa Law Journal*
Sanh.	*Sanhedrin*
Shab.	*Shabbat*
Shebi.	*Shebi'it*
Shebu.	*Shebuot*
Shek.	*Shekalim*
Sot.	*Sotah*
Suk.	*Sukkah*
R. Tam.	*Jacob b. Meir*
Tan.	*Ta'anit*
Tashbetz	*Simeon b. Zemah Duran*
Taz	*Turei Zahav by David halevi*
Tem.	*Temurah*
Ter.	*Terumah*
Tosafot Rid	*Commentary to the Talmud by Isaiah b. Mali di Trani*
Yale L.J.	*Yale Law Journal*
Zev.	*Zevahim*

Acknowledgements

I am grateful to Joseph Raz and Bernard Jackson. From both I have greatly profited. I also would like to thank Mordecai Rabello for his support and encouragement, Shmuel Wosner for his linguistic suggestions, and Edith Schimmel for her skilled assistance in proofreading. Finally, I am indebted to Neil Hecht for choosing to inaugurate this series with my volume, and for his painstaking work in editing this book.

My intellectual debt to my parents, Ayala and Elyakim Ben-Menahem, exceeds adequate acknowledgement.

For Yemima
מאשר יקרת, בעיני נכבדת.

Foreword

With the publication of this book, we inaugurate a new series at the Institute of Jewish Law. In recent years there has been a growing interest in Jewish law in American law schools. In turn, this casts an obligation on those involved in Jewish law to make available in the English language publications which focus on contemporary issues and their analysis in traditional Jewish sources. *Jewish Law in Context* will attempt to do precisely this by presenting Jewish law in its own context as well as in the context of our milieu.

The analysis of legal sources always reflects to a certain degree the intellectual climate of the outside world. This is even more so in our own generation when scholars of Jewish law are familiar with general legal concepts, and therefore bring to their analysis concepts and tools which were developed in general jurisprudence. As in any intellectual enterprise, the analysis of Jewish law both within (halakhic authorities) and without (those who reflect upon it), is not pursued in a vacuum. Rather, the contemporary, intellectual world has always had an important impact upon the study of Jewish law: the way Jewish law was presented, analyzed, formulated, discussed and perceived. Accordingly, in developing *Jewish Law in Context*, we have sought to present the reader with a series of studies which clearly reflect this relationship. In this way it is hoped that those who have an interest in Jewish law, as well as those who have a larger interest in legal studies in general, will find it enriching to examine the material in this series.

This inaugural volume deals with the judicial process in Talmudic law. More specifically, it addresses the issue of self-declared judicial deviation. That is, it analyzes cases recorded in the Talmud in which judges explicitly claimed to have deviated from the law on the basis of extra-legal considerations. Moreover, it demonstrates that this judicial policy was accepted by the communities in which these judges officiated.

The notions "judicial deviation" and "extra-legal consideration" seem to presuppose a positivistic framework. In fact, the conclusion which emerges from this study significantly exceeds the positivistic model, for the author shows that the legal philosophy of Talmudic law is not characterized by the Western ideal of "governed by laws, not by men." Instead, the author argues that Talmudic law is epitomized by the very reverse: "governed by men, not by laws." This does not mean that rules and norms lose their role in regulating the behavior of individuals and officials. Rather, it signifies that the political and moral dimension of law have been recognized.

In its jurisprudential approach to Talmudic law, this book is both pioneering and provocative; it will surely encourage further works in this direction. However, its contribution is not confined to its jurisprudential import. Thus, for example, in chapter 4 we are presented with an extensive comparison of the Babylonian and Jerusalem Talmuds with regard to their respective attitudes toward judicial policy. The systematic difference discovered here will be of interest not only to the lawyer but to anyone interested in Talmud.

This volume is a pioneering one in that until now the tendency has been to approach Jewish law in a historical perspective by tracing legal institutions and rules from Biblical times to the present day or by focusing on legal institutions in a particular period. By contrast, this work is a jurisprudential analysis which employs conceptual tools developed by legal positivists and applies them to Talmudic legal material. This enables us to approach Jewish law in more general terms and to formulate the issues appearing in Jewish legal sources in terms familiar to us in current legal analysis, such as the rule of law and judicial discretion in decision-making.

In addition, this book introduces us to a remarkable and unique contribution of Jewish jurists: the power of judges to deviate from the law, that is, to ignore precedent in order to do justice in particular cases. One of the points emerging from this study is that the supremacy of law, or the integrity of the legal system itself, is not the ultimate goal of Jewish law. Rather, in each case, Jewish law seeks the attainment of justice as understood by those who have to apply the legal principles to the facts and parties of the particular case before them.

Finally, a reading of Jewish legal sources, which are very formalistic in style, may lead one to conclude that Jewish law is rigid and pedantic. Indeed, many scholars have expressed this opinion.

However, as this book continually demonstrates, this view is a serious misconception. It confuses legal formalism (the method of formulating legal rules in a precise, specific and detailed manner rather than in a general, abstract way) with the method of applying those rules in practice. Jewish law was extremely flexible and liberal in interpreting legal precedents and applying them to factual situations. As this seminal study conclusively demonstrates, when circumstances required it, judges were even willing to ignore precedents in order to do justice in particular cases.

This type of research raises the necessity for additional analysis concerning the nature of acceptance of legal authority in Jewish law. We are hopeful that this volume will stimulate further research in this rich and important area of Jewish law.

Neil S. Hecht
The Institute of Jewish Law
Boston University School of Law

CHAPTER 1

INTRODUCTION

1.1 Judicial Deviation from the Law

The judicial process has been studied both in general terms and with regard to particular legal systems, and a vast amount of literature has been written on the subject by classical as well as by contemporary jurists.[1] Notwithstanding a few partial historical descriptions,[2] little attempt has been made thus far to analyze the judicial process within the context of Talmudic law. This book will examine the judicial activity of the Rabbis. More specifically, it will focus on the concept of judicial deviation from the law as reflected in Talmudic sources.

The central question of this volume is not whether a given decision is legally correct. Rather it is concerned with whether judges conceived of their role as requiring strict adherence to the law, or whether judges occasionally exercised or recognized a measure of freedom to depart from it. The problem is similar, but not identical, to the current debate concerning judges' discretion. Contemporary legal philosophers discuss the issue of judges' discretion with reference to what has been termed "hard cases." Their discussions focus on allegedly

---

[1] The literature is too vast to be listed. Apart from general works dealing with the subject there are many studies specifically devoted to the judicial process, among which the following can be singled out: B.N. Cardozo, *The Nature of the Judicial Process*, (New Haven, 1921); J. Stone, *Legal System and Lawyer's Reasoning*, (Stanford, 1964); E.H. Levi, *An Introduction to Legal Reasoning*, (Chicago, 1949); R.A. Wasserstrom, *The Judicial Decision, Towards a Theory of Legal Justification*, (Stanford, 1961). For an historical survey of the main trends see E. Bodenheimer, "Hart, Dworkin and the Problem of Judicial Lawmaking Discretion," 11 *GLR* (1977) 1143.

[2] See the literature cited in Chapter 2, note 53. See also S. Zucrow, *Adjustment of Law to Life in Rabbinic Literature*, (Boston, 1928); W. Greene, "Extra-Legal Juridical Prerogatives" 7 *JSJ* (1976) 152.

rare cases where the law is felt to be obscure, where it seems that the law does not provide sufficient instructions to warrant a legal solution, or where more than one solution seems to follow from the law.[3] In so doing, commentators consider whether it is appropriate for a judge to assume the role of a legislator by creating new rules to be applied retrospectively to the case at hand.

Even those who concede that judges are entitled, in legal terms, to exercise discretion by deciding cases through an appeal to extra-legal considerations, restrict this discretionary power to hard cases only. Proponents of this view maintain that this discretionary power is a legal power, either explicitly granted to judges or inferred from a proper analysis of the true nature of a legal system. Thus, the proposition that judges have discretion in hard cases is rendered compatible with the proposition that judges always adhere to the law.

The question posed in this book is more radical. Namely, whether despite allegedly clear law, judges would ever allow themselves to deviate explicitly from the prescriptions of the law on the basis of extra-legal considerations.

If an affirmative answer emerges, then any explanation of the judicial process must account for this extra-legal activity of judges. Our understanding of the judicial process will thereby be enlarged by an examination of Talmudic law, for it is the peculiarities of particular legal systems which demonstrate the limits of abstract analysis and which force us to modify the rather dogmatic conceptions depicted by general jurisprudence.[4]

---

[3] See H.L.A. Hart, *The Concept of Law* (Oxford, 1961) 138-144. J. Raz, "Legal Principles and the Limits of Law" 81 *Yale L.J.* 823; R. Dworkin, *Taking Rights Seriously* (Duckworth, 1977) 31-39, 68-71; R. Sartorious, *Individual Conduct and Social Norms*, (California, 1975) 181-204.

[4] On the relation between general jurisprudence and particular jurisprudence, see J. Bentham, *An Introduction to the Principles of Morals and Legislation* (edited by W. Harrison) (Oxford, 1948) 424-426; J. Austin, "The Uses of the Study of Jurisprudence," in *The Province of Jurisprudence Determined* (London, 1955) 365-373; C.K. Allen, *Legal Duties and Other Essays in Jurisprudence*, (Oxford, 1931) 1-77; W.W. Buckland, *Some Reflections on Jurisprudence* (Cambridge, 1945) 67-72.

1.2 A Jurisprudential Analysis Rather Than a Historical Reconstruction.

Though the sources that will be examined in this book are ancient, this is not a study in legal history. Its primary aim is not to establish historical veracity, nor is it an attempt to discover hitherto unknown sources. Rather, this study seeks to present a jurisprudential reading of Talmudic material by means of conceptual tools developed by analytic positivists.[5] It is not suggested that the conceptual tools which will be employed to analyze Talmudic material have themselves ever been articulated as part of Talmudic law or of the legal thinking of the Rabbis. In order to enter the minds of the original authors, a legal historian attempting to reconstruct Talmudic law or any other ancient legal system must establish that the concepts being used to describe the legal system in question are themselves contemporary with the ancient sources, or he would justly be charged with being anachronistic.[6]

This is not so in the case of a jurisprudential analysis where one may project a given conceptual framework upon a given legal system, the intellectual process being that of reading the ancient sources from the perspective of that conceptual framework.[7]

---

5   B. Cohen, *Jewish and Roman Law* (New York, 1966) vol. 1, p. 14, defines this as "the philosophic approach." Salmond, *On Jurisprudence* (11th ed.) 4, refers to it as "analytical jurisprudence." See also B. S. Jackson, *Essays in Jewish and Comparative Legal History* (Leiden, 1975) 7 and I. Englard, "Research in Jewish Law -- Its Nature and Function," in *Modern Research in Jewish Law (The Jewish Law Annual, Supplement One*, edited by B.S. Jackson, Leiden, 1980) 21.
6   *Cf.* Englard, *op. cit.* p.34.
7   What does require a justification, however, is the choice made of a particular conceptual framework among various alternatives. But such a justification would require the evaluation of all the alternatives, a task for which a separate discussion is required. For the present purposes, the following will suffice: In the course of this work it is argued that the notion of judicial deviation based on extra-legal considerations is detrimental to the understanding of Talmudic law. Explicit judicial statements that the ruling reached is not based on the law cannot, if we take these statements seriously, be accounted for in terms of a legal theory which does not accept any variation of Raz's thesis of the limits of law (Raz, *op.cit.*). The thesis of the limits of law is a typical positivist thesis.

A historical reconstruction of Talmudic law must take into consideration external evidence found in extra-Talmudic sources whenever available. A jurisprudential analysis, by contrast, is concerned exclusively with that material which is considered by the system itself as having a normative value. To be sure, the determination of what constitutes a binding source might itself require some jurisprudential deliberation. For the present purpose, the criterion of relevance determining the material to be discussed is meta-jurisprudential: all of the halakhic material found in the standard Rabbinic sources. The claim of a jurisprudential study is that the account given represents the best rationale one can make when the material discussed is conceived of as representing a complete description of a legal system.

Chapter 4 of this volume provides a good illustration of how the concept of extra-legal considerations helps to elucidate the material discussed. A number of apparently unrelated passages are analyzed in terms of this conceptual tool, which leads, in turn, to the discovery of a systematic difference between the two Talmudim, Bavli and Yerushalmi, concerning their respective conception of the role and power of judges. The Jerusalem Talmud seems to hold that the judge's power is strictly limited to the application of the halakhah; it does not consider extra-legal considerations as an acceptable justification for judicial decisions. The Babylonian Talmud, on the other hand, is more flexible on this issue; it sometimes accepts the view that the judge's power exceeds the limits of the law. This discovery is significant in view of the fact that historical reconstruction has thus far pointed out only sporadic differences between these two Talmudim, lacking any systematic or conceptual organization.

1.3 Judges' Self-Awareness of the Judicial Process

The Rabbinic sources, Mishnah and Talmud, may correctly be regarded as representing the formative years of Jewish law. The tremendous activity of exegetical exposition of Scripture which flourished in the Tannaitic era, and its subsequent interpretation and elab-

---

It should be made clear, however, that using this conceptual framework does not imply an adoption of the positivist *Weltanschauung*.

INTRODUCTION

oration in the Amoraic era, is a unique phenomenon without parallel in the history of Jewish law.

A direct result of this intensive development was the emergence of a pluralistic legal community. The Rabbis present a great range of opinions about the content of the law, and it is by no means rare that these opinions contradict each other. It might therefore be argued that in the context of Talmudic law one cannot speak of judicial deviation, since there is no single shared convention of what the law dictated. Even to the extent that there was, one cannot simply compare a given judge's decision with the prevailing rule and thereby conclude that he has deviated from the law, since the judge could have maintained that his decision accorded with the law as understood by him.[8]

The following case is illustrative:

> Resh Lakish said: He who lifts his hand against his neighbor, even if he did not smite him, is called a wicked man ...; Zeiri said in the name of R. Hanina: He is called a sinner ...; R. Huna said: His arm should be cut off, as it is written, *Let the uplifted arm be broken.*[9]
> R. Huna had the hand cut off [of an habitual offender].[10]

R. Huna's position was not shared by his colleagues. Yet he put his view into practice and ordered that the hand of a certain man who was brought before him be cut off. Did R. Huna deviate from the law? Surely he enforced the law as he best understood it. This is emphasized by his reported view, based on a Biblical verse, which precedes the recorded case.[11] Thus even this extreme case cannot be cited as an example of judicial deviation from the law.

While the content of the law was sometimes disputed, its very existence was never challenged. The Written Law, Torah, had long been recognized as a normative and binding source from which all particulars of the law could and should be derived. Indeed, the intensive halakhic activity which characterizes Jewish law's formative period

---

8 See, for example: b.Jev.121a; bB.B.174a; bGit.19a; yKet.9:2 (33,1); but see also yKid.3:12 (64,4) and parallels.
9 Job 38:15. Ginzberg, *Mishpatim Leisrael* (Jerusalem, 1956) p. 27, was misled by the erroneous reference to Job 31 in *Tora Or ad loc.*, and consequently engaged in a lengthy superfluous argument.
10 bSanh.58b.
11 See also bNid.13b where R. Huna's view is cited as an example of *dina*.

originated in the attempt to interpret the one common source which was accepted by all members of the legal community as a binding code. The view that the law was there to be interpreted and applied was thus well-rooted in the legal commitment of the Sages.

Despite this commitment to the law, one finds that when officiating as judges, or when commenting on court decisions, Rabbis would sometimes openly declare that the decision reached was not derived from the law as understood by them but was based on extra-legal considerations.[12] Cases falling under this category are crucial for an analysis of the judicial process and are the core of this study. They reveal, without requiring any resort to external evidence, the judges' own perception of their role.

Dworkin claims that American judges do not regard their role as allowing them to exercise any measure of "strong discretion," leaning heavily on judicial expressions which he interprets to that effect.[13] Without commenting on Dworkin's analysis, the same method of investigation leads to the opposite conclusion when applied to Talmudic law.

John Dewey distinguished between two types of logic operating in the judicial process: "The logic of exposition is different from that of search and inquiry."[14] The former is needed because "courts not only reach decisions, they expound them and the exposition must state justifying reasons."[15] Courts have to account to the concerned parties, the legal community and the public at large, for their decisions. Our concern here is with the logic of exposition, and it is significant that an overt declaration that the ruling reached is not based on the law does not jeopardize the task of accounting for the ruling. It signifies that the judge's conception of a power either to follow the legal rule or some other rule of his choosing was shared by the community at large. Furthermore, the inclusion of these cases in the Talmud attests that these sentiments were endorsed even after an opportunity for considered reflection. Thus, the Talmudic image of a judge's activity

---

[12] These cases are fully discussed in this study. The following is a partial list: bKet.49a; bKet.50b; bKet.86a; bJev.110a; bB.K.96b; bB.M.83a; bB.B.22a.
[13] Dworkin, *op. cit.*
[14] J. Dewey, "Logical Method and Law," 10 *Cornell L.Q.* (1924) 17,24.
[15] *Ibid.*

is not confined to the application and interpretation of pre-existing rules. Rather, it embodies the notion that judges sometimes act explicitly and overtly without resorting to existing halakhic rules or principles. However, some Talmudic passages imply that objections to this judicial policy were occasionally voiced. Chapter 5 examines these passages, and it will be seen that while objections were occasionally raised against types of judicial deviation, the concept itself was never rejected as such.

The necessity to restrict our analysis to those cases where judges openly concede their deviation from the law is also dictated by the aim of this study. A case in which a judge deviates from the law, but conceals his deviation by presenting the ruling as derived from legal interpretation, will not qualify for the present analysis which seeks to examine whether judges conceived of their role as allowing occasional departure from the law rather than whether departures actually occurred. Judicial expressions which concede that the decision reached is not derived from the law reveal judges' self-awareness of a role in the judicial process which allows them to depart from precedents. They also indicate that the Rabbis endorsed a notion similar to Hart's rule of recognition,[16] which distinguishes what is law from what is not.[17]

These judicial expressions destroy the myth that the judicial process falls completely within the domain of legal reasoning. It is only if one approaches these pronouncements with preconceptions of how judicial decisions ought to be reached and expounded that one is likely to distort their significance by reading into them fictitious legal argumentation contrary to the judges' own explicit statements.

---

16 Hart, *op. cit.*
17 Opinions may differ as to the exact formulation of that rule, which is intricate and complicated. But the exact formulation of the rule is of no immediate interest here. What is significant is that some allusion to its existence is manifested by these judicial statements. Allusions to this notion can be also found in other Talmudic maxims. For example: "Repayment of a debt to a creditor is a religious duty as distinct from a legal duty" (bKet.86a;bB.B.174a; bArkh.22a); "Not culpable by the law of man but culpable by the law of heaven" (mB.K.6:4; tB.K.6:16-17; bB.K.55b-56a); "Halakha that should not be practiced" (bShab.12b; bErub.7a; bBez.28b; bB.K.30b.).

"Legal interpretation" and "application of legal principles" are notions that are habitually called upon to rationalize decisions which seem to be contrary to pre-established juridical practices. In this manner the myth that all judicial decisions fall within the limits of the law is sustained. When judges are not clear about the process which led them to their decisions, there is room for jurisprudential speculations in accord with these notions. Sometimes contemporary judges are unclear about the process of reaching a decision partly because they want to conform to artificial constructs proposed by legal philosophers. Apparently, Talmudic judges did not have to conform to any articulated legal philosophy and could therefore express themselves on the judicial process more clearly and more freely, thereby obviating jurisprudential speculation about their decisions.

Consider a case where a judge renders a decision contrary to established juridical practice, but without indicating the process which led to the decision. Would it be correct to say that the judge "made new law?"

A positive conclusion can be reached only after subsequent decisions demonstrate that the judge's innovation was followed. It is only then that we can determine whether the innovation actually became "law." There is, however, another difficulty. The proposition that the judge made new law might be correct only in the sense that his ruling stimulated a change in the law, but the proposition might be quite inaccurate if it seeks to describe the actual process in which the judge had been engaged. The judge might well have been attempting to enforce the law to the best of his jurisprudential understanding (such as R. Huna's decision above) without intending to "make new law."

The same applies with even greater force to the opposite case, where the judge renders a decision contrary to the law and openly declares it to be so. Suppose that his deviant ruling were followed in subsequent cases. Here, again, the product of the judge's decision might be that a new interpretation is assigned to the violated legal rule, but from this it does not follow that the judge was engaged in interpreting the law. The judicial process and the judicial product must be separated and kept apart.

Chapter 6 examines various possible power-conferring rules that could be invoked to justify a departure from generally practiced rule. It is demonstrated that the range of permitted departures authorized by these power-conferring rules is rather limited in comparison with

INTRODUCTION 13

the deviation practiced by Talmudic judges as discussed in the preceding chapters. Judicial expressions appearing in the decisions discussed in this book clearly reveal that the judicial process through which the decisions were reached cannot be accounted for in terms of interpretation or in terms of application of legal principles, though their product might well be a new interpretation or the crystallization of a new legal principle.

Indeed, most, though by no means all, of the rulings based on extra-legal considerations have been incorporated into the halakhah by post-Talmudic authorities, notably the Codifiers,[18] as special stipulations of the law. The rule violated by the Talmudic judge was later reformulated so that it contained a clause which warranted the ruling. This "restatement of the law" was designed to harmonize the various sources and to exclude contradictions. If we now re-examine the decisions in view of the later formulation of the rule it appears that the judge never violated the law. However, this is historically inaccurate as well as conceptually misleading. Reading the ruling in the light of its subsequent presentation distorts the jurisprudential significance of the ruling.[19]

The Codifier's activity, however, bears out an important aspect of extra-legal considerations. Many extra-legal considerations upon which judges base their rulings penetrate the halakhah and become legal ones, thereby playing an important role in the evolutionary process of the law.

In one case at least, this transformation from the extra-legal to the legal domain is documented in the Talmud itself. In discussing the law of monopoly of trade, which bans merchants from settling in places which are not their domiciles, the Talmud states:

> If however, the seller is a scholar (*zurba merabanan*) he may also settle, following a ruling issued by Rava allowing R. Joshia and R. Obadiah to settle contrary to the law, the reason being that as they are Rabbis they might be disturbed in their studies.[20]

---

18 On the codification literature in Jewish Law, see C. Chernowitz, *Toledoth Haposkim* (New York, 1946-7, 3 vols.); Elon, *Jewish Law*, p. 938ff.
19 *Cf.* Kadish & Kadish, *Discretion to Disobey* (Stanford, 1973), 69-70.
20 bB.B.22a.

The incorporation of Rava's ruling into the halakhah does not change the fact that originally it was contrary to the law, and the ruling is referred to as such by the Talmud.

1.4 Extra-Legal Considerations in Judicial Decisions

Extra-legal considerations are discussed here only within the context of the judicial process, as distinct from the context of legislative activity. Within the latter, the notion signifies considerations with which the law ought to have no concern; hence no legislation should be enacted on their basis. For example, it has been claimed that moral considerations do not justify legislation prohibiting consensual homosexual acts between adults.[21] That is to say, moral considerations banning homosexuality are extra-legal in the sense that the immorality of the behavior provides no justification for rendering such behavior illegal.

It is clear, however, that if we remain within the framework of the positivist model (that is, any legal theory which determines the validity of a law not by reference to its content but by reference to the procedure of its enactment), then any law duly passed would be valid, including a law prohibiting homosexuality.

The question whether the legislator ought or ought not to make use of a certain consideration is thus a question of policy, not of legality. The distinction between a legislative act and a judicial pronouncement should be borne in mind throughout, and it is only to the latter that this book is directed.

Since this study is concerned with judicial activity, it commences in Chapter 2 with a short descriptive survey of case reports in the Talmud and reviews some of the major problems involved in their analysis. Chief among them are their identification, which is problematic due to the casuistic formulation of the Talmud, and the absence of a requirement for judges to state reasons for a decision.

Economic, sociological, scientific, ethical, and psychological considerations that figure in legal reasoning, in attempting to delineate the scope of legal rules and principles and their applicability to the case at hand, are not extra-legal in the sense that the term is used in

---

21   H.L.A. Hart, *Law, Liberty and Morality* (Oxford, 1963).

this work. Two examples will suffice to make this point clear. The first is the ruling of R. Hisda in the dispute over an inheritance, quoted in full in the next chapter. When required to provide evidence for his position, a powerful defendant exclaimed: "Is that the law?" [The burden of proof lies on the claimant.] To which R. Hisda retorted: "Thus do I judge your case and for all who are powerful men like you."[22]

Now it is clear that R. Hisda deviated from the general practice of placing the burden of proof on the claimant. However, R. Hisda does not indicate that he deviated from the law. Rather, he employs a socio-psychological consideration to determine the scope of the legal principle.

A contemporary authority provides a second example. A ruling given by Rabbi Kook, permitting the use on Passover of specially prepared oil derived from legumes, caused much agitation at the time the ruling was rendered and various objections were raised against it. One such argument was that the Hatam Sofer, an unquestionable halakhic authority, had been very strict on such matters. In order to deflect the opposition to his ruling, Rabbi Kook advanced the following sociological consideration: "Let me tell you that the reason for the strict attitude taken by the Hatam Sofer in these matters was the needs of the time, since the reform movement, aiming for a reform in the Jewish religion, was in its prime. Any ruling against the prevailing custom would thus supply the rebellious with ammunition. Therefore, the Hatam Sofer was not willing to introduce a new custom lest it encourage further reforms. However in our time this fear no longer exists, since those who wish to break off from religion do not seek any authority. Rather, they do as it pleases them, reforms no longer being an issue. There is therefore no fear in sanctioning that which is halakhically permissible although it is against the prevailing custom. On the contrary, knowing perfectly well the inclinations of our generation, I know that, by permitting what may be permitted, people will realize that what we do not allow cannot possibly be permitted."[23]

It is evident from this ruling that the sociological consideration, differentiating between Hatam Sofer's period and Rabbi Kook's per-

---

22   bB.M.39b and parallels.
23   A.I. Kook, *Orakh Mishpat* (Jerusalem, 1937) 126.

iod, does not involve any departure from the law; rather, it is used as a means of maintaining the true intent of the halakhah as expounded by Rabbi Kook. By contrast, extra-legal considerations in the sense that the term is used in this book have to be so regarded by the judge who employs them. That is to say, the judge is not claiming that his decision is based on a true interpretation of the legal rule or is a careful individuation of it.

Chapter 3 seeks to familiarize the reader with the notion of extra-legal considerations by means of illustration. Two suggestive cases are discussed, which demonstrate the concept at work.

1.5 Social and Individual Extra-Legal Considerations

Whether a consideration is legal or not depends on the content of a given legal system at a given time, and we have seen that an extra-legal consideration may subsequently become a legal one by virtue of its perpetuation or by a direct act of legislation. A consideration which was identified as extra-legal was thus identified not because it possessed some intrinsic features which distinguished it from others, but simply because it had not been incorporated into the law.

Since extra-legal considerations have nothing in common, apart from being non-legal, any attempt to classify them seems pointless, unless it is based on collected data of actual application of extra-legal considerations in a given legal system. It is possible, however, to introduce at the outset an *a priori* distinction which is peculiar to the way extra-legal considerations function. It is proposed to distinguish between social considerations and individual considerations, the difference between them being that of their respective objects. The object of a consideration is to be understood as the idea, aim or person(s) towards which the consideration is directed.

In determining the object of the court's consideration, the justifying reasoning of the court should be the only criterion. This is not because it always represents the actual object that the judge had in mind, but because we are concerned here with the judge's "logic of exposition."

Social considerations have as their object the welfare of society at large or of a certain segment of it. The deviation from the law comes about as a result of the judge considering the case in the light of some fact which is not controlled by any of the litigants (as, for example, the frequency of a crime or the current moral standards of society) when according to the rule of recognition these considerations ought to be excluded from the decision-making process, and aiming at affecting the social phenomenon considered (that is, reducing the frequency of a crime or improving current moral standards).

Individual considerations, on the other hand, have as their object the litigants themselves. Acts which are not performed by any of the litigants or acts not controlled by them do not figure in the reasoning. The deviation from the law comes about as a result of the judge considering the character, status, past behavior, economic position, or any other personal feature that one or both of the litigants may have. Individual considerations do not necessarily imply that they are applicable only to the individuals standing before the court. The judge may indicate his intention to employ them in subsequent similar cases. As long as the judge realizes that these considerations are not authorized by the law, his intention to perpetuate their employment, as distinct from their actual perpetuation, does not change their extra-legal status. Compare, for example, the following two case reports:

In a reported case recorded in the Babylonian Talmud, it is related that a certain man who had sexual intercourse with his wife in public was brought to court and flogged, though according to the law he did not deserve such punishment.[24] The reason given for the flogging was "not because he merited it but because of the needs of the time." Presumably the court viewed the moral standards of the time as low, and ordered the man flogged in order to deter others from behaving similarly. By contrast, the reasoning provided in the Yerushalmi's report of the case of the public fornicator is substantially different: "He conducted himself shamefully."[25]

In both reports of the case the judges imposed a penalty contrary to the law, but the reasoning invoked in each reported case was significantly different. In the Bavli's report the reasoning refers to a social phenomenon, the "needs of the time," and it clearly implies that had the defendant been brought to court in some other period he might have escaped punishment. Social considerations have a dimension of

---

24 bJev.90b and parallels.
25 yHag.2:2 (78,1).

time and are to be applied not only with reference to the facts of the case at hand but also with reference to social conditions. In the Yerushalmi's report the judge deviated from the law on the basis of considerations applying directly and exclusively to the defendant. The fact taken into account was intrinsic to the case. According to this reasoning the punishment was not a function of unusual circumstances but of the behavior itself, even though it was not punishable according to the halakhah. Thus, the aim of the court was not to safeguard society but to reform the offender.

A characteristic feature of most cases based on social considerations is that the prevailing social situation which justified the deviation from the law existed prior to the occurrence of the particular case. An efficient legislator could address the problem by means of legislation and the matter would not be left to the judiciary. Where changing social conditions are met with timely and adequate legislation, judges are less frequently faced with a situation demanding a judicial response to novel social phenomena. Indeed, in Babylon, where local legislation without complicated procedures was practiced by the Rabbis, all recorded cases of extra-legal considerations are based on individual considerations.

Within the context of the judicial process the distinction between social considerations and individual considerations as two kinds of judicial justification is peculiar to cases based on extra-legal considerations. When a decision is said to be based on the law, its ultimate justification is that the law so provides. The legal rule applied by the judge might be based on social or individual considerations, but this is not a decisive factor in reaching the decision. It is only when the judge deviates from the law that he is called upon to justify his deviation by relying upon either social or individual considerations.

CHAPTER 2

CASE REPORTS IN TALMUDIC LAW

2.1 Introduction

Since this study is concerned with judicial activity it commences with a short descriptive survey of judicial cases in Talmudic law. Thereafter, it reviews some of the major problems involved in their analysis.

A judicial case is defined here either as a procedure initiated by a party to a civil dispute aimed at obtaining a binding judgment settling the dispute, or as a procedure initiated by a court (or one of its agents) as a result of an offense allegedly committed.

Two sorts of cases are thereby excluded. First, what might be called cases of "moral advice." In this situation, an opinion given by an authority concerning a pending issue lacks the main features of a judicial decision: coercion and rules of procedure. One of the criteria for determining that a given passage represents moral advice rather than a judicial decision is the identification of one of the parties as a relative of the judge.[1] The principle forbidding judges to try their own or their relative's case (*nemo iudex in re sua*) was very strictly obeyed,[2] and there can be no doubt that the decision reached in such

---

1   See for example bKet.52b; bKet.54b; bKet.84a; bKet.84b; bKet.85b; bGit.37a; b B.M.44b; bB.B.5a.
2   See tSanh.5:4 (Lieberman, *Tosafoth Rishonim ad loc.*); see also Midrash Devarim Rabba, p. alef; ySanh.3:9 (21,3), yShebu.4.1 (35,2), bKet.105b, bSanh.28b-29a. The principle of self-help is consistent with this concept since the act of self-help is a temporary remedy subject to judicial review. See Y.Dinari, "Self-Help in Jewish Law," *Dine Israel* vol.4 (Tel Aviv, 1973) p. 91 at p. 103. For a different account of the principle of self-help, see S. Albeck, *Law Courts in Talmudic Times* (Hebrew) (Bar Ilan University, 1980) Chapter 4. For a novel solution to this problem, see E. Quint & N. Hecht, *Jewish Jurisprudence: Its Sources and Modern Applications*, vol.2, p.128 (New York, 1986).

a matter was not judicially binding. Another criterion, again sufficient but not necessary, is the indication that there was no one, other than the person seeking moral advice, interested in bringing the issue before the judge.

Moral advice is distinguishable from a judicial decision by its concern with ethical and conscientious deliberations which need not be strictly required by the law. Hence, in this context, the problems of extra-legal considerations do not apply.

Second, there are cases of "declaratory judgments." Here a binding judgment is given by an authority in response to an halakhic query, involving only one party. The halakhic term denoting this kind of judgment is *sheilat haham*, and it is usually concerned with matters pertaining to ritual law (i.e., *issur veheter, kashrut*, vows and Shabbat).[3]

One who requests a *sheilat haham* is entitled to a decision based upon halakhic reasons.[4] Hence the problematics of extra-legal considerations do apply here. Therefore, it will occasionally be referred to in the course of this study although, strictly speaking, it is excluded from the foregoing definition of a judicial case.

In analyzing judicial cases in the Talmud, one is faced with a difficulty caused by the extreme brevity with which most cases are reported. The oral delivery of the verdict, coupled with the absence of a requirement to state reasons for the decision, might account for this abbreviated style. Accordingly, these two elements will now be considered in some detail.

2.2 Absence of a Requirement for a Written Decision

Nowhere in the Mishnah is it stated that the decision of a court must be in writing. In describing the process of a trial, the Mishnah says:

---

3   On the distinction between *sheilat haham* and judicial decisions see mYev.2:10; see also tEd.1:5; yShab.19.1 (16,4); bA.Z.7a; bHul.44b; bNid.20b; bBer.53b; Bamidbar Rabba 11:3; and H. Mantel, *Studies of the History of the Sanhedrin*, (Cambridge, Mass. 1961) p. 221.

4   See for example mBek.4:4 and parallels; bB.M.91a.

1   When the verdict is arrived at ... the senior judge says, "So and So you are not liable, So and So you are liable."[5]

According to this account the decision of the court was delivered orally. This does not exclude the possibility that the decision was later documented, but there is no evidence whatsoever that documentation was required by law.

Weingreen infers from mSanh.4:3 that "the verdicts reached by the judges were recorded by professional court clerks."[6] However, it seems that Gerhardsson is right in questioning the correctness of such a view.[7] mSanh4:3 refers exclusively to the deliberations of the court and not to its final decision. Moreover, the reason for writing down the court's deliberations, as provided by mSanh.5:5, is related to court procedure and is not applicable to writing down the final decision.

Likewise, there is no reason to accept Waxman's view that "if there was a controversy (among the judges) the judgment was written down."[8] The passage on which Waxman relies is presumably the controversy between R. Johanan and Resh Lakish in bSanh.30a.[9] That debate, however, refers to how a non-unanimous decision should be written down if it were demanded by one of the parties. There is thus no basis for inferring a general requirement for written court decisions in case of a controversy, unless specifically requested by a party.[10]

---

5   mSanh.3:7. See also Sifra Kedoshim, parasha 4 and tSanh.6:3. For further indications that the decision of the court was delivered orally see bB.K.68b-69a; bB.M.17a and the frequent Tannaitic term *amru hahamim* (e.g. mA.Z.1:4; mB.M.8:8; tA.Z.3:7) and see also Epstein, "Amru Hahamim" in *Studies in Memory of Asher Gulak and Samuel Klein* (Jerusalem, 1942) p. 252 at p. 254.
6   Weingreen, *From Bible to Mishnah* (Manchester University Press, 1976) p. 78. See also J. Kaplan, *The Redaction of the Babylonian Talmud* (New York, 1933) p. 266.
7   Gerhardsson, *Memory and Manuscript* (Uppsala, 1961) p. 162. See also Falk, *Introduction to Jewish Law* (Hebrew) (Tel Aviv, 1969) p.90ff.
8   M. Waxman, "Civil and Criminal Procedure" in *Studies in Jewish Jurisprudence* (ed. E.M. Gershfield, New York, 1971) p. 226. On oral versus written opinion in general, see J.J. George, *Judicial Opinion Writing Handbook*, (Buffalo, 1984).
9   See also ySanh.3:10 (21.4).
10 See A. Weiss, *Court Procedure* (Hebrew) (New York, 1957) p. 125.

Nevertheless, some Amoraic sources refer in passing to written documents constituting judicial pronouncements.[11] This might indicate that in practice, commencing at least with the Amoraic period, judicial decisions were written down, even though there was no legal obligation to do so.

The discrepancy between the earlier rule and the later practice is brought out by the Talmudic treatment of a certain ruling in the Tosefta. The Tosefta rules:

2   A judge is believed when he says: I have ruled in favor of this one; I have ruled against that one. When is that, only if the litigants are still standing before him; but if they are no longer standing before him he is not believed.[12]

This ruling contemplates a case in which some doubt has arisen about the decision, and it regards the judge, in certain circumstances, as the sole authority to clarify the doubt. The ruling evidently contemplates a case in which the decision was delivered orally without written documentation, a procedure which is in line with the Mishnaic rule. The Talmud, however, accustomed to the practice of writing down judicial decisions, raises the question of why we do not consult the written document.[13]

The Talmud even finds it more appropriate to restrict the application of the ruling to an exceptional case in which the document was destroyed rather than answering simply that no written document had been issued at all.

In any event, even if we assert that there was a tendency in the later Talmudic period towards writing down judicial decisions, they still remained extremely brief due to the absence of a requirement to state reasons for a decision.

---

11   See for example bKid.74a; bB.B.130b; bB.B.153a; bSanh.30a; bSanh.31a; yGit.9:8 (50,3). But see also tB.M.1:9 and Epstein, "Notes on Talmudic Lexicography," 1 *Tarbiz* (1923-30) part 3, p. 131.
12   tB.M.1:12
13   bKid.74a.

2.3 Absence of a Requirement to State Reasons for a Decision

Since a proper and public evaluation of a judicial decision can be pursued only if the reasons underlying the decision are available, it seems only reasonable to oblige judges to state the reasons for the decision reached.[14] Providing reasons is essential in order to address two types of criticism, formal and informal. Formal criticism arises when a decision is challenged before an appellate court and is subject to a fresh examination which might result in its overruling, modification or the like. Informal criticism, in addition to the above and even if the decision is final, refers to criticism by the parties concerned, by professional lawyers, or, if the decision involves a point of general interest, by the public at large.

In the former case the requirement of specifying reasons is meant to serve a practical aim: to facilitate the task of the appellate court. In the latter situation, the requirement of providing reasons serves the principle that justice should not only be done but should manifestly and undoubtedly be seen to be done. Indeed, in recent times, the requirement of giving reasons, even if the decision is final, has come to be regarded as a principle of natural justice.[15]

In addition to the practical considerations and the desire to manifest justice, the requirement of giving reasons has another significant aspect. If reasons are given, members of the community are able to regulate their affairs more easily in a lawful way because they can predict the probable ruling of a court on the basis of a previously stated legal explanation.[16] In other words, when a judicial decision contains the reasoning of the court, it can serve more effectively as a legal guide for future conduct. However, Talmudic law was reluctant to disclose

---

14 See J. Frank, *Courts on Trial* (Princeton, 1950) pp. 165ff; G.A. Flick, *Natural Justice* (Butterworths 1979) pp. 86-111.

15 See P. Stein & J. Shand, *Legal Values in Western Society* (Edinburgh, 1974), pp. 78-79. Regulation 104, of the *Regulations of Procedure in Rabbinic Courts in Israel*, 1960, stipulates that the Rabbinical court has to state the reasons for its decision.

16 The publication of judicial decisions plays a further important role. If the final ruling over controversial issues were made known it might help reinforce one trend and suppress another. See tSanh.6:6 and parallels; bGit.35a; bJev.15a; bEr.41a; bKid.14a.

the reasons for a judicial decision because of diametrically opposed considerations.

Although Mishnah and Tosefta give a relatively detailed account of the various stages of a trial, they do not make even the slightest allusion to any requirement of stating the reasons for a court's decision. On the contrary, the laconic formula in which the verdict was delivered ("So and So you are liable") suggests that the concerned parties were not provided the reasons which led to the decision. Notwithstanding the general trend in the Mishnaic and Talmudic eras to spread knowledge of the law and to facilitate its accessibility to the general public, the process of the trial, as described in Tannaitic sources, had some elements of secrecy.

For example, if a decision were not unanimous, the Mishnah forbids the judges from revealing the positions they took in the deliberations preceding the decision.[17]

To ensure that this secrecy would be maintained, the trial had to be conducted *in camera*.[18] It appears that providing reasons was regarded as dangerous in that it exposed the court's internal reasoning and decision-making process to the outside world.[19] Many presumptions (especially those dealing with credibility) and legal constructions made by the judges in seeking a correct solution for a given dispute would lose their persuasive power and be rendered useless if they were known in advance by the litigants.[20] If judicial reasoning were revealed, then justice would suffer. Litigants would be in a position to shape the presentation of their case in a way that would affect the outcome at the expense of accuracy to the actual facts.[21]

Furthermore, it is related that in Palestine the custom was to withhold the reasons underlying new legislation (*gezerah*) for twelve

---

17 MSanh.3:7 and parallels.
18 Sifra Kedoshim, parasha 4, and the Talmudic discussion in bSanh.30a. Falk *op. cit.* p. 93 is mistaken when saying that the trial was conducted in the presence of the public.
19 See bSanh.31a. See also bShab.153b and bSanh.21b.
20 Notably the legal presumption known as *miggo*; see I. Herzog, *The Main Institutions of Jewish Law* (The Soncino Press, sec. ed. 1965) p. 250; M.D. Cohen, "Letorat Hamiggo Bamishpat Haivri," 11 *Sinai* (1942-3) pp. 247-253.
21 See mAv.1:9; yB.B.9:4 (17,1).

months after its enactment, in order to prevent public disputation lest some people disagree with the reasons and consequently refuse to observe the new law.[22] This desire to preclude informal criticism of the legislative process might have played a similar role in the judicial process and reinforced the practice of withholding the reasons underlying judicial decisions.

In light of what has been said thus far, we can interpret the following passage of Sifra:[23]

3   *Thou shalt not go about as a talebearer among thy people* (Lev.19:16): That you shall not be soft in words to one and harsh to another; Another interpretation: That you shall not be as a peddler (mat'im)[24] who is verbose.

These lines are taken from a passage dealing with the duties and conduct of judges. The first interpretation clearly relates to the judiciary. It instructs the judge to treat both sides equally. The second interpretation, however, seems puzzling. The Ravad, Malbim, and other commentators explain this second exegesis as referring to the general prohibition against gossip, and this rendering is supported by yPeah 1:1 (16,1). The difficulty with such an analysis, however, is that it is out of the immediate context of Sifra. Although it is not inconceivable that an alternative interpretation of a Biblical verse should be introduced by the term *davar aher*, even though the content is out of the prevailing context, it is nevertheless desirable to relate the alternative, if possible, to the context within which it occurs.

The notion of *mat'im* appears in other Tannaitic sources related to court procedure, and it refers to explaining one's case thoroughly.[25] Moreover, the peddler imagery is used in the Talmud to denote someone who enumerates in detail all of his wares in order to persuade

---

22   bA.Z.35a. See also S. Lieberman, *Hellenism in Jewish Palestine* (New York 1950) p. 139.
23   Sifra Kedoshim, parasha 4.
24   In the Venice edition (1545) and in *Codex Assemani* LXVI (ed. Finkelstein) the reading is *mat'in* and so it is also in yPeah 1:1 (16,1); in most of the printed editions, however, the reading is *mat'im*.
25   bSanh.7b; bShebu.31a.

others to purchase.²⁶ Finally, the interpretation in the Sifra is directly followed by its recording of the previously mentioned short formula in which the decision of the court was delivered ("So and So you are not liable, So and So you are liable").

In view of these observations, it is probable that the alternative exegesis addresses itself to the judge, as does the whole pericope, instructing him not to specify the reasons underlying his decision.²⁷

From two Amoraic sources it appears that a requirement of providing reasons was recognized under certain circumstances, the nature of which, however, is not very clear.²⁸ This first is a passage dealing with formal criticism of a judicial decision, which requires analysis.

---

26 bGit.33a; bNaz.21a; bB.K.36b; b.Arakh.23b.
27 See R. Hillel and Korban Aharon (in their commentaries *ad loc.*) who also relate the second exegesis to court procedure, though in a different way. See also A. Goldberg, "Leshonot Davar Aher Bemidreshe Halakah," *Studies in Rabbinic Literature, Bible and Jewish History*, (Hebrew) ed., Gilat et al. (Bar Ilan University 1982) p. 99.
28 Reference should also be made to the Sheiltoth's version of bM.K.16a which might be a source for the requirement of giving reasons under defined circumstances. The Talmud in bM.K.16a discusses the procedure initiated by the court in case one of the litigants fails to appear before the court though requested to do so. One of the means that the court may invoke is to pronounce a *shamta* on the disobedient litigant: *umenalan demeshamtinan ... dehakhi sevara degavra raba dekhtiv amar mal'akh hashem*. The common interpretation of these rather obscure lines is that they refer to the duty of the court's messenger to inform the concerned litigant that he is put under a *shamta* according to the instruction of the court. (See Rashi, Meiri, Ran, Nimukey Yoseph *ad loc.*) The Sheiltoth, however, has a different reading: *vekhi meshamtinan lo haya zarikh lemymar sevara dedayana leshamute* (*Sheiltoth De Rav Ahai Gaon*, edited by S.K. Mirsky, Jerusalem, 1977, vol.5, p. 53, section 147). According to this reading, these lines refer to the duty of informing the concerned party of the reasons for putting him under a *shamta*, and not merely that it was pronounced according to the court's order. For a possible source for this view, see Sifre on Num. (ed. Horovitz) p. 102. On the Sheiltoth's reading, see Ginzberg, *Geonica*, (2nd ed. New York, 1968) vol. I, pp. 83-84. On the requirement of giving reasons, in post-Talmudic literature, in special cases such as the imposition of a fine not stipulated by law, or a decision contrary to the prevailing law, see *Sdei Hemed* by H. Medini (rep. Tel-Aviv 1963) vol. 2, pp. 337-338; vol. 7,

4 I. R. Safra said in the name of R. Johanan:
   II. If two litigants are in obstinate disagreement with respect to a lawsuit and one says: Let us be tried here, and the other says: Let us go to the place of the Assembly, he must attend the court in his home town.
   III. And if it is necessary to consult, the matter is written down and forwarded to them.
   IV. And if the litigant says: Write down the grounds on which you made your decision and give them to me, they must write them down and give him the document.[29]

This passage confirms by implication the view presented above that as a rule the parties to a case were not given the reason for the decision. But the direct significance of this passage is unclear. Does IV depend on II? In other words, is it the case that if, and only if, a litigant is compelled to be tried in his local court (II), then he is entitled to demand a written document with the grounds for the decision (IV)? Most Rabbinical authorities maintain that this indeed is the case. Accordingly, they hold that if both parties have willingly submitted themselves to the jurisdiction of the court, then neither of them has the right to demand the reasons upon which the decision is based.[30]

This view, however, is questionable. The procedure referred to in III is a well established one, known from other sources,[31] and it is independent of II. It is mentioned in this passage to demonstrate how to overcome a possible disadvantage which might otherwise result from trying a case in a local court. Similarly, IV provides another means by which the rights of the litigants may be secured: by requiring judges to state their reasons upon request by a party. An unhappy liti-

---

p. 373ff. See also E. Shochetman, "Obligation to State Reasons for Legal Decisions in Jewish Law" (Hebrew) *Shenaton Ha-Mishpat Ha-Ivri* vol. VI-VII (1979-80), p. 319.

29 bSanh.31b, see also ySanh.3:2 (21,1). bSanh.31b records two contradictory accounts of the view of R. Johanan. For proposed solutions see Rashal and Rema *ad loc.*; Finkelstein, *Jewish Self-Government in the Middle Ages*, (New York, 1964), p. 379.

30 See Meiri on Sanh. *ad loc.*; Rashba on bB.M.69a; Tosafoth and Nimukey Yoseph on Sanh. *ad loc.*

31 tSanh.7:1; tHag.2:9.

gant may thus challenge the decision before the Assembly, and the stated reasons provided by the local court may facilitate the task of the superior court. Thus conceived, the above quoted source imposes an obligation on judges to provide reasons upon request, provided their decision can still be appealed to a higher court.[32]

But what if the decision is final? Does not the manifestation of justice element dictate that reasons should nevertheless be given? The notion that justice should not only be done but should manifestly and undoubtedly be seen to be done is not unknown in Talmudic law. The Biblical verse to which this view was attached is Numbers 32:22: "And you shall be quit of your obligation to the Lord and to Israel." The concept was applied to a wide range of different matters. For example, because of this reason treasurers were instructed not to collect money unless at least two of them were present,[33] nor to change coins of public funds for themselves.[34] Various Temple officials were praised for having considered the possible effect of public opinion and for having therefore refrained from conducting themselves in a manner that could have been mistakenly regarded as corrupt.[35] There was a general directive that a person should behave not only in a lawful manner, but also in such a way that his conduct be regarded as lawful by his neighbors.[36] Of special interest is the ruling of tJev.4:7, which is related to judges:

5   A judge who decides an issue, or who pronounces aught to be unclean or clean, or forbidden or permissible, may (in law) buy the object that was in dispute, but the Sages have said: Keep aloof from anything hideous and from whatever appears to be hideous.[37]

A judge who rendered a decision concerning the ownership of an article may, legally speaking, purchase the article from the party who acquired title through his ruling. The purchase is legal and valid, but

---

32   See Rosh on bB.M.69a, but see also R. Yehuda Almadari on Sanh. *ad loc.*
33   tPeah 4:15.
34   bPes.13a.
35   tYoma 2:5-6; bYoma 38a.
36   mShek.3:2; yShek.3:2 (47,3); tHul.2:24; Midrash Tannaim (ed. Hoffman) p. 134; Avot de R. Natan, ch. 2.
37   bHul.44b. See also tBek.3:9; 3:19.

it is somehow tainted by an appearance of corruption. The sages therefore advised the judge to withdraw from such unseemly conduct, since it might be rumored that the judge's ruling was motivated by his desire to buy the article.

In view of all these Tannaitic sources it seems remarkable that the Talmud never invoked this principle in order to oblige judges to specify the reasons for their opinions.[38] The apparent conclusion is that the Talmud, while endorsing the principle of the manifestation of justice, felt that it was inappropriate to apply it to the case of proclaiming reasons for a decision because of more important overriding considerations. Namely, the possible exploitation of institutional judicial reasoning by potential litigants, and the possible disrespect to judges due to a misunderstanding or a disapproval of their reasons, seem to have tipped the scales against the manifestation of justice element in this particular instance.

Another passage, in bB.M., has been traditionally interpreted as implying a qualified obligation to state reasons in a decision so that justice should manifestly be seen to be done.

6   Two Cutheans entered into a shared partnership. Then one went and divided the money without his partner's knowledge. So they came before R. Papa. Said he to him: What difference does it make to you? Thus did R. Nahman rule: Money is considered to be already divided. The following year they bought wine in partnership. Thereupon the other arose and divided it without his partner's knowledge. Again they came before R. Papa. Said he to him: Who divided it for you (i.e. your division is not legal). I see, the other replied, that you are biased in my partner's favor. Said R. Papa: In such a case it is certainly necessary to inform him. As for coins would he take good coins and leave short-weighted ones? No, he replied. Said R. Papa: In the case of wine however, everybody knows that some wine is sweet and some is not.[39]

The common view, shared by most Rabbinical authorities, is that the opening words of R. Papa's reply ("In such a case it is certainly

---

38 On this notion in general see Alon, "The Halakha in Barnabae Epistula," *Studies in Jewish History* (Hebrew) (2nd ed.), Tel-Aviv (1967) vol. 1, p. 275 at p. 282; S. Lieberman, *Tosefta Ki-Fshutah*, Jevamoth, pp. 33-34.
39 bB.M.69a and see Dik.Sof. *ad loc.* For a similar case, see bB.M.31b.

necessary to inform him") refer to the requirement of giving reasons.[40] According to the dominant view, the suspicion raised by one of the parties concerning R. Papa's partiality constitutes the unique feature of the case, and it was this suspicion that dictated the obligation to state a reason. Thus a rule was formulated on the basis of this case specifying that whenever the impartiality of a judge is questioned the judge is under an obligation to remove the doubt by providing the reasons which led to the decision.

However, as has been pointed out, it might well be that R. Papa did not refer to the obligation of informing the parties about the reasons underlying the decision. Rather, he indicated that whenever the nature of a partnership is such that its dissolution requires an expert's assessment of the value of each partner's share, as in the second case, one is not entitled to divide the assets without the partner's knowledge. That is, "the necessity to inform him" does not refer to judicial procedure. Rather, it refers to a stipulation governing the law of partnership.[41] Support for this interpretation can be found in the fact that R. Papa gave his reason for the earlier decision as well ("Thus did R. Nahman rule . . .") though no complaint had been voiced. Apparently R. Papa's stated reason was not connected with the complaint.

Even if we accept the view shared by most Rabbinical authorities that R. Papa refers to the requirement of giving reasons, the circumstances in which the duty arises are still questionable. The impartiality of the judge was challenged in other instances as well but no parallel reaction is recorded. On the contrary, the sources report firm and even punitive reaction from the court when its motives were challenged by the losing party.[42]

Moreover, it is hard to understand the point of a rule which stipulates that judges are not obliged to render an opinion unless doubt is cast upon their impartiality. Any unhappy litigant could claim that he was discriminated against and thereby would force the judge to state his reasons. A criterion determining whether judges should provide reasons must have a more objective basis, and cannot depend on the expression of a disappointed litigant's feelings. It therefore seems that

---

40 Meiri, Ran, Rashba and Ramban *ad loc.*
41 Ritba *ad loc.*
42 bGit.35a; bNed.50b; bKet.63b-64a; bKet.84b.

if one wants to maintain the view that R. Papa refers to the requirement of giving reasons, one has to focus attention on a different feature of the case.

What distinguishes this case from all other recorded cases in the Talmud is that both litigants were gentiles. Neusner "find(s) this story difficult" because he can "find no other examples of non-Jews resorting to the Jewish judiciary."[43] However, various sources contemplate the appearance of gentiles before a Jewish court.[44] In such cases the basis of the jurisdiction may have been no more than arbitral. There is no reason to assume that the Jewish court had the power to enforce its decision on the gentiles, even if they submitted themselves to its jurisdiction.

In one of the Tannaitic sources contemplating the appearance of gentiles before a Jewish court, the judge is warned not to subvert the case of a gentile in order to "sanctify the Name."[45] The accumulation of these two elements, the arbitral basis of the court and the desire to show gentiles how good Jewish law was,[46] apparently motivated R. Papa's verbosity.

While in theory judges were not obliged to state opinions, and indeed the bulk of recorded decisions are reported without the underlying reasons, cases are also reported in which the reasons for the deci-

---

43   Neusner, *A History of the Jews in Babylonia*, vol. 5. (Leiden, 1970), p. 304. See also Heiman, *Toledot Tannaim Veamoraim* (London, 1910, repr. Jerusalem, 1954) pp. 966-9. Nachmanides, in his Responsa (ed. Z. Schwall, Jerusalem, 1975) resp. 2, suggests that the Cutheans were in fact apostates.

44   tB.K.4:2; Mekhilta (ed. Horovitz) p. 246; yB.K.4:3 (4,2); bB.K.113a; bArkh.22a. See also Alon, *Toledot Hayehudim Betekufat Hamishnah Vehatalmud*, (Tel Aviv, 1954) vol. 1, p. 133 note 177; B. Cohen, *Jewish and Roman Law*, (New York, 1966) p. 157; B. Jackson, "Liability for Animals in Roman Law" 37 *C.I..J* (1978) 122 at p. 139.

45   Sifre ad Deut. (ed. Finkelstein) pp. 26-27. See also bB.K. 113a.

46   That this was indeed a factor is supported by the fact that the Talmud, in commenting on the Mishnaic source (mB.K.4:3) to which the Tosefta adds the rule concerning two gentiles submitting themselves to Jewish jurisdiction (tB.K.4:2), introduces the story of the Roman commission which inspected Jewish law and concluded that "it was correct with one exception ..." bB.K.38a; yB.K.4:3 (4,2). See also Jackson, *op. cit.* p. 140.

sions were given.⁴⁷ Here, however, a distinction must be introduced between original reasoning and ascribed reasoning.

Occasionally, a decision in a reported case is not compatible with the prevailing law, and either the Mishnah or the Talmud seeks to reconcile the decision with the prevailing law. Sometimes the decision is compatible with the prevailing law but incompatible with a minority view, in which case proponents of that view attempt to reconcile the recorded decision with their view.

Basically three different methods are employed to achieve this end, with a combination of these methods often being utilized.⁴⁸ Occasionally, the claim is made that a recorded decision is based on a mistake of law.⁴⁹ Alternatively, the tradition reporting the disputed case is simply rejected as being an erroneous report, and it is not accepted that such a decision was actually rendered.⁵⁰

The third method employed, which is most relevant for this study, is to explain that the recorded case is based on extra-legal reasoning, thereby asserting that the recorded case does not represent the law.⁵¹ A reasoning assigned to the original court by a later authority will hereafter be referred to as ascribed reasoning.

While the distinction between ascribed reasoning and original reasoning might be crucial for an historical reconstruction of the case, it is less relevant if a normative acccount is sought. The Talmudic conception regards ascribed reasoning as binding as an authentic account of the case, even if historically inaccurate.

---

47 See, for example, bGit.14a; bKet.85b; bB.B.29b; bB.B.88a; and see Judolowitz, *Pumbedita* (rep. Jerusalem, 1971) p. 100. Rabinowitz in his *Mavo Hatalmud* (Vilna, 1894, rep. Jerusalem, 1971) p. 51, wants to infer from bB.B.173b, which juxtaposes the Persian courts with the Jewish ones, that Jewish judges always gave reasons for their decisions. This is, no doubt, a sweeping statement. The only significance of bB.B.173b is that, according to the Talmud, Persian courts gave arbitrary judgments whereas Jewish courts did not, but nothing is said there concerning the obligation to state opinions. Moreover, it is likely that the passage deals with legislative enactments and not with reasons underlying judicial pronouncements. *Cf.* bGit.14a (bB.B.144a) and bKer.20a.
48 *Cf.* Epstein, *Mavo Lenusach Hamishnah* (Jerusalem, 1948) p. 154ff.
49 mNaz.5:4; mSanh.7:2; bSan.52b.
50 tSanh.9:11; bSanh.52b: bMeg.20a.
51 mB.B.9:9; bJev.107b; bJev.110a.

2.4 What Should be Viewed as a Judicial Case?

Another difficulty in analyzing judicial cases in the Talmud stems from its casuistic formulation. It is sometimes difficult to determine whether a given passage represents a report of an actual case or is an hypothetical discussion presented in the casuistic style.

As early as 1905 Weiszburg called attention to the fact that actual cases recorded in the Talmud provide the most reliable historical data at our disposal.[52] Sixty years later, Neusner attempted to compile a list of all actual cases recorded in the Talmud.[53] The list, however, suffers from several shortcomings which limit its usefulness for this study.[54] The data collected by Neusner is limited to Babylonian cases,

---

52   Y.Weiszburg, "Odot Bate Hadin Bizeman Hatalmud," *Festschrift zu M.A. Bloch* (Budapest, 1905) pp. 76-82. See also Y.M. Guttman "Sheeloth Academiyoth Batalmud," *Dvir*, vol. 1 (Berlin, 1923) p. 38 at p. 43.

53   J. Neusner, *A History of the Jews in Babylonia*, vol. 1. (Leiden, 1965), vol. 2 (Leiden, 1966), vol. 3 (Leiden, 1968), vol. 4 (Leiden, 1969), vol. 5 (Leiden, 1970); vol. 3 pp. 319-334; vol. 4 pp. 257-277; vol. 5 pp. 329-342. For further studies specifically devoted to the analysis of court cases, see: H.P. Chajes, "Les Juges Juifs en Palestine de l'an 70 a' l'an 500," *REJ* 39 (1899) 39-52; A. Kaminka, "Hama'ase Betor Makor Lehalakha", *Mehequarim Batalmud* (Tel Aviv, 1950) pp. 1-41; E.Z. Melamed, "Hama'ase Bamishnah Kemakor Lahalakha," 46 *Sinai* (1954-60) p. 152-166; B. De Vries, "Hauveda Kegorem Lehidush Hahalakha," *Festschrift zu L. Jung* (New York, 1962) pp. 143-148; A. Weiss, *Studies in the Literature of the Amoraim* (Hebrew) (New York, 1962), pp. 313-334; S. Zuri, "Hamassim Bebeit Dino Shel R. Ami," 6 *Sinai* (1960) pp. 26-35, pp. 193-201. The opposite task of collecting hypothetical questions was carried out by Y.M. Guttman, *op. cit.* (continued in *Dvir*, vol. 2, Berlin, 1924, pp. 101-163).

54   The list is also full of typographical errors which further limit its practical value. An example chosen at random will suffice. The list of court cases in B.M. vol. 5, p. 336 contains the following errors:
   For bB.M.77b, R. Papa, re sale of land, read bB.M.67b;
   For bB.M.76a-76b, R. Ashi, re collection of debt, read bB.M.67a-67b;
   For bB.M.73a, R. Ashi, re interest, read bB.M.73b;
   For bB.M.83b, R. Papa, re negligence, is non-existent;
   For bB.M.104, Rabina, re lease of field, read bB.M.104b;
   For bB.M.104, R. Kahana, re lease of field, read bB.M.104b;
   For bB.M.106b, R. Nahman b. Isaac, re lease of vineyard, is non-

excluding all Tannaitic and Palestinian cases recorded in the Babylonian Talmud. While this might be a sound approach for one interested in a historical description of the day-to-day life among Babylonian Jewry, it surely distorts the normative account of Talmudic law. Palestinian, let alone Tannaitic decisions, were often relied upon and formed an integral part of Babylonian Talmudic law. The locality of their origin (Palestine or Babylon) was not a factor in accepting or rejecting their binding or even persuasive status. Their very presence in the Babylonian Talmud testifies to this fact.

Furthermore, Neusner does not seem to be fully aware of the difficulty posed by the casuistic formulation of the Talmud, and hypothetical discussions appear in his list as reports of actual[55] cases. This confusion stems from a failure on Neusner's part to construct a set of criteria for distinguishing hypothetical discussions from actual cases at the outset of his endeavor.

The distinction between hypothetical discussion and halakhic derivation from an actual case is well rooted in the Talmud, and the grouping of given passages into the former or the latter category is of legal consequence.[56] For our analysis the distinction is crucial. When expressing a legal view on an hypothetical case, the Rabbi is not under the same legal constraints as when delivering an authoritative and binding judgment in a concrete case. In the hypothetical case the Rabbi resembles the legislator in not having to address himself exclusively to the application of pre-existing legal standards.[57]

---

existent, and probably should be R. Kahana.
In addition to printing mistakes, the report of the ruling is sometimes mistaken: for example, vol. 4, p. 266, for bBK 117b. Abaye ruled on misappropriation of bailment, read Rava (Abaye only commented on the ruling); vol. 4, p. 261 for bJev.122a, R. Joseph permitted woman to remarry, read forbade woman to remarry.

55 See Neusner *op. cit.* vol. 3, p. 317, note 5, and vol. 4, p. 253; also see note 76 below.
56 tSanh.7:7 (ySanh.3:10 (21,4)); yPeah 2:4 (17,1); yBez.2:1 (61,2); yM.K.3:5 (82,4); yNid.2:7(50,2); bJev.77a; bB.K.59b; bB.B.83a; bB.B.130b; bNid.7b.
57 This consideration might be the basis for the distinction between judicial decision and hypothetical discussion; see Elon, *Jewish Law*, pp. 1215-1218.

Talmudic case reports basically follow two forms:
i) as a reference fully integrated into the *sugya*, without retaining its independent meaning;
ii) as an independent unit, which can be isolated from the context within which it occurs, without losing its significance.

Corresponding to these two forms, two types of criteria can be formulated in order to identify a report of an actual case:
i) a criterion based on external evidence, that is, terminology employed by the Talmud when referring to a given tradition;[58]
ii) a criterion based on internal evidence, that is, terminology occurring within a given passage or its internal structure.

To the extent that reasons are reported, it is mainly in the latter that they occur. We shall therefore discuss this form in some detail.

The most frequent and most distinct term indicating a report of an actual case is *ata lekameh ledina* or its shortened form *ata lekameh*, which is the Aramaic equivalent of the Hebrew *u'va ma'aseh lifneh hahamim*. Most of the rulings occurring in the *ata lekameh* passages are preserved in the direct speech form in which they were delivered.

The following example is illustrative:

7   There came a brother to Mari b.Isak from Be Hozai, saying to him: Divide (my father's estate) with me. I do not know you, he replied. It came before (*ata lekameh*) R.Hisda. Said he to him: He (Mari) speaks truly to you, for it is written, *And Joseph knew his brethren, but they knew him not*, which teaches that he had gone forth without the stamp of a beard and came (before them) with one. Go then, he continued, and produce witnesses that you are his brother. I have witnesses, he replied, but they are afraid of him because he is a powerful man. Thereupon R. Hisda said to the other (Mari): Go you and bring witnesses that he is not your brother. Is that justice?, he exclaimed, the onus of proof lies on the claim-

---

58   The most frequent terms are *ma'ase* and *uveda*. See, for example, bB.K.59b; bB.B.13b; bKet.49b for the former, and bD.K.27b; bB.B.51a; bKet.50b for the latter. See also B. Hoenig, *The Great Sanhedrin*, (Philadephia, 1953) p. 27; Lieberman, "Sefer Hama'assim" 2 *Tarbiz* (1930-31) p. 377; S. Zuri, *Mishpat Hatalmud* (Warsaw, 1921) Book 7, p.21. In addition, there is also evidence relating to usages or customs of a particular Beth Din or courts in general: e.g., bKet.19a; bKet.105a; bSanh.6b; bKid.12b; bKid.81a; bBk95b; bBk113a. The term *dilma* which occurs in the Palestinian Talmud does not refer to a judicial case but to a story relating an episode in the life of the Amoraim.

ant. He replied: Thus do I judge your case and for all who are powerful men like you.[59]

This is a classic example containing all the main characteristics of a case report, such as, the names of the litigants, the term *ata lekameh* denoting appearance before a court, the direct speech form reporting the ruling as it was delivered, and the reasoning of the court.

All of these elements do not always appear in case reports. Often the names of the litigants are missing and the anonymous formula "a person" (*hahu gavra*)[60] replaces them. Occasionally, the ruling is reported in indirect speech in the third person singular past tense, as in the following case:

8   A certain man had a silver cup which had been deposited with him and, being attacked by thieves, he took it and handed it over to them.
    It came before Rabbah who declared him exempt. (*u'fatre*).[61]

In other cases the same structure is retained but without the typical term *ata lekameh*:

9   A certain woman once entered the house of another person for the purpose of baking bread there, and a goat of the owner of the house came and ate up the dough, from which it became sick and died. (In rendering judgment) Rava ordered the woman to pay damages for the value of the goat (*hiyve Rava leshelume*).[62]

Here, and in similar instances, the identification of an actual case is facilitated by the accusative inflection of the recorded ruling (for example, *hiyve*), which means that it is related to a concrete case or person.

The main difficulty lies in characterizing passages with the following structure: a set of facts related to "a person" (*hahu gavra*) is first

---

59   bB.M.39b (bKet.27b). In this case the ruling of R.Hisda is contrary to the well-established principle of *hamozti mehavero alav hare'aya*.
60   *Hahu gavra* is sometimes used as a circumlocution for 'I' or for 'you' (see G. Vermes, *Post Biblical Jewish Studies*, (Leiden, 1975) pp. 156-57), but this usage is not relevant in this context.
61   bBK.117b.
62   bBK.48a.

described, followed by a ruling ascribed to a named authority, but without directly relating it to the "parties" concerned. For example:

10 A certain shepherd was entrusted with cattle every day in the presence of witnesses. One day people handed cattle over to him without witnesses. Subsequently he issued a complete denial (of the receipt of the cattle). But witnesses came and testified that he had eaten two of the cattle. Said R. Zera: If the first law of R. Hiyya is valid, (the shepherd) ought to swear regarding the remainder.[63]

This structure seems to suggest a case report, and so it was regarded by Neusner.[64] However, this is by no means conclusive.

When, as here, the opinion is given without indicating a concrete addressee, there is no certainty that it is more than a proposed solution to an hypothetical construct. The "person" to whom the facts are related might be no more than a casuistic expression of a contingency. To be sure, the factual situation discussed might be derived from an actual case, but the ruling which follows is not that of the original court but of some authority engaged in an academic discourse.[65]

A detailed analysis of all passages of this type would take us far beyond the scope of this study. Suffice it to demonstrate by a few examples that *"hahu gavra"* as such, or the literary structure stated above, does not necessarily denote an actual judicial decision. Thus, in the last passage quoted above the ruling of R. Zera is conditional: "If the first law of R. Hiyya is valid." A judicial ruling by its very nature cannot be presented as conditional, since that would leave the controversy unresolved.[66]

---

63   bBM 5a.
64   Neusner *op. cit.* vol. 4, p. 267, and see below note 76.
65   See, for example, bKid.45b concerning a certain man who insisted that "our daughter must be married to my relative," etc., which is a hypothetical discussion based on an incident which actually happened to Abaye, recorded in bNed.23a and referred to in bBer.56a.
66   For another example of a conditional ruling, and hence not a judicial one, see bGit.63b. See also bB.B.6b-7a. The Talmud comments on two "cases" recorded by R. Hama: "Is not this (the second) case the same as the other, why then this repetition?" This comment clearly demonstrates that the Talmud takes these two statements to be hypothetical statements (despite the *hahu gavra* formula in the second case) and hence the problem of redundancy arises.

A similar consideration also prevents the following passage from being regarded as a judicial decision:

11 A certain man kicked another's money-box into the river. The owner came and said: So much and so much did I have in it. R. Ashi was sitting and pondering on it. What should the law be in such a case? Rabina said to R. Aha the son of Raba, or, as others report, R. Aha the son of Raba said to R. Ashi: Is this not exactly what was stated in the Mishnah? For we learnt: The Sages agree with R. Judah in the case of one who set fire to a mansion, that payment should be for all that was kept therein, as it is surely the custom of men to keep (valuables) in (their) homes. He, however, said to him: If he would have pleaded that he had money there, it would indeed have been the same. But we are dealing with a case where he pleads that he had jewels there. What should then be the legal position? Do people keep jewels in a money-box or not? Let this remain undecided (*teyku*).[67]

The *teyku* which is declared at the end of the passage manifests that at issue is an hypothetical question that can, unlike concrete disputes, be left unsolved.[68]

The proposition that R. Ashi deliberated on a hypothetical case is attested by Ms.M. (the Munich Manuscript) which reads here *ve'ka mibaye le* instead of *ve'ka me'ayen be*. It has been convincingly shown by Guttman that *ba'ye* is a technical term denoting hypothetical questions or "academic questions."[69]

Another example of an academic question is the following:

12 A certain man borrowed a cat from his neighbor. The mice then formed a united party and killed it. R. Ashi was sitting and pondering on it: How is it in such a case? Is it as though it had died through its work or not? R. Mordecai said to R. Ashi: Thus did Abimi of Hagronia say in Raba's name: A man whom women killed there is no judgment nor judge... [70]

Both the literary form and R. Mordecai's analogy manifest the hypo-

---

67 bB.K.62a. See Guttman *op. cit.* vol. 2, p. 146, and Epstein's comment there in note 1.
68 On *teyku*, see Guttman *ibid.* pp. 140-164.
69 Guttman, *op. cit.*, *Dvir* vol. 1, p. 41.
70 bB.M.97a see also bB.M.77b.

thetical nature of this passage.[71]

Another term denoting academic discourse is "come and hear," by which a solution based on a recorded tradition or a Biblical verse is introduced.[72]

Consider the following example:

13 A certain (person) said: My estate (shall be given) to my sons. He had a son and a daughter. Do people call a son 'sons' or perhaps they do not call a son 'sons', and his intention was to include his daughter in the gift? Abaye said: Come and hear: *And the sons of Dan: Hushim* (Gen. 46:23).[73]

The reformulation of the legal problem involved, in terms of a question[74] and a reply introduced by "come and hear," clearly demonstrates that the passage deals with an academic question.

In many cases the set of facts related to "a person" is followed by controversial rulings reported in the traditional form of a dispute:

14 A certain (person) said: My estate (shall be given) to my sons. He had a son and a grandson. Do people call a grandson 'son' or not? R. Habiba said: People call a grandson 'son'. Mar b.R.Ashi said: People do not call a grandson 'son.'[75]

It is clear that unless a final, unequivocal ruling terminating the litigation is reported, a passage cannot be regarded as a judicial decision, since the "parties" are not left with a ruling.

---

71 The above account is immediately followed by "another version" according to which the cat "ate many mice whereby it became sick and died." For the significance of "another version," see text accompanying note 33 in Chapter 5 below.
72 On "come and hear", see Guttman *op.cit.*, *Dvlr*, vol. 2, p. 117.
73 bB.B.143b. See also yKet.13:1 (35,4). The formula, "what ruling shall judges give in this case," which occurs in bB.M.42a-b as the opening of legal deliberation and which is used by three different Amoraim, also signifies academic discussions. But cf. bB.B.33b-34a (bShebu.32b and 47a) where it is used by yet a fourth Amora; the context and terminology there suggests an actual judicial decision.
74 See also bB.B.34a. See also Weiss, *op. cit.* p. 325 and p. 327.
75 bB.B.143b. This form is to be distinguished from a master-disciple dialogue that sometimes follows a judicial decision; see, for example, bB.K.11a; bB.K.84a; bB.K.93a; bB.K.96b.

It seems safe to conclude on the basis of the foregoing illustrations that a set of facts followed by a ruling not directed to a concrete addressee is not necessarily a report of a judicial case. Unless there are indications to the contrary, passages of this structure will not be regarded in this book as case reports.[76] It is possible that some actual case reports will thus go unidentified; however, authenticity of the data discussed will thereby be enhanced.

As a result of the preceding analysis, the number of judicial decisions reported in the Talmud is dramatically reduced. This directly affects the view that Talmudic law is a case law system developed primarily through judicial activity.[77] If the evidence concerning judicial activity is much more limited than is generally assumed, and the role academic discourse plays in the development of the law is much more significant, then the view regarding Talmudic law as a case law system should be substantially moderated.[78]

The concern of this study, however, is with judicial deviation as it is reflected and documented in judicial cases. The next chapter illustrates two such cases which serve in post-Talmudic literature as paradigm cases of judicial deviation.

---

[76] All the passages here discussed are listed by Neusner as reports of actual cases. See Neusner *op. cit.*, vol. 5, p. 336; vol. 4, p. 270; vol. 5, p. 337 respectively.

[77] Elon, *Jewish Law*, p. 772.

[78] C. Chernowitz, *Toledoth Ha-halakah* (New York, 1945, 2nd ed.) vol. 1, p. 173; S. Rozenboim, "Common Errors" (Hebrew) 4, *Hamishpat Haivri* (1933) 113, at p. 115; Y. Gafni, "Maasei Beth Din Ba-Talmud Ha-Bavli," *American Academy for Jewish Research Proceedings*, vol XLIX (1982) p. 32.

CHAPTER 3

TWO PROTOTYPE CASES OF EXTRA-LEGAL CONSIDERATIONS

This chapter seeks to familiarize the reader with the notion of extra-legal considerations by means of illustration. Two suggestive cases will be discussed here, demonstrating the concept of extra-legal considerations at work.

In the course of this study further types and examples of extra-legal considerations will be presented and discussed. The cases chosen here have been singled out because they contain the most explicit recognition that the decision reached is not derived from the law but is based upon extra-legal considerations.

3.1 The Case of the Kidnapper

The Talmud in Jevamoth discusses the view of Rav concerning the validity of the marriage of a minor who has been married off by her mother or brothers.[1] According to Rav, the marriage becomes valid only if on attaining majority the girl cohabits with her husband. If the girl was betrothed to another man, then the second marriage is null *ab initio* and the girl need not obtain a letter of divorce (*get*) to dissolve it. If, however, the girl married another after attaining majority but before the first marriage was consummated, the second marriage is valid and a letter of divorce is needed to dissolve it.[2]

The Talmud proceeds to examine whether Rav actually holds that the validity of the marriage of a minor depends on its consummation after attaining majority. A case is cited from which it appears that

---

[1] bJev.109b. Although according to Biblical law as understood by the Rabbis, a fatherless minor girl cannot be married, the Sages legalized her marriage; see bJev.112b.
[2] See bJev.109b for the dissenting view of Samuel.

Rav's disciples ruled that such a marriage was valid although cohabitation had not taken place.

15 It once happened in Naresh[3] that a man betrothed a girl while she was a minor, and when she attained her majority and he placed her upon the bridal chair[4] another man came and snatched her away from him; and Rav's disciples, R. Beruna and R. Hananel, were there and they did not require the girl to obtain a letter of divorce from the second man.[5]

A fatherless minor was married off by her mother (or brothers) to a certain man who betrothed her. When the girl attained her majority and apparently was prepared for the *huppah*, another man snatched[6] the girl away and convinced her to marry him.[7] Though we are not told so we may assume that later on the girl regretted her consent to marry the second man and wished to dissolve the marriage. Thereupon she came before R. Beruna and R. Hananel and they declared the second marriage to be invalid and did not require her to obtain a letter of divorce from the second man, which under the circumstances would probably have been difficult.

The ruling in this case apparently contradicts the alleged view of Rav. According to Rav's view, as presented above, the second mar-

---

3 On the town Naresh, see M.D. Judolowitz, "Hair Naresh Bizeman Hatalmud," 14 *Sinai* (1944) pp. 94-99. See also bHul.127a for a rather negative evaluation of its inhabitants.
4 *Cf.* bSot.12b; see also A.S. Hershberg, "Minhage Haerussin Vehanessuin Bizeman Hatalmud", *Haatid*, vol. 5 (Berlin, 1923) p. 75, 89.
5 bJev. 110a.
6 The Hebrew text is *veata ah'rina vehatfa*. A similar situation is discussed in the Alexandrian case recorded in Tosefta though the ruling is different; see tKet.4:9; yJev.15:3 (14,4); yKet.4:8 (28,4); bB.M.104a. The common usage of the verb *hatof* in both cases is probably an influence of Judges 21:21. For the Tosefta case, see S. Lieberman, *Tosefta Kefshutah ad loc.*; B. Cohen, *Jewish and Roman Law*, (New York, 1966) p. 304ff.; Freiman, *Seder Kiddushin veNessuin* (Jerusalem, 1945) p. 11; Falk, *Nessuin veGerushin* (Jerusalem, 1961) 40-41; Compare also with bKid.45b and bNed.23a.
7 But see W. Greene, "Extra-Legal Juridical Prerogatives," 7 *JSJ* (1976) p. 152 at p. 165, who mistakenly assumes that the girl did not assent to the second marriage. But if that was the case no legal issue would have been involved, since no marriage can be effected against or without the will of both sides. See also Freiman, *op. cit.* p. 13.

riage should have been considered valid since the first took place while the girl was a minor and was not consummated after the girl had attained her majority. According to the alleged view of Rav, the girl should have been required to obtain a letter of divorce to dissolve the second marriage. Since Rav's disciples did not require the girl to obtain a letter of divorce, the Talmud infers that Rav did not hold the view previously ascribed to him. In an attempt to reconcile the ruling in the Naresh case with the alleged view of Rav, R. Ashi maintains that the second marriage was not annulled by Rav's disciples because the first was valid. Rather, it was annulled because the second man, the kidnapper, had behaved improperly.[8]

> R. Ashi said: He acted improperly, therefore they [Beth Din] treated him improperly and deprived him of the right to a valid betrothal.[9]

The decision in the Naresh case is reported without its underlying reasons. R. Ashi fills in the gap by ascribing an extra-legal considera-

---

8   R. Ashi's attempt is preceded by another attempt made by R. Papa. R. Papa, who was himself from the town of Naresh, held that according to the custom in his own town the placing on the bridal chair was not a preparation for the *huppah*, as was assumed by the questioner, but a ceremony which succeeded the actual marriage. It follows that the second marriage in the Naresh case took place after the first had been completed and hence never came into effect and was void *ab initio*. Weiss, (*The Talmud and its Development* (Hebrew, New York, 1954) p. 393) argues that once R. Papa reported the custom in his home town, there was no need for further attempts to reconcile Rav's view with the ruling in the Naresh case. Weiss therefore suggests that R. Ashi's formula is out of place in the present context and that its original source is bB.B.48b from which it is taken. This suggestion, however, has no basis. Very often the Talmud provides us with several answers to a particular question, of which some may be superfluous if others are accepted. It should also be remembered that R. Papa and R. Ashi are considering an early case, one which did not occur in their presence or time. R. Ashi may have been discontent with R. Papa's attempt on the ground that the custom referred to by R. Papa might not yet have been in practice at the time of the Naresh case. Moreover, it is argued below that bB.B.48b. cannot be the source of R. Ashi's formula; see below note 29.

9   bJev.110a. See also bKet.86a and Ritba *ad loc.* The Hebrew text is *hu as'a shelo ka'hogen lefikakh asu imo shelo kahogen.* Heilperin, *Teshuvoth Beanshei On,* (Frankfurt A.M.1845) p. 68 reads here *hu-as'a ima shelo*

tion to the original court, that the decision annulling the second marriage was not based on the law but was rendered because of the improper behavior of the kidnapper.

The Talmud does not specify what constitutes the improperness of the act. Since the first marriage was not yet consummated, the kidnapper may be viewed as one who betrothed a woman knowing that another was already preparing to marry her.[10] This behavior is condemned by R. Ashi, but what, if any, are its legal consequences? Is such a marriage deemed valid? The issue is whether the impropriety involved in a given act affects its legal consequences.

In order to obtain a better assessment of R. Ashi's reasoning it is necessary to consider briefly the more extreme case, the validity of an illegal act. Talmudic law distinguishes between acts forbidden by the Torah (*mideorayta*) and acts forbidden by the Sages (*miderabanan*).[11]

In the former case, the illegality of the act renders it invalid and deprives it of any legal consequence.[12] In the latter case the act committed is considered valid in spite of its illegality. Numerous examples attest to the fact that Talmudic law regarded the transgression of Rabbinical injunctions as an irrelevant factor in determining the legal validity of the act.[13] It follows *a fortiori* that the principle of validity

---

    ka-hogen.... as'ta imo shelo ka-hogen. This reading, which is not supported by any of the Mss. or printed editions of the Talmud (nor is it found in any of the Rishonim), is a typical attempt of the apologetic school to "reconstruct" the Talmud so that a recorded deviation from the law might be suppressed.

10 See Ran on bKid.58b and mKid.3:1.

11 For a full analysis of the problem, see E. Shochetman, *Illegal Act in Jewish Law, Ma'ase Haba Beavera* (Hebrew) (1981).

12 This is the view of Rava in his controversy over this issue with Abaye; see bTem.4b. The *sugya* there deals only with Biblical injunctions; see Shochetman *ibid.* Legal issues that are debated by Abaye and Rava are decided as a rule according to Rava (with the exception of very few cases; see bSanh.27a and parallels).

13 tBez.4:4; tB.K.7:19; mTer.3:6 (tTer.4:10). A Talmudic dictum holds that a "sinner should not profit from his sin"(mShebi.9:9; mHal.2:7; Sifre ad Num. §110; bJev.92b; bKet.11a; bKet.36b; bGit.25b; bSot.15a; bB.K.19a; bA.Z.2b; bMen.6a; bNid.4b). At first glance, this saying indicates an opposite approach, namely one which invalidates illegal acts in

EXTRA-LEGAL CONSIDERATIONS 45

in spite of illegality, applies to acts of a less objectionable nature such as acts involving merely improper conduct.[14]

Notwithstanding this well-established doctrine, the marriage of the kidnapper, though valid, was annulled because of the impropriety involved in it. R. Ashi's courageous statement that the kidnapper was "treated improperly" constitutes an explicit admission of the possibility of judicial deviation from the law.[15] In fact, R. Ashi's use of the terminology "The Beth Din treated him improperly," was not an innovation. Rather, it constituted an Amoraic formulation of a Tannaitic notion expressing the same idea.[16]

The foregoing exposition of R. Ashi's reasoning, as being based on extra-legal considerations, can be attacked along two different lines. First, perhaps one should not interpret R. Ashi's formula literally; perhaps one should attribute to R. Ashi a more moderate view and regard the formulation only as a manner of speech. According to this restricted interpretation, R. Ashi maintains that due to the improper behavior of the kidnapper the court was strict with him but remained within the limits of the law.[17] The implication of the proposed interpretation is that R. Ashi qualifies the view of Rav. R. Ashi claims that Rav would agree that in an exceptional situation such as the Naresh case, the marriage of a minor becomes valid even though not consummated. Reading such a qualification into the formula would be a great

---

      order to deprive the sinner of any benefit he might have derived from his illegal act. However, this dictum appears exclusively as a principle justifying pre-existing *takkanoth* and not as a guiding principle directing the court how to deal with offenders.

14   See mB.B.8:5; tJev.4:4; bKid.59a.

15   Elon (*Jewish Law*, pp. 427, 519) regards the reasoning of R. Ashi as representing a *takkanah* but gives no justification for this view. See below note 29. See also Freiman, *op. cit. supra*, note 6, p. 13.

16   See bJev.107b; yJev.13:1(13:3), which is another example of a decision protecting a fatherless minor who has been married off. A parallel structure: The formula there also removes a difficulty posed by an early recorded case by ascribing to the early case an extra-legal consideration. See below Chapter 4, section 4.1. S. Zuri, *System of Actions* (London, 1933) p. 68 mistakenly assumes that this principle is an innovation made by the last generation of the Amoraim in Babylon.

17   *Cf.* Tosafoth Rid on bKet.86a.

distortion of its plain meaning, however, since R. Ashi does not imply the existence of any discretion accorded by the law to hold the marriage valid in exceptional circumstances.[18]

In fact, the Naresh case (according to R. Ashi's reasoning) is only one manifestation of a policy to deviate from the law and to treat a wrongful litigant with a particular severity not warranted by the law. In most cases the result obtained by deviating from the law could be achieved by reinterpreting the existing rules so that the desired solution follows from it and is within the limits of the law. The technique of reinterpreting an existing rule so that a particular solution, corresponding to the moral conviction of the judge, can be presented as corresponding to the legal rule is not unknown to Talmudic law.[19] Therefore, if judges took a different path and chose explicitly to depart from the law, it was not necessarily because they had no alternative means to impose their will. Rather, it was because they apparently believed that explicit deviation from the law was a more appropriate technique in the prevailing circumstances. Strict adherence to the law and to its formalities ensures legal stability. At the same time, however, it enables wrongdoers to rely on the court's strict adherence to the law and to calculate their affairs accordingly. By contrast, if it is possible that the court may depart from the law, then potential wrongdoers can neither anticipate the conduct of their eventual trial nor prepare for it in advance. The reasoning employed by the courts in the cases involving extra-legal considerations demonstrates that the judges were not merely attempting to overcome the difficulty of reaching a solution that was otherwise unobtainable through legal means. They were not only seeking to frustrate the purpose of and deny any benefit to the blameful litigant. Rather, the reasoning was motivated by the desire to proclaim that he who attempts to use the law to

---

18 Any attempt to determine the precise meaning of R. Ashi's formula on a linguistic basis is bound to fail since the linguistic evidence is insufficient to warrant any conclusion. See, however, mB.B.8:5 and tB.K.8:15 (and parallels). See also Sifre ad Deut. (ed. Finkelstein) p. 326; bA.Z.55a; bHul.95a; bTan.4a.

19 Compare, in particular, the legal reasoning invoked by Hillel in the Alexandrian case (note 6 above), which demonstrates how a desired solution can be obtained by reinterpreting the law.

achieve an improper aim cannot rely on that very law he himself has exploited.[20]

It is important to realize that there is a misleading gap between the theoretical discussion of the halakhah and its actual application in the judicial process. Legal formalism, the specific, precise, and detailed formulation of halakhic rules on the theoretical plane, the extensive use of minutely defined measures and standards, the shunning of abstract terms such as "reasonable," "good faith," and the like, may create the impression that, in practice, Talmudic halakhah is a pedantic, legalistic system, where rights and obligations are determined by the breadth of a hair. This impression, however, is fundamentally wrong. In most cases a judge's ruling will of course be presented as corresponding to the theoretical formulation. However, the Talmudic judge does not feel chained to the legal norm, and does not hesitate to deviate from it when, in his opinion, circumstances of the case warrant such a deviation. Obviously, we are not dealing here with an arbitrary, wanton deviation. When a judge deviates from the law, he does so in order to enforce the spirit of the Torah as he understands it. But this is a concept that is not susceptible to an objective definition.

The second possible objection to our interpretation of R. Ashi's reasoning is internal, based on the continuation of the *sugya* in Jevamoth 110a. R. Ashi's analysis is followed by this dialogue:

> Said Rabina to R. Ashi: [Your explanation is] satisfactory where the man betrothed [her] with money; what, however, can be said where he betrothed her by cohabitation? The rabbis have considered his cohabitation as an act of mere fornication.[21]

---

20   In all the cases in which such a reasoning was invoked, the improper behavior causing the court to deviate from the law was directly linked with the subject-matter of the case. The case of the sons of Rokhel (mB.B.9:7, bB.B.156; below ch.4.1.iii) is an exception. There, the improper behavior was a violation of one of the laws of *kilayim* and the subject-matter of the case was the ownership of a veil. Should one dismiss this case as being an anomalous instance and generalize on the basis of all the other cases that Talmudic judges would deviate from the law only on the basis of improper behaviour which is directly connected with the subject-matter of the case? I leave this question open.

21   b.Jev. 110a.

This dialogue demonstrates that R. Ashi himself[22] was engaged in an attempt to base the annulment of the second marriage on legal grounds. Hence it cannot be said that the court deviated from the law.

To meet this objection and to gain a better understanding of the Rabina-R. Ashi dialogue, this passage must be considered in conjunction with five other passages where this dialogue also occurs. In four places in the Talmud the Rabina-R. Ashi dialogue follows different attempts to validate a letter of divorce (*get*) which according to Biblical law is invalid.[23] In the fifth passage the dialogue follows a recorded norm annulling the consent of a woman to a marriage where that consent was obtained by duress.[24]

The common feature of these passages is that they all deal with various attempts to cancel a marriage which according to Biblical law is valid. In four of the passages, those dealing with the ratification of the *get*, the dialogue is preceded by another, anonymous dialogue:

16 And is it possible then that where a *get* according to Biblical law is cancelled we should ... declare it valid and so allow a married woman to marry another? Yes, when a man betroths a woman he does so under the conditions laid down by the Rabbis and ... the Rabbis annul his betrothal.

The question refers to the power of the Sages to enact new rules contrary to Biblical law.[25] If Biblical law prescribes that a certain *get* is not valid, from where do the Sages derive the power to declare it valid? The answer given is that anyone betrothing a woman does so subject to the conditions laid down by the Sages. The legal transaction between bride and groom includes an implied clause that the validity of the transaction is subject to its conformity with the conditions laid

---

22 Though the question is referred to R. Ashi, the answer is anonymous and does not follow the usual introductory clause *amar le*. However, in bB.B.48b and bGit.73a, it does. See J. Kaplan, *The Redaction of the Babylonian Talmud* (New York, 1933) p. 35 and p. 40.
23 b.Jev.90b; bGit.33a; bGit.73a; bKet.3a.
24 b.B.B.48b.
25 On this power see Y.D. Gilat, "A Rabbinical Court may Decree on the Abrogation of a Law of the Torah" (Hebrew) *7-8 Bar Ilan Annual*, (1970), p. 117; Elon, *Jewish Law*, vol. 2, p. 413.

EXTRA-LEGAL CONSIDERATIONS 49

down by the Sages.[26] It should be noted that the power referred to is not the intrinsic power of the Sages, but a conferred power, a power conferred upon the Sages by those who benefit from the institution of marriage.[27] The power of the Sages is derived from the implied clause inserted into the contract of marriage. This legal construction empowers the Sages to annul betrothals which do not conform to the conditions laid down by the Sages prior to the betrothal. Conditions laid down or made known after the betrothal took place do not provide a legal ground for invalidating the betrothal even when it does not conform to them, because the betrothal was not made subject to these conditions.

Various suggestions have been made why this latter dialogue does not occur in the passage containing the Naresh case.[28] The clue is perhaps provided by an important distinction, so far overlooked, which exists between Jevamoth 110a and the other passages. Jevamoth 110a is the only passage among the six mentioned above which records an actual court case; all the other passages deal with different types of legislation (*takkanah* or *gezerah*). Whereas Jevamoth 110a describes an actual event that took place in the past, the other sources describe a hypothetical event that may occur in the future.[29] The power conferred upon the Sages by the implied clause allows the Sages to enact new rules and to lay down new conditions for the validity of a marriage from the day of the enactment onwards but not to enact new conditions retroactively so as to affect marriages made prior to the time of the enactment. The conferred power excludes any retroactive effect from the conditions laid down by the Sages. It follows that whereas the conferred power referred to in the anonymous dialogue does empower the Sages to enact new rules with regard to future mar-

---

26 The legal construction of inserting an implied clause into the contract of marriage was also used by Hillel in the Alexandrian case. See Cohen, note 6 above; S. Atlas, "Kol Demekadesh Adeata Derabanan Mekadesh," 75 *Sinai* (1974) p. 119.
27 The distinction between the intrinsic power and the conferred power is indicated by the Tosafoth on bJev.110a; See Elon, *op. cit.* p. 524.
28 Tosafoth on bB.B.48b; Elon, *op. cit.* p. 519; Atlas, *op. cit. ibid.*
29 Concerning bB.B.48b (which also has the formula "He acted improperly") and its relation to bJev 110a, see H. Ben Menahem, "Hu Assa Shelo Kahogen," 81 *Sinai*, (1977) p. 156. See also D. Weiss Halivni, *Sources and Traditions on Seder Nashim* (Tel-Aviv, 1968) p.530, n.2.

riages, it does not allow the judges in the Naresh case to annul retroactively the marriage of the kidnapper. Hence, the dialogue is not relevant to the ruling in the Naresh case, and consequently it does not appear in Jevamoth 110a.

While the anonymous dialogue seeks the authority-granting rules which empower the Sages to enact new legislation contrary to Biblical law, the Rabina-Rav Ashi dialogue seeks the validity-determining rules which enable the court to annul the marriage by cohabitation of the kidnapper.[30] Rabina argues that the second marriage could have been effectively annulled if the betrothal had been done with money, in which case the court could have confiscated the money and consequently the marriage would have been cancelled. But, asks Rabina, what if the betrothal had been done through cohabitation? Rabina's question refers to the effectiveness of the decision and not to its rightfulness.[31] Hence, the Rabina-R. Ashi dialogue does not warrant the conclusion that R. Ashi considered the ruling to be based on legal grounds; it was effective, even though not rightful.[32]

3.2 The Case of the Fictitious Transaction

The concept of extra-legal judicial reaction to wrongful conduct similarly appears in the following case:

17   I. A certain slave was owned by two, and one of them emancipated his half. The other thereupon thought to himself: If the Rabbis hear of that,

---

30 On the distinction between "authority-granting rule" and "validity-determining rule," see text accompanying note 74 in Chapter 6 below.

31 This is also indicated by the answer given, which is that the court would have to employ a legal fiction regarding the cohabitation as fornication. On legal fiction in Talmudic law, see S. Atlas, "Haarama Mishpatit Batalmud," *Festschrift fur Levi Ginzburg*, (New York, 1946) pp. 1-24; S. Zuri, "Hahashava Hahukit Batalmud," *Festschrift fur B. Levin*, (Jerusalem, 1939) p. 174; C. Chernowitz, *Toledoth haHalakhah* (New York (1945) vol. 1, pp. 179-84; Zeitlin, "The Halakhah," 39 *J.Q.R.* (N.S. 1948-9) p. 28; S. Shilo, "Circumvention of the Law in Talmudic Literature," *Israel L.R.* vol. 17 (1982) p.151.

32 Greene seems to contradict himself when equating the term *shelo kahogen* with the term *shelo kadin* (*op. cit. supra* note 7, p. 165) and then, a few lines later claiming that "Rabbis Beruna and Hananel were apparently acting according to the Halakhah."

they will force me to give him up. So he went and transferred him to his son who was still under age.

II. R. Joseph b. Raba submitted the case before R. Papa. He sent back:

IIIa. As he has done so it shall be done to him; his dealing shall return upon his head.

IIIb. We all know that a child is fond of money; we shall therefore appoint for him a guardian and he will rattle some coins before the child; and he will write out a deed of emancipation for the slave in his name.[33]

The master's fear that he would be compelled to set his slave free was based on the Mishnaic ruling that "One who is half-free and half-slave ... his master is compelled to liberate him"[34] (and the free man is now indebted to his former master for the value of his half-share). To avoid this dire consequence the master transferred his slave to his minor son. As a result of this fictitious transaction the slave became the property of the minor,[35] and would have to remain in slavery since minors are not subject to any coercive orders.[36]

This transfer presented a dilemma which is characteristic of many other fictitious transactions. On the one hand, the transaction, if considered valid, would frustrate a legal rule (that is, the Mishnaic rule of requiring the half-slave to be emancipated). Yet no offense was committed in making the transaction. When faced with this dilemma, R. Joseph b. Rava sent the case to R. Papa.

Passage III (a & b) constitutes R. Papa's reply. Internal considerations suggest that the passage is composed of two parts: R. Papa's original reply (IIIa) and an explanation that was later attached to it (IIIb). The distinctions between the two are clear and can easily be drawn: R. Papa's reply is in Hebrew, while the explanation attached to it is in Aramaic. Part IIIa is a general formula with no direct reference to

---

33 bGit.40a-b. See Dik. Sof. on Gittin (ed. Feldblum, New York 1966) *ad loc.*

34 mGit.4:5.

35 Minors have power, granted to them by the Sages, to become the owners of property, if that property was given to them by others. See mB.B.9:7; tKet.10:2; bB.M.72a.

36 For a similar fictitious transaction of transferring property to a minor, see bB.M.72a; but see also bB.M.90b, where such a fictitious transferring is recommended.

the case under consideration; part IIIb refers directly to the case under consideration, showing how the formula can effectively be applied to it.[37]

The formula in IIIa is an adaptation of a Biblical verse[38] which expresses the idea of measure for measure and resembles the formula of "he acted improperly therefore he was treated improperly."[39]

---

37   The proposition that IIIb does not form a part of R. Papa's original reply is supported by the following arguments:
   1.   The Meiri (on Gittin 40b; see also *Ozar Hageonim ad loc.*) reports that he found in an "old and exact manuscript of the Talmud" that R. Papa's reply contained only part IIIa.
   2.   In contrast with part IIIa, part IIIb has many variant readings in the various MSS and Rishonim. See Dik. Sof. *ad loc.* On the significance of variant readings in determining the literary development of the *sugya*, see S. Friedman, "A Critical Study of Yevamoth X with a Methodological Introduction," *Text and Studies* (ed. H.Z. Dimetrovsky, The Jewish Theological Seminary of America, New York, 1977) p. 275 at p. 301 ff.
   3.   Part IIIb has the following elements:
        a. The appointment of a guardian.
        b. The rattling of some coins before the child.
        c. The writing of a deed of emancipation for the slave. This part is rather obscure and a good indication of its obscurity is the great number of contradictory interpretations given to it by the Rishonim. It does not specify who is the agent in element 3. Moreover, it is not clear why all these elements are required. The obscurity of the passage also indicates a later insertion. In fact, the passage is a citation from bB.B.156a.
38   Obadias 15. See also bB.M.101b; Bamidbar Rabba 11; see also bB.M90a-b.
39   Commenting on the above case, Neusner (*History of the Jews in Babylonia* (Leiden, 1970) vol. 5, p. 305) has the following to say: "Technicalities of property law and not considerations of humanitarianism governed their (the Rabbis') actions. The fact that the Rabbis would force a man to allow his slave to purchase the unfree part of himself tells us merely that the Rabbis disliked an anomalous situation, not that on principle they made the effort to help the slave to free himself." However, the reasoning of the case which is embodied in the formula "As he has done so it shall be done to him," clearly negates Neusner's argument. The emphasis is placed on the improper conduct of the master towards his slave. Clearly it was not a mere dislike of legal anomaly. The principle enunicated in mGit.4:5, which R. Papa attempted to preserve, even though in this particular case it was contrary to law, was predicated exclusively on humanitarian grounds.

EXTRA-LEGAL CONSIDERATIONS

The question is whether the difference between the two formulas is merely verbal or whether the distinction is more fundamental. R. Tam is of the opinion that the difference is fundamental. He explicitly distinguishes between the "As he has done so it shall be done to him" formula and the "He acted improperly therefore he was treated improperly" formula, arguing that had R. Papa meant to deviate from the law he would have employed the latter formula which is used in the Naresh case. Because a different formula is employed in the present case, R. Tam infers that R. Papa's ruling was intended to be in accordance with the law.[40]

However, the formula in the present case plays a different role than the one employed in the Naresh case. In Naresh, the formula provides an explanation for an already decided case; hence it uses the past tense, "therefore they treated him improperly" (*lefikakh asu imo*). In the present (half-slave) case, the formula is introduced as a proposed ruling for a case not yet decided, and aims at directing the court in its decision-making process. Hence it uses the future tense, "so it shall be done to him" (*ken ye'ase lo*). It follows that the "He acted improperly" formula in its exact form could not be employed by R. Papa in the present case. Consequently not much weight can be assigned to the verbal difference between the two formulas.[41]

According to R. Tam, part IIIb demonstrates how the intention of the father may be frustrated by legal means. This view however is difficult to maintain. The Tosefta in Terumoth records a dispute between the Sages and Rabbi concerning the power of a guardian to emancipate the slave of one who is under his guardianship.[42] R. Tam is correct in stating that once a guardian is appointed he can emancipate the slave either directly (according to Rabbi) or through selling him to others who would liberate him (according to the Sages).[43] The

---

40 Tosafoth on Git.40b. The argument may derive *prima facie* support from bKet.86a where it appears that R. Papa was indeed familiar with the "He acted improperly" formula. Among others who share this view are the Meiri *ad loc.* and Ritba *ad loc.*
41 See Tashbetz, Responsa, Part 2, §3, and Maharik, Responsa, §29. See also Zuri, *op. cit.* p. 68.
42 tTer.1:10; tB.B.8:14; bGit.52a.
43 For an explanation of the Sages' view, see Rashi on Git. *ad loc.*; Tosafoth on Gittin 38b.

difficulty, however, is why a guardian should be appointed in the first place. The child's father was still alive and he did not act against the financial interests of his son, which would justify the appointment of a guardian.[44] Indeed, the appointment of a guardian is regarded by some traditional commentators as the court's deviation from the law.[45]

Further support to the view that the two formulas merely differ in their verbal formulation is provided by Rashbam. In his commentary to the *sugya*, Rashbam explicitly refers to the "He acted improperly" formula, equating it with the "As he has done" formula.

The cases discussed in this chapter demonstrate a Talmudic conception that the judge's role is not confined to applying or interpreting existing legal principles. Rather, on occasion, judges are empowered to render judicial rulings with an overt declaration that their decision is not based on traditional sources, texts, precedents and practices, or even on conventional morality. The famous saying, "Governed by rules and not by men," which reflects the ideal of Western civilization, does not accord with this Talmudic conception. It has been suggested that at the base of the classical Western conception is a litigant who has come to court to claim his due rather than to plead for succor from the judges. The Western litigant claims that he is entitled to a favorable ruling. By necessity, such a claim is based on the court's subordination to an integrated set of standards from which no departure is permitted, and which, in the litigant's view, entitles him as a matter of right to a favorable ruling. In a Talmudic court, a litigant cannot by right claim a favorable ruling, even though a legal rule exists in his favor. He is in a position of merely requesting the judges to come to his aid because his situation merits such relief. In a real sense, the maxim reading "Governed by men and not by rules" would more faithfully express the Talmudic conception. But this viewpoint and the judicial conduct which it generates were not universally accepted by Talmudic Sages. The next chapter proposes that a fundamental difference exists between the Palestinian and the Babylonian Talmudim regarding the acceptability of this practice of judicial deviation from the law based upon extra-legal considerations.

---

44 See Tur Hoshen Mishpat, ch. 290, §§ 5 and 9, and the accompanying commentary of Beth Yoseph; Gulak, *Jesodoth Hamishpat Haivri* (Berlin 1922) vol. 3, p. 147; *ET*, vol. 2, p. 129.
45 See Ran *ad loc.* and Rashbam in Tosafoth on bGit.40b.

CHAPTER 4

TWO CONCEPTS OF JUDICIAL POWER: YERUSHALMI VERSUS BAVLI

4.1 Introduction

This chapter seeks to demonstrate that the two Talmudim differ fundamentally in their view of the concept of judicial power. The Yerushalmi seems to hold that the power of a judge is strictly limited to applying the halakhah proper to the facts of the case before him; it does not consider extra-legal reasons as acceptable grounds for a judicial decision. The Bavli, by contrast, adopts a more flexible attitude; occasionally it recognizes the power of a judge to exceed the limits of the law.

This difference in attitude is manifested on two levels. First, the legal notion of judicial power endorsed by the Yerushalmi is narrower than that endorsed by the Bavli. This will be shown by analyzing power-conferring rules which grant judges the authority to deviate from the law. As will be seen, such an analysis reveals that the Yerushalmi limits the scope of these power-conferring rules much more than does the Bavli.

But a legal notion of limited judicial power does not in itself imply that the Yerushalmi does not permit judges to deviate from the law. By definition, deviations cannot be authorized by a norm or they cease to be deviations. Hence, in order to defend the assertion that the Yerushalmi does not consider extra-legal reasons to be acceptable grounds for judicial decisions, one must look for supporting evidence outside the framework of legal norms. Such supporting evidence may be found in the discrepancies between parallel traditions reporting judicial decisions. Judicial decisions which are presented by the Bavli as being based on extra-legal considerations are reported by the Yerushalmi with no reference to extra-legal considerations. It is not the aim of this study to establish the comparative veracity of competing accounts. Rather, it seeks to demonstrate that the different versions reflect different concepts of judicial power, formed by those responsible for the Talmudim. For the purpose of the present discussion, this chapter ignores the issue of textual analysis and the problem of the different layers of which both Talmudim are composed. Rather, it provides an analysis of the material from a synoptic point of view.

The first section of this chapter presents a detailed comparative analysis of cases recorded in the two Talmudim and demonstrates that the Yerushalmi systematically excludes any allusion to extra-legal reasoning from its exposition of the cases. The second section shows how power-conferring rules bearing on the issue are limited by the Yerushalmi, with no parallel restrictions in the Bavli. The concluding section presents further supporting evidence for the claim that the Yerushalmi insists on strict adherence to the law, and offers a historical explanation for this phenomenon.

To be sure, the analysis that follows establishes only that there is disagreement between the two sources in all the cases discussed. However, one cannot resist the suggestion that these apparently unrelated dissimilarities, rather than being incidental and due to the imperfections of oral transmission, reflect a common basic difference in the conceptualization of judicial power.

A. *The Case of Pishon*

The Mishnah in Jev.13:1 records a dispute between Beth Shammai and Beth Hillel with regard to the scope and procedure of the right of refusal, *meun*.[1]

18 Beth Shammai ruled: Only those who are betrothed may exercise the right of refusal;[2] but Beth Hillel ruled both those who are betrothed and

---

1 A fatherless minor girl who was married off by her mother or brothers has the right to declare, upon attaining majority, that she does not wish to be married to her husband. This declaration is called *meun*. See *Judaica* vol. 5, p. 425.
2 Traditional commentators such as Ramban, Ritba, Rosh and Meiri infer, from the fact that the Mishnah uses the masculine gender *mema'nin* and not the feminine gender *mema'not*, that the Mishnah refers to the Beth Din and not to the minors themselves; that is to say, Beth Din is entitled to accept a declaration of refusal only from those who are betrothed, etc.

those who are married ... Beth Shammai ruled: The declaration of refusal must be made in the presence of the husband;³ but Beth Hillel ruled whether in his presence or not in his presence. Beth Shammai ruled: The declaration must be made before Beth Din; but Beth Hillel ruled whether before Beth Din or not before Beth Din.

In an attempt to invalidate the view of Beth Shammai, that the right of refusal may be exercised only by the betrothed and must be made in the presence of the husband, Beth Hillel cite a recorded case from which it appears that a declaration of refusal need not be made in the presence of the husband and may be exercised by a married minor as well as by a betrothed.

19 It was taught. Beth Hillel said to Beth Shammai: Did not the wife of Pishon the camel driver make her declaration in his absence?⁴

---

3   A betrothed is sometimes referred to as the husband; see Meiri on the Mishnah.
4   bJev.107b; yJev.13:1 (13,3). mJev.13:1 is composed of four disputes and one debate between the Schools. The debate is not related to any of the antecedent disputes. The Baraita concerning Pishon directly refers to the third dispute listed in the Mishnah. One would assume that had the Baraita been available it would have made a better debate to attach to the Mishnah than the existing one. Moreover, Neusner comments on the tradition concerning Pishon that "it looks to me like an artificial construction, showing what each House theoretically might make of a known case. Pishon looks like a name formed of KPYSH, and the story seems a play on words." (Neusner, *The Rabbinic Tradition About the Pharisees before 70*, (Leiden, 1971) vol. 2, p. 200). These and the additional fact that the case of Pishon does not occur elsewhere (Neusner, *ibid.* vol. 3, p. 196) would suggest that the Baraita was formed later than the compilation of the Mishnah. However, the tradition does not include any novel issue apart from the position of Beth Shammai (as expressed in their reply; see below), and even this is restricted to a particular case. I can see no reason for inventing such a Baraita when the halakhah had already been fixed according to Beth Hillel. As to Neusner's point, the identification of Pishon as a camel driver, which has nothing in common with "kpysha," clearly indicates that an actual human being is referred to. If there is any play on words it must be in the other direction, that the name Pishon inspired Beth Shammai to formulate their reply in the way they did. On *kfysha* see also Tanhuma (Buber) Tazria, 8.

The case of Pishon the camel driver is reported without giving the court's reasons for its ruling. However, it explicitly states that a declaration of refusal was made in the absence of the husband. In order to reconcile their view with this recorded case, Beth Shammai argue that Pishon the camel driver acted unfairly towards his wife and therefore the court dealt with him with unusual severity. In other words, in this case the court deviated from the established rule. Consequently, the case is an exception which does not represent the law.

> Beth Shammai answered Beth Hillel: Pishon the camel driver used a reversible measure, therefore, they also used a reversible measure against him.

The Baraita does not reveal the exact nature of Pishon's unfair act, and this is discussed in the Talmud.[5] Suffice it to observe that, according to Beth Shammai, Pishon's unfair act provided sufficient justification for the court to deviate from the law. As previously mentioned, Pishon's case is reported without the reasons for the court's decision. Beth Shammai fill the gap by ascribing extra-legal reasoning to the court. It should be noted that the need for ascribing extra-legal reasoning arises only according to Beth Shammai; Beth Hillel would argue that Pishon's case is based on the law without any extra-legal reasoning being involved. Nevertheless, Beth Hillel accept Beth Shammai's answer as a legitimate one. This can be deduced from the fact that Beth Shammai's response is not followed by any further comment.[6] This acceptance of Beth Shammai's reply as legitimate also emerges from the Bavli. The *sugya* in bJev. contains no comment on Beth Shammai's answer, and we may thus conclude that the compiler of the *sugya* considered the technique of ascribing extra-legal reasoning

---

5 bJev.107b. Apparently he was encroaching upon his wife's *melog* property.
6 Silence is significant in Tannaitic and Amoraic discourse in that it implies assent. See bBer.11a; bNidda 52b; bNazir 32a; bShab.15a; *ibid.* 29b, and especially bB.K.11a. See also S. Zeitlin, "Spurious Interpretations of Rabbinic Sources in the Studies of the Pharisees and Pharisaism," 65 *J.Q.R.* (1974-75) p. 122 at p. 133; R. Margalioth, *Mehqarim Bedarke ha-Talmud ve-Hidotav*, (Jerusalem, 1967) pp. 90-96 and the comment of R. Fishman in *Azqara to Rav Kook* (Jerusalem, 1938) vol. 3, p. 219. See further bB.K20b; bB.M.37b; bJev.87b.

to recorded cases, in order to remove the difficulty which they pose, as an acceptable approach.

In the Yerushalmi, the same dialogue between Beth Shammai and Beth Hillel is reported with some slight variations. Unlike the Bavli, however, the Yerushalmi is not content with Beth Shammai's answer. The Yerushalmi records the dialogue in the following way:

20 Said Beth Hillel to Beth Shammai: It once happened with the wife of Pishon the camel driver that the Sages exercised on her behalf the right of refusal in the absence of her husband. Said Beth Shammai to Beth Hillel: Is there proof from there? He used a reversible measure; the Sages therefore also used a reversible measure against him.[7]

The Yerushalmi, as opposed to the Bavli, continues with the following comment:

And [Beth Shammai's answer] is objectionable; should one act blamefully, would we liberate his wife?

That is, if the declaration of refusal made by Pishon's wife was not legally valid, as Beth Shammai argue, how did the court permit her to remarry without a letter of divorce?

This objection does not occur in the Bavli. On the contrary, we saw that the Bavli justified a previous case involving the validity of a marriage on extra-legal grounds: that the court may deviate from the law if one of the litigants acted unfairly.[8] But this principle, employed here by Beth Shammai, is not accepted by the Yerushalmi, whose tendency is to limit the power of the court to that of strict enforcement of the law. Hence its objection that Pishon's unfair act cannot justify any deviation from the law.

To meet this objection, the Yerushalmi modifies the view of Beth Shammai, saying in the name of R. Hisda[9] that even Beth Shammai agree that a declaration of refusal made either by a married minor or by a betrothed in the absence of her husband,[10] is valid in spite of the

---

7 yJev.13:1 (13,3).
8 bJev.110a. See text accompanying note 9 in Chapter 3 above.
9 Rashba on bJev.107b reads here R. Isaac.
10 According to Aruch (v. *kafash*) and Tosafoth (on bJev.107b) who insert "and not in his [husband's] presence."

prohibition. That is to say, the Mishnah quoted above presents only the view of Beth Shammai in the first instance (*l'chatchilah*). After the fact however (that is, if a declaration of refusal actually was made), it would be valid even if it took place under imperfect conditions (in the absence of the betrothed or after the marriage). It follows that even according to Beth Shammai[11] the court in Pishon's case based its decision on the law and not on extra-legal considerations.

The Yerushalmi's modification of the view of Beth Shammai demonstrates its objection to extra-legal reasoning, but it also raises the following difficulty: If the court followed the law in accepting the declaration of Pishon's wife, what is the meaning of Beth Shammai's answer? To what does "the court dealt with him unfairly" refer? To answer this question, we must look at another difference between the Bavli version of the Baraita and that of the Yerushalmi. In the Yerushalmi we read:

> It once happened with the wife of Pishon the camel driver that the Sages exercised on her behalf the right of refusal ...

That the Sages exercised the right of refusal on behalf of Pishon's wife is not mentioned in the Bavli. It is clear that the declaration must be made by the minor in person.[12] Apparently the Yerushalmi means that the Sages informed Pishon's wife that should she declare her refusal, the declaration would be valid. The policy of the Sages was to minimize the exercise of the right of refusal.[13] Only in a very limited number of cases would the Sages inform minors about their right of refusal. In the case of Pishon it was his unfair behavior that induced the Sages to inform his wife that she could declare her refusal. Thus, according to the Yerushalmi, the court's unfair treatment of Pishon consists in its deviation from the accepted policy, not in its employment of extra-legal considerations to arrive at its decision.

---

11 Traditional commentators (see note 2 above) in their attempt to harmonize the two Talmudim argue that this is the case also according to the Bavli.
12 mJev.13:7, 11; mEd. 6:1.
13 bJev.109a; but see note 2 above.

B. *The Case of the Needy Father*

The Mishnah in BB.8:7 deals with a situation in which a person in good health desires to transfer ownership of his estate to his sons but wishes to retain the income from it during his lifetime. A case in point is one who intends to marry for a second time and wants to protect the sons from his first marriage from a possible seizure of his estate by his second wife in payment of her *kethubah*. The Mishnah states:

21 Whoever assigns his goods to his sons must write: "From today and after death." These are the words of R. Judah. R. Jose says: He need not do so [i.e., the words "from today" are not necessary].

The Talmud concludes that the halakhah is according to R. Jose. A person who desires to leave his estate to his son after his death and to retain the income from it during his lifetime need only write, "This estate is assigned after my death."[14]

If a person assigns his estate to his son, but does not write the words "after my death," the estate becomes the property of the son as soon as the written document is delivered to him. The father is then excluded from the present income from the estate, which no longer belongs to him. But is the father entitled to maintenance from the estate? The Talmud in Kethuboth records the following tradition:

22 R. Elai stated in the name of Resh Lakish: It was enacted in Usha that if a person assigned all his goods to his sons in writing, he [the father] and his wife are nevertheless maintained out of it.[15]

According to the Usha regulations, a father who assigned his estate to his sons in writing without adding the crucial words "after my death"[16] is nevertheless entitled to be maintained from the estate.

---

14 bB.B.136a; Yaron, *Gifts in Contemplation of Death in Jewish and Roman Law* (Oxford, 1960) p. 114; G. Blidstein, *Honor Thy Father and Mother. Filial Responsibility in Jewish Laws and Ethics* (New York, 1975) p. 62.
15 bKet. 49b; yKet. 4:8 (28,4).
16 See R. Nissim on Kethuboth *ad loc.*

62   DEVIATION IN TALMUDIC LAW

After reporting the tradition of R. Elai, the Talmud asks whether the law is in agreement with the Usha regulations. To answer this question,[17] the following story is cited:

23 R. Hanina and R. Jonathan[18] were once standing together when a man approached them and bending down kissed R. Jonathan on his foot.[19] "What is the meaning of this?" said R. Hanina to R. Jonathan. The other replied, "This man assigned his estate to his sons in writing and I made them (*asitinhu*) maintain him."

The Talmud infers from this story that the law is not in agreement with the Usha regulations.[20]

> Now if it be conceded that this was not in accordance with the law one can well understand why he had to "make" them, but if it be contended that this is the law would it have been necessary for him to "make" them?

What does "to make" mean? Does it involve coercion or does it merely refer to persuasion? This is debated by Tosafoth and Rashi. The Tosafoth explain that *asitinhu* means "I persuaded them [to support him]."[21] The above passage should accordingly be understood as

---

17   According to the accepted view, the Usha regulations were enacted by the Sanhedrin when it was sitting in Usha after the Bar-Kokhba Revolt (middle of the second century C.E.). According to this view the question whether the law is in agreement with the Usha regulation seems strange. Rif and Rosh omit the opening "It was enacted at Usha," thereby removing the difficulty. Mantel argues that these regulations were enacted at Usha by a local court at a later period, and hence were not necessarily in accordance with the law. See "Zemanan shel Takanot Usha," 34, *Tarbiz* (1964-65) pp. 281-3.

18   Both Amoraim, who lived in Palestine at the beginning of the third century, were pupils of R. Judah Hanasi.

19   Bending down and kissing one's foot appears to be a form of gratitude especially in matters connected with trials and courts; see bSanh.27b; see also bB.B.16a.

20   This is the final view of the Talmud. In accordance with this we read in bB.M.75b: "Our Rabbis taught: Three cry out and are not answered . . . he who acquires a master for himself. What does this mean? He who transfers his property to his children during his lifetime . . . ."

21   Tosafoth on bKet. *ad loc*. Tosafoth's interpretation is probably inspired by yKid.1:7 (61,1), "He came and tried to persuade him but to no avail." This passage, however, clearly shows that a different and a more

follows: If the law is that they are not bound to support him, then R. Jonathan had to persuade them; but if the law requires them to support their father, what necessity was there to persuade them? It follows that the law is not in agreement with the Usha regulations. According to this interpretation, R. Jonathan did not deviate from the law since he did not use any coercion to compel the sons to support their father. As will be seen below, however, the difficulty with this interpretation is that *ase* has a different meaning than "to persuade."[22] Rashi explains that *ase* means "I compelled them," that is, R. Jonathan used coercion to compel the sons to maintain their father. But since coercion, in itself, does not indicate that the ruling is not in accordance with the law,[23] Rashi explains that the Talmud's inference that the law is not in agreement with the Usha regulations [R. Jonathan's ruling] is based on the fact that the father bent down and kissed R. Jonathan upon his foot as a form of gratitude. Had R. Jonathan ruled according to the strict law, the father would not have thanked R. Jonathan[24] so profusely. The crucial question, then, hinges on the correct meaning of *ase*.

From a close examination of the various sources in which *ase* occurs it appears that this is a technical term denoting compulsion, especially compulsory enforcement by a court of law.[25] The linguistic

---

    direct term is used when persuasion is at issue. See also Jastrow, s.v. *ase*, who reads "I persuaded them to support him" though he himself renders *ase* "to force." See also N. Berggruen "Talmudic Dictionary," *Lesonenu*, vol. 32 (1968) p. 117.

22 The Tosafoth (*ibid.*) are aware of this difficulty. The Tosafoth cite bKet.53a as an example of using *ase* as mere persuasion. But this is not at all clear. In any event this Talmudic passage does not adhere to common terminology; it uses the term *kafa* for persuasion, whereas it usually denotes coercion.

23 *Cf.* Soncino edition (Kethuboth 49b) and Yaron (*op. cit. supra* note 14, p. 28) who apparently dismiss the possibility of the law being enforced by coercion.

24 Rashi on Ket. *ad loc.*: "R. Jonathan ruled *lifhtm mishurat hadin*."

25 A few examples will suffice to show the connection between *ase* and coercion by a court:

evidence seems to support Rashi's view that *ase* means to "compel." R. Jonathan, in response to R. Hanina's query why a certain man kissed his foot, replies that he forced the man's sons to maintain him and that the man, knowing that coercion under the prevailing circumstances was not prescribed by law, kissed his foot as a token of gratitude. The Talmud concludes from this reply and from the setting of the story that R. Jonathan's ruling, albeit complying with the Usha regulations, was not in accordance with the law. It should be noted that the Bavli is not troubled by the conclusion that a particular judicial decision was not made in accordance with the law, and it does not seek to harmonize it with the prevailing law.

The Yerushalmi's version of the incident is significantly different:[26]

25 R. Jonathan and R. Yanai were sitting. A certain man came up and kissed R. Jonathan upon his feet. R. Yanai asked: What does he owe you?[27] R. Jonathan answered: Once this man came before me complaining about his son that he does not support him. I told him to announce this in the Synagogue in public in order to shame him. R. Yanai asked: And why did you not compel the son to support his father? R. Jonathan said: Can one compel thus? R. Yanai answered: And do you still ponder on that?[28]

---

1) "And Thou Shalt Do:" this is an instruction to the Beth Din to make thee (*sheyiasukh*) do it. bR.H.6a.
2) The judge decides the law and the officer enforces (*mease*) the law. Peskita Rabbati 33.
3) A letter of divorce given under force (*hameuse*) if forced by a Jewish court is valid. Mekhilta, ed. Horovitz, p. 246; mGit.9:8; see also tJev.12:13.
4) We do not force (*measin*) a man to divorce his wife except in the case of those who are disqualified to their husbands. bKet.77a. See also bGit.88b and bKet.53a. The Hebrew sources for the examples cited in this footnote appear in Appendix, no. 24.

26 Yerushalmi Pea 1:1 (15,4); Kid.1:7 (61,3). See M. Ratner, *Ahavat Zion Veyerushalim* on Pea p. 10. A slightly different version is recorded in Pesikta Rabbati 23. Tosafoth on bKid.32a seems to be a paraphrase of yPea rather than a different version of it. See, however, Yalkut Shimoni 297, which differs substantially from the Yerushalmi.

27 According to S. Lieberman, *Hayerushalmi Kiphshuto* (Jerusalem, 1934) p. 11 (*mavo*).

28 See Z. Frankel, *Mevo Hayerushalami* (Breslau, 1870 rep. Jerusalem, 1967) p. 143b.

From that day onward R. Jonathan stated that the law was that sons should be compelled to support their father.

From the detailed dialogue between R. Jonathan and R. Yanai it is evident that the former did not compel the son to support his father because he thought that compulsion under the prevailing circumstances was not warranted by the law. This dialogue displays an entirely different attitude of R. Jonathan from the one ascribed to him in the Bavli. The "Babylonian" R. Jonathan does not hesitate to compel the son to maintain his father although he is aware of the fact that the law does not authorize him to do so. The "Palestinian" R. Jonathan, on the other hand, is reluctant to deviate from the law, and instructs the father to use social pressure in order to persuade the son to support him. Assaf has pointed out that not a single instance of such social pressure can be found in the Bavli.[29] Apparently, according to their concept of judicial power, Babylonian Amoraim would use their authority to penalize or to coerce whenever they deemed it appropriate and did not need to resort to the device of social pressure.[30]

In the Yerushalmi the circumstances of the case are slightly different from those in the Bavli. According to the Bavli the complaining father had assigned his estate to his son in writing but wanted nevertheless to be supported out of it. In the Yerushalmi, the father's claim was apparently based on the precept of *tsedakah*, charity.

Yaron notes that the Usha regulations, which provide that one who assigns his property to his sons is nevertheless entitled to be supported out of it, "was accepted as a good law by the Palestinian Talmud."[31] This observation would help to explain the difference

---

29 See S. Assaf, *Batei Din Vesidrehem Aharei Tekufat Hatalmud* (Jerusalem, 1925) pp. 25-26. On the significance and procedure of this social pressure, see also L. Finkelstein, *Jewish Self-Government In the Middle Ages*, (New York, 1964) p. 16, note 1 and p. 382; D. Patterson, "Ancient Hebrew Law in Modern Hebrew Literature," in *Daube Festschrift* (Oxford, 1974) 169, 173; A. Grossman, "The Origins and Essence of the Custom of Stopping the Service" (Hebrew) in Milet, *Everyman's University Studies in Jewish History and Culture*, vol. 1 (Tel-Aviv, 1983) p. 199, and the literature cited there.
30 *Cf.* Assaf, *op. cit.* p. 25, n. 1.
31 Yaron *op. cit. supra* note 14, p. 28. See yKet.4:8 (28,4).

between the two Talmudim with regard to the ground for the claim. The Yerushalmi is anxious to emphasize that R. Jonathan refrained from using coercion where he thought the law did not sanction it (as evidenced from the dialogue between R. Jonathan and R. Yanai). Had the Yerushalmi reported the case according to the Babylonian version, the story would have been superfluous since according to the Yerushalmi R. Jonathan was allowed, in fact was obliged, to compel the son to support his father. The Usha regulations could not possibly have slipped R. Jonathan's mind and he could not credibly have been presented as ignorant of the sons' duty to support their father.

By contrast, the obligation to support a needy father which is derived from the precept of *tsedakah* was not regulated and was probably less known.[32] Hence it is a more likely candidate for a law with which R. Jonathan might not be familiar, and it makes it possible to interpret his decision as illustrating his adherence to the law.

C. *The Case of the Sons of Rokhel*

The Mishnah in B.B.9:7 reads as follows:

26 If a person distributed his possessions orally, R. Eliezer said: Whether he was healthy or dangerously ill, goods for which there is security [i.e., real property] are acquired by money or by deed or by *hazaqa* while those for which there is no security [personal property] are acquired only by drawing. They said to him: It once happened that the mother of the sons of Rokhel was sick and said, "Let my veil be given to my daughter," and it was worth twelve hundred denars, and she died and they fulfilled (*vkeymu*) her words. He said to them: May their mother bury the sons of Rokhel.

The Mishnah records a dispute between the Sages and R. Eliezer[33] concerning the modes of acquisition which must be employed in order to effectuate a disposition of property by a sick person in contempla-

---

32 See yGit.9:9 (50,4) and Tosafoth on bKid.32a. See also G. Blidstein, *op. cit., supra* note 14, Chapter 3.
33 The correct reading is R. Eliezer and not R. Eleazar; see Albeck *ad loc.*; Schachter, *The Babylonian and Yerushalmi Mishnah*, (Jerusalem, 1959) p. 255; Epstein, *Mavo Lenussach Hamishnah* (Jerusalem, 1940) pp. 134, 1179.

tion of death. The opening of the second sentence implies that a statement by the Sages has already been made, although it is omitted from the present text. The sequence, however, makes it clear that the Sages hold the view that, in the case of a sick donor, verbal instruction is sufficient to effectuate his transfer in contemplation of death.[34] R. Eliezer, on the other hand, maintains that the traditional, formal modes of acquisition are required whether the gift is made by a healthy person or by one who is dying.

Although it is not explcitly stated, it is clear that the case of Rokhel's sons was brought before a court and it was the court's ruling which gave effect to the mother's will. This is evident from two things. First, *kayem* is a technical term, denoting in Tannaitic sources a kind of judicial ratification, especially of deeds and transfers in contemplation of death.[35] In addition, had the sons transferred the veil to their sister without being compelled to do so by the court, the incident could not have served to support the view of the Sages. Only if the sons were deprived of the veil by a judicial decision would the story be relevant in the present context, that is, as an attempt to refute R. Eliezer's view.

R. Eliezer defended his position by tersely dismissing the cited case: "May their mother bury the sons of Rokhel."[36] Many of the traditional commentators point out that the terse dismissal of the case by R. Eliezer is based on the postulate that the case was not decided according to the law but on the basis of an extra-legal consideration. The sons of Rokhel were wicked and therefore the court deviated from the law by granting the veil to the daughter rather than to the sons despite their legal right to it.[37] The case, in R. Eliezer's view, does

---

34 See Yaron, *op. cit.* pp. 49-50.
35 See tB.B.10:6; yJev.2:11 (4,2); bKid.26b.
36 Compare with R. Eliezer's curse in tKellim 1:1; bPes.69a; bAZ.46b; bB.B.121b; bSanh.68a. See also Finkelstein, *The Pharisees* (Philadelphia, 1946) p. 48. Compare also with bB.K.80a and bNaz.57b (Albeck, "Leheker Hatalmud," 3 *Tarbiz* (1931-2) p. 13).
37 See Rashbam, Rabenu Gershom, Bartenura, Rema and Meiri *ad loc.*; Melechet Shelomo, *ad loc.* For a different interpretation see Rashi on bGit.15a. The Meiri apparently qualifies the principle that the court may base its decision on extra-legal considerations to the effect that one who is not formally a litigant in a trial should not benefit from the court's decision. This qualification is meant to preserve the principle of the

not represent the general rule regulating disposition of transfers in contemplation of death, and therefore the normative law cannot be inferred from it.

So presented, the pattern of the above Mishnah closely resembles that of the Baraita concerning Pishon the camel driver.[38] Both cases provide proof that the technique of ascribing extra-legal reasoning originated in Tannaitic sources. In both instances an antecedent case is cited in order to refute a certain opinion, after which the author of the attacked opinion rejects the cited case as being atypical by ascribing extra-legal reasoning to the original decision. In both cases, neither the Mishnah nor the Bavli question the technique or raise an objection to it.

As it emerges from the Mishnah, the dispute between the Sages and R. Eliezer in the case of the sons of Rokhel centers on whether the wickedness of the sons provided sufficient grounds to warrant a deviation from the law. R. Eliezer maintains that the court ruled contrary to the law on the basis of the litigants' behavior; whereas the Sages maintain that, *in spite* of their wickedness, the sons of Rokhel were treated according to the law, and that the case represents the halakhah.

The Mishnah, as usual, is very brief and does not indicate what the censurable behavior of the sons of Rokhel was. It must have been a serious violation of the halakhah to incite the use of such strong

---

impartiality of the court. This seems to be the significance of the following comment: "And although they [the court] had to avoid partiality, it appears that the sons did not summon her [their sister] for the veil."

According to the Talmud the improper behavior of the sons of Rokhel involved a violation of one of the laws of *kilayim* (see discussion in text below). From mShekalim 1:2 it appears that the only sanction for violating the laws of *kilayim* is the confiscation of the field itself. The decision also disregards the instruction of Samuel in bB.B.133b, "Keep away from transfers of inheritance even [if they be] from a bad son to a good son, much more so when they are from a son to a daughter." (See also mB.B.8:5). Finally, the decision is opposed to Mekilta (ed. Horovitz) p. 326, which is discussed in Chapter 5 below in the text accompanying note 69. (On this last point see Tiferet Yisrael on the Mishnah *ad loc.*)

38   bJev.107b; yJev.13:1 (13,3).

language by R. Eliezer. The Bavli reports a tradition that the censurable behavior of the sons of Rokhel was their violation of the laws of *kilayim*.

27 Why did R. Eliezer curse them? Rav Judah said in the name of Samuel: They [the sons of Rokhel] allowed thistles to grow in their vineyard.[39]

Allowing thistles to grow in a vineyard is a violation of the laws of *kilayim* only according to R. Eliezer; the Sages do not consider the practice forbidden.[40] The attribution of this controversial behavior to the sons of Rokhel introduces a new element. The dispute between the Sages and R. Eliezer with regard to the case of the sons of Rokhel now appears to originate in their different evaluations of the sons' behavior. According to R. Eliezer their behavior constitutes an offense, whereas according to the Sages it does not.

Why should the Babylonian Talmud attribute such a controversial and strange offense to the sons of Rokhel, who were cursed so vehemently by R. Eliezer? It seems that the Bavli is anxious to dispel the impression that is likely to be gained from the Mishnah, and which was stated above, that the Sages rejected the principle that improper conduct of a litigant may justify a deviation from the law. The Babylonian Talmud stresses that according to the Sages the sons were treated according to the law not in spite of their wickedness (a conclusion that would stand against the principle), but because they were not wicked at all (in which case the decision is compatible with the principle). The Bavli therefore seeks an act which is evaluated differently by the Sages and R. Eliezer and which could be attributed to the sons of Rokhel. mKilayim 5:8 provides such an example. One cannot conclude, then, that the Sages were in disagreement with the principle that the wicked behavior of a litigant may justify a deviation from the law. The Sages would maintain that there was no need to apply the principle in this case.

The Yerushalmi, however, as opposed to the Bavli, attributes to the sons of Rokhel a practice which is an offense not only according to R. Eliezer but also according to the Sages:

---

39 bB.B.156b.
40 mKilayim 5:8.

28 Said R. Yossi b. R. Bun: A pretext; he wanted to curse them because they were sowing saffron in their vineyard.[41]

Sowing saffron in a vineyard, as distinct from growing thistles, is a violation of the laws of *kilayim* according to the Sages as well as according to R. Eliezer.[42] It follows that the Sages who maintain that the case of the sons of Rokhel represents the halakhah (that is, that the sons were treated according to the law), must also maintain that the sons' offense, sowing saffron in their vineyard, was not an acceptable reason for deviating from the law. Thus the Sages' attitude is seen as hostile to the concept that judicial decisions may be justified on the basis of extra-legal considerations. By attributing only to R. Eliezer the view which assumes that extra-legal reasoning may justify a deviation from the law while at the same time showing that the Sages do not share this view, the Yerushalmi displays its disapproval of the use of extra-legal reasoning in judicial decisions.

D. *The Case of Maintenance of Orphans*

The following two case reports are recorded by the Bavli and the Yerushalmi respectively:

29 R. Eleazar intended to allow maintenance out of movable property. Said R. Simeon b. Eliakim to him: Master, I know that in your decision you are not acting on the line of law but on the line of mercy, but [the possibility] ought to be considered that the students might observe this ruling and fix it as an halakhah for future generations.[43]

---

41 Yerushalmi B.B.9:7 (17,2). Levy, *Worterbuch uber die Talmudim*, (Berlin, 1924) vol. 2, p. 406, reads here "Ulla wolte denjenigen fluchen . . . ." *Cf.* Lieberman, *Talmuda shel Kessarin* (Supplement to *Tarbiz*, vol. 2, Jerusalem, 1931) who does not have Ulla in his list of Amoraim in yB.B. Yerushalmi clearly differs from the Bavli in its description of the censurable behavior of the sons of Rokhel (see below). Daiches, however, in his *Netivot Yerushalim* (London, 1928) suggests that the reading in the Yerushalmi should be *kubin* instead of *kurkemin*. *Kubin* is a kind of thistle (see J. Felix, *Agriculture in Palestine in the Period of the Mishnah and Talmud* (Hebrew) (Tel Aviv,1963) p. 43) and thus the two Talmudim are in harmony.
42 mKil.5:8; bB.B.156b; *Netivot Yerushalim, ibid.*
43 bKet.50b.

30 R. Yossa had in his possession orphans' movable property.[44] The daughters of the deceased father claimed their marriage outfit. The case was brought before R. Eleazar and R. Simeon b. Yakim. Said R. Simeon b. Yakim: Is it not better that the daughters would be maintained out of their father's estate rather than from *tsedakah*? Said R. Eleazar:[45] Such a claim if brought before our Masters would be dismissed, are we going to accept it?[46]

It is rather difficult to determine the exact nature of the legal issue involved in this case, since the following two different terms must be distinguished.

1. *Mezonot* (Maintenance). According to the Biblical law, the daughters of a deceased person are not entitled to be supported out of the estate. The Rabbis, however, enacted a *takanah* to the effect that the sons who inherited the estate are obliged to support the daughters out of the estate.[47] The daughters' right to support according to this *takanah* is referred to as the right to *mezonot*.
2. *Parnasah* (Marriage Outfit). According to another *takanah*, the daughters are entitled to a certain portion of the estate when they get married.[48] According to the prevailing law, both *takanoth* entitle the daughters to be paid only out of real property.[49]

The Talmud, however, does not adhere consistently to this terminology; *mezonot* sometimes denotes *parnasah*, and vice versa.[50] As a result, it is almost impossible to determine the subject matter of the case on the basis of linguistic considerations. The fact that the Bavli speaks about *mezonot* as the subject matter of the case, while the Yerushalmi speaks about *parnasah*, does not in itself indicate that two

---

44   See S. Lieberman, *Hayerushalmi Kiphshuto*, (Jerusalem, 1934), p. 20 (*mavo*).
45   In the latter source, R Eleazer's retort indicates that R. Simon b. Yakim was his master (Rabbi); see note 56 below, and bKet.50b.
46   yKet.6:6 (30,4); yGit.5:3 (46,4).
47   mKet.4:11; bKet.52b; B. Schereschewsky, *Family Law in Israel* (Hebrew) (Jerusalem, 1958) p. 352.
48   bKet.68b; Schereschewsky *ibid.*
49   bKet.51a.
50   bKet.50b; 68a. In addition to this, the terms are also used to denote duty of the husband to supply his wife with food and clothing; see bKet.48a.

different cases are recorded. In any event, at this stage the nature of the exact claim of the daughters (*mezonot* or *parnasah*) is not significant, since in either event the daughters are entitled to claim only from real estate.

From the Bavli R. Eleazar emerges as a liberal judge who is willing to depart from the law and "to act on the line of mercy,"[51] whereas R. Simeon b. Eliakim appears as a conservative judge anxious to apply the law literally. The Yerushalmi reverses the roles: R. Simeon b. Yakim intends to depart from the law, whereas R. Eleazar refuses to countenance such a ruling. In both versions the heart of the discussion between the two Rabbis is the right of judges to depart from the law.

It could be argued that the "liberal judge" (R. Eleazar in the Bavli and R. Simeon b. Yakim in the Yerushalmi) does not intend to depart from the law, but rather expresses an opinion on what the law is or should be. That this is not the case can be shown from R. Simeon b. Yakim's own words. Since he must be credited with understanding R. Eleazar's intention, we may learn about the latter's intent from the former's argument. In his argument against R. Eleazar, R. Simeon states, "I know that in your decision you are not acting on the line of law but on the line of mercy." This clearly shows that R. Eleazar did not pretend that his intention to allow support out of personal property was in accordance with the law. From the Yerushalmi it is less clear that R. Simeon b. Yakim intended to depart from the law. However, the style in which R. Simeon's argument is presented ("Is it not better") suggests a challenge to an established rule, and R. Eleazar's response implies that R. Simeon's argument is against the law.

In reporting the Palestinian case, the Bavli puts the following objection in the mouth of the conservative judge, "The possibility ought to be considered that the students might observe this ruling and fix it as an halakhah for future generations." The argument does not state that the court has no power to rule on the basis of extra-legal considerations. On the contrary, the argument implies that the court does in fact have such power. The sole objection to the proposed rul-

---

51 Compare yB.K.8:4 (6,3). On R. Eleazer's approach to mercy see bR.H.17b; yPea 1:1 (16,2); Urbach, *The Sages: Their Concepts and Beliefs*, (Jerusalem, 1975) p. 495.

ing is the fear of a possible undesirable side effect; students might derive a false conclusion of the normative law from the decision.

This latter kind of argument is very often found in Tannaitic discourses,[52] and it reflects awareness of the great importance that students attached to the actions of their Masters. The Rabbis were constantly reminded that their behavior might determine the halakhah in the sense that their student observers might emulate and so perpetuate their modes of conduct.[53] The fear of false deduction is easily understood if we remember that the daily conduct of the Rabbis was not usually accompanied by explanations or reasons. Thus, even if a Rabbi had a good reason in a particular situation to depart from the normal manner of behavior, he was nevertheless advised not to do so in order to prevent the mistaken identification of the exceptional behavior with the actual state of the halakhah.

In the domain of judicial decisions, however, this concern seems misplaced. The daily life of the Rabbis could be considered as a model to be adopted and followed unquestioningly; not so their judicial decisions which are case specific. The judges did not usually reveal the reasons underlying their decisions, but this was a custom from which they could easily depart if they felt a need to do so. In the courtroom a judge was aware of the precedent-setting potential of his ruling, so that when it departed from the accepted law he would be likely to point out the exceptional features of the case in order to eliminate the risk of misconstruction. Indeed, the dialogue between R. Eleazar and R. Simeon b. Eliakim is the only recorded instance in which such a consideration is applied to a judicial decision; in all other cases where this concern is mentioned it refers to the daily behavior of the Rabbis. That this argument did not play, or at least ceased to play, an important role in the process of judicial decisions can be shown from a case recorded in the Bavli, in which R. Nahman was thought to have ruled contrary to the law.[54] R. Huna b. Hiyya, who was present in the court room, asked R. Nahman whether his ruling was in accordance with

---

52 mHalla 4:11; tBer.1:6; 5:2; tPes.8:10; Sifre ad Deut. (ed. Finkelstein) p. 63; yBer.1:3 (3,2); yHalla 4:5 (60,2); yPes.10:1 (37,2); bBer.11a; bPes.100a.
53 mAvot 1:11 and see also E.Z. Melamed, "Hamase Bamishnah Kemakor Lahalakha," 46 *Sinai* (1959-60) 152.
54 bB.K.116b-117a.

the law. Later he explained his question as referring to the possibility of using this ruling as a precedent; had R. Nahman ruled contrary to the law, R. Huna b. Hiyya would simply have concluded that a general principle could not be inferred from the ruling. Notably, there was no objection to the ruling on the ground that it might lead to an incorrect generalization.

To summarize, the objection to ruling against the law which the Bavli attributes to the conservative judge focuses on strategy and not on principle. Furthermore, as was seen, there are ways of meeting this tactical objection, especially where judicial decisions are concerned.

Turning to the Yerushalmi's report, an entirely different approach is encountered. R. Eleazar, who plays the role of the conservative judge in the Yerushalmi, expresses complete and unqualified opposition to judicial departure from the law: "Such a claim if brought before our Masters would be dismissed, are we going to accept it?"[55] Implied in R. Eleazar's question is the authoritarian argument that we are not entitled, or perhaps have no power, to rule against the view of our Masters.

By objecting so absolutely to the idea of departing from the law, the Yerushalmi once again manifests its hostility to extra-legal considerations. It should also be noted that the Yerushalmi adds to the weight of conservative view by ascribing it to R. Eleazar, who was a higher authority than R. Simeon b. Eliakim.[56]

E. *The Case of the Negligent Porters*

The final case to be discussed in this section deals with employer-employee relations. The following are its two versions as reported in

---

[55] yJev.1:2 (3,1); yKid.1:1 (58,4); See also yNid.1:3 (49,1). For R. Eleazer's approach compare yTan.2:14 (66,1). On *maase* see Lieberman, "Sefer Hamasaim," 2 *Tarbiz* (1930-31) 377. In this form the argument appears only in the Yerushalmi; in the Bavli it appears in a less categorical form; see bKet.50b.

[56] Weiss, *Dor Dor veDorshav* (Wien, 1883) vol. 3, pp. 76-8; Halevy, *Doroth Rishonim* (Berlin, 1923) vol. 2, pp. 327-332. The term *amar lefanav* always indicates that the addressee is the master of the addressor; see bHul.98a; bShebu.30b. See, however, the version in yGit.5:3 (46,4). But see Z. Frankel, *Mevo Hayerushalmi* (Breslau 1870, rep. Jerusalem, 1967) p. 129a, and note 45 above.

the Yerushalmi and in the Bavli respectively:

31 It was taught in the name of R. Nehemia:[57] A potter gave his pots to someone who eventually broke them. The potter seized the garment [of the porter]. He came before R. Yossi b. Hanina. Said he to the porter: "Go and tell him *thou shalt walk in the way of the good*."[58] He went and told him; thereupon he returned the garment. He [R. Yossi b. Hanina] asked [the porter]: "Did he pay your wages?" "No", said the other. [R. Yossi b. Hanina] said: "Go and tell him *and the paths of the just shouldst thou keep*." So he went and told him; thereupon he paid his wages.[59]

32 Some porters broke a barrel of wine belonging to Rabba bar Bar Hanan. Thereupon he seized their garments; so they went and complained to Rav. "Return them their garments," he ordered. "Is that the law?"[60] he asked. "Yes," he replied, *Thou shalt walk in the way of the good*. Their garments having been returned, they said: "We are poor men, having worked all day, and are in need; are we to get nothing?" "Go and pay them," he ordered. "Is that the law?" he asked. "Yes," was the reply, *And the paths of the just shouldst thou keep*.[61]

Two legal issues are involved in this case. First, is an employee who caused damages to his employer in the course of his employment liable for the damages? Second, is the employer entitled to set-off the employee's wages against the amount of the damages?

---

57 As it stands the passage poses an historical difficulty. R. Nehemia was a Tanna and therefore could not have reported a case which had been brought before R. Jossi b. Hanina who was an Amora. Various suggestions have been made to avoid this difficulty: *Netivoth Yerushalmi* (London, 1927) *ad loc.*; Rabinowitz, *Sharei Torat Eretz Ysrael* (Jerusalem, 1941) p. 492; Hyman, *Toledoth Tannaim Veamoraim* (London, 1910) p. 976; S. Lieberman, *Talmuda Shel Kessarin*, p. 108; *Yerushalmi Neziqin Escorial Manuscript* (ed. E.S. Rosental, Jerusalem, 1983) *ad loc.*

58 Proverbs 2:20.

59 yB.M. 6:8 (11.1).

60 The question *dina haki* was presented to Rav by one of his disciples in another case, to which Rav did not reply. The Talmud infers from Rav's silence that the law was not in accordance with his ruling, bB.K.11a (bB.M.96b). In another case a litigant asked R. Hisda *dina haki*, bB.M.39b. See also bB.B.29b.

61 bB.M.83a. Rif and Rosh read Rabba b. Rav Huna; see Dik.Sof. *ad loc.*; M. Silberg, *Talmudic Law and the Modern State* (New York 1973), pp. 119-120. The word "Yes" in Rav's reply is missing in some of the early manuscripts of the Talmud. See Dik.Sof. *ad loc.*

On the second issue, the Talmudic principle is that whenever an employee is legally liable to compensate his employer, the latter may set-off the amount of the wages.[62] The crucial question then is the first issue, whether the employee, the porters in our case, was liable to the employer.

As to this first issue, the *sugya* in bB.M.82b-83a suggests the following legal principles: (1) If the porters were negligent, then they are liable for damages to the owner of the barrels; (2) If the porters maintain that the barrels had been broken due to *force majeure* and the accident occurred in a place where people were frequently present, then the porters would have to produce witnesses to that effect in order to avoid liability; (3) If the accident occurred in a place that was ordinarily unfrequented, and the porters were therefore unlikely to be able to produce witnesses, then they would have to take an oath and swear to the truth of their claim in order to be exempted from liability for damages.[63] These rules apply in the absence of any other private arrangement agreed upon by the parties concerned.[64]

The Talmud does not give a detailed account of the incident. However, it is evident from the reasoning invoked by Rav that the incident occurred under circumstances that rendered the porters legally liable to the owner for the barrels, and that the latter was consequently exempt from paying them their wages.[65] Had the incident occurred under circumstances that would have exempted the porters from liability, then Rav could have referred to the legal rules already formulated in Tannaitic times.[66] The fact that Rav had to refer to a verse in Proverbs in order to justify his decision implies that on purely legal grounds the porters would have lost the case. The question whether the owner of the barrels had the right of distraint over the bailees' property was not raised. Apparently it was assumed that if the porters

---

62 bB.M.58a; S. Warhaftig, *Jewish Labor Law* (Hebrew) (Jerusalem, 1969) vol. 2, p. 864, 896.
63 Warhaftig, *ibid.* pp. 831-41; 924-8.
64 See tKid.3:7-8; Elon, *Jewish Law: History, Sources, Principles* (Jerusalem, 1973) vol. 1, pp. 159-63.
65 For different reconstructions of the case, see Rif and Rashi *ad loc.*
66 See mB.M.6:8; bB.M.82b, and discussion accompanying note 63 above.

were liable, then the owner was within his rights in seizing their garments as a means of recovering his damages.[67]

We may assume that both the account in the Yerushalmi and that in the Bavli are based on the same tradition. The similarity between the two stories cannot be mere coincidence. The common features of the two accounts (the same legal issue, the seizure of the porters' garments and the ensuing dialogue including the quotation of the same verse in Proverbs) indicate that the two traditions have a common source.[68]

There is, however, one notable difference between the two Talmudim with respect to the presentation of the incident, and this difference reflects the difference in their respective attitudes towards judicial deviation from the law.

In the Babylonian version, the case is recorded in the precise stylistic form used in recording court cases. According to MS.M in which the technical term *ata lekame* occurs, the form is exactly that of a case report of the first order.[69] Both the plaintiffs and the defendant are present in court, and the judge speaks directly to the defendant. The initiative throughout the trial is in the hands of the plaintiffs, as is to be expected in court cases. The judge orders the defendant to return the garments and then to pay the porters' wages only after the porters presented their claim to the judge.

Rabba bar Bar Hanan (or the defendant)[70] protested after having heard the decision: "Is that the law?" In the opening of Rav's reply, the current editions of the Talmud read "Yes." Early manuscripts and

---

67   On the problem of distraint, see B. Cohen, *Jewish and Roman Law* (New York, 1966) pp. 637, 642ff; Falk, *Introduction to Jewish Law* (Hebrew) (Tel Aviv, 1969) 83ff. See also S. Shilo, "On One Aspect of Law and Morals in Jewish Law: Lifnim Mishurat Hadin," 13 *Isr. L.R.* (1978) 359, 385.
68   L. Ginzberg, *A Commentary on the Palestinian Talmud* (New York, 1941) Introduction (Hebrew) p. 93; Silberg, *op. cit.* p. 119; Urbach, *The Sages, op. cit. supra* note 51, p. 331. Zuri has observed that some traditions that are reported in the Bavli in the name of Rav are attributed in the Yerushalmi to R. Jossi b. Hanina. See Zuri, *R. Jossi b. Hanina* (Jerusalem, 1927) pp. 61-2; *Rav* (Jerusalem, 1925) pp. 132-3.
69   See text acccompanying note 59 in Chapter 2 above.
70   See note 61 above.

78   DEVIATION IN TALMUDIC LAW

Rishonim suggest that the word "Yes" ought to be deleted.[71] Thus, Rav did not claim to base his decision on the law as is suggested by the later insertion, which was probably inspired by a desire to present Rav's ruling as being harmonious with the law.

Silberg wanted to infer from the fact that Rav chose to quote a verse from the Hagiographa, rather than from the Pentateuch, that Rav's words were in the nature of a moral instruction rather than a judicial pronouncement.[72] The fact that Rav did not refer to the verse in Exodus 18:21, or to the exegetical interpretation based upon it,[73] suggests that he did not base his decision on the principle of *lifnim mishurat hadin* as later commentators, notably Rashi, have suggested.[74] Moreover, there is no reason to assume that Rav's ruling was merely a moral instruction. The Talmud records other incidents in which judicial decisions were based on verses from parts of the Bible other than the Pentateuch.[75] The principle on which Silberg based his argument, that legal norms cannot be derived from Biblical verses other than those in the Pentateuch, is often ignored and may therefore be disregarded.[76] The literary form in which the incident is presented leaves no doubt that the Babylonian Talmud reports a judicial decision. Yet the Bavli is not disturbed by the fact that the decision deviates from the law.

In the parallel version in the Yerushalmi, the incident is not recorded as a court case. There are several elements in the passage which indicate that the judge is employing only moral persuasion. Only the complaining porter is explicitly mentioned as coming before

---

71   See Dik. Sof. *ad loc.*; Urbach *op. cit.* p. 330. See also M. Eschelbacher "Recht und Billigkeit im der Jurisprudenz des Talmud," *Festschrift Hermann Cohen* (1912) 501, 511ff.
72   Silberg, *op. cit.* p. 122.
73   Mekhilta (ed. Horvitz) p. 198.
74   See Rashi on bB.M.83a; but *cf.* Tosafoth on bB.M.24b. On *lifnim mishurat hadin*, see S. Berman, "Lifnim Mishurat Hadin," 25 *JJS* (1975-6) p. 86; 28 (1977) p. 181. Shilo, *op. cit. supra* note 67. The reason for equating the ruling in bB.M.83a with the principle of *lifnim mishurat hadin*, though the latter does not occur there, might be Rav's dictum in yShebi.10:4 (39,4).
75   bSanh.58b on Job 38:15; bGit.40a-b on Ob.15; bB.M.101b on Ob.15.
76   For a detailed discussion of this principle, see Urbach, "Halakhah Venevua," 18 *Tarbiz* (1946-48) 1 on p. 13.

R. Yossi b. Hanina, which suggests that the other party is absent from the court. This absence is further established by the reported fact that the porter had to leave the "court" in order to go and inform the potter about the instruction of R. Yossi b. Hanina.

R. Yossi b. Hanina at his own initiative asked the porter when he came back, probably to thank him,[77] whether he had been paid. Upon hearing that he had not been paid, R. Yossi b. Hanina instructed him to return to the potter and to claim his wages on the ground of *the paths of the just shouldst thou keep*. The fact that R. Yossi b. Hanina at his own initiative advised the porter to claim his wages shows that he was not acting in his capacity as judge. Had R. Yossi b. Hanina been officiating as a judge in a trial, he would have been forbidden to advise either side on how to act in court.[78] By stressing that some basic rules of legal procedure were not followed, the Yerushalmi makes it clear that this incident does not involve a court case. R. Yossi b. Hanina, who in his instruction deviated from the law, is presented by the Yerushalmi as a moral authority dispensing moral advice rather than as a judge pronouncing a judicial decision.[79]

The common feature in all the preceding cases is a discrepancy between their exposition in the two Talmudim. It has been shown that judicial decisions that are reported in the Bavli as indicating resort to extra-legal considerations are presented by the Yerushalmi in such a way as to make the ruling consistent with the law or to be regarded as a non-judicial incident. In fact, the Yerushalmi does not hesitate to introduce artificial constructs in order to avoid any allusion to extra-legal considerations.

The Yerushalmi's recoil from extra-legal considerations also finds expression in the relatively narrow scope allowed in the Yerushalmi to principles governing judicial discretion. The next section examines this aspect.

---

[77] Compare with the case of the needy father, in text accompanying note 15 above.

[78] See mAvot 1:8; yKct.4:10 (29,1); ySanh.3:8 (21,3); yB.B.9:4 (17,1); bKet.52b; 86a; Zuri, *The System of Action* (Hebrew) (London, 1933) pp. 140-57.

[79] *Cf.* yShebi.10:4 (39,4). See also L.I. Levine, *Caesaria Under Roman Rule* (Leiden, 1975), p. 98.

80   DEVIATION IN TALMUDIC LAW

4.2 Power-Conferring Rules

We proceed now to examine some power-conferring rules which allow judges to deviate from the generally accepted law and to exercise their discretion.

A. *Samuel's Rule: Shuda Dedaynee (Discretion of the Judges)*

Samuel's rule relates to the discretionary power of judges. It maintains, *inter alia*, that whenever the evidence in a trial concerning a deed of gift is equally balanced between the two sides, the judge may use his own discretion to decide the case, and may allocate the land specified in the deed to whomever he sees fit.[80]

This rule is potentially disruptive to the stability required for commercial life, and grants judges a power that cannot be controlled by legal means. A legal system that tends to limit the power of the court to strict enforcement of the law and insists on providing legal grounds for all judicial decisions cannot accommodate such a rule. And, indeed, it can be demonstrated on the basis of internal evidence that Samuel's rule was not accepted in Palestine as a valid law.

Samuel's rule contradicts a certain Tannaitic ruling. In attempting to meet this difficulty, the Talmud in bKet.94b seeks Tannaitic support for Samuel's (Amoraic) rule and finds it in a Baraita which deals with the dilemma of an agent who has been left with a sum of money in his possession but has not been given instructions as to what to do with the money. The Baraita considers various possible solutions and concludes with the following:

33   The Sages say [that the money] must be divided [between the claimants]. While here [in Babylon] it was ruled that the agent shall use his own discretion [i.e., he can give the sum in full to either of the claimants].[81]

Although the Baraita explicitly and exclusively deals with an agent, the Talmud applies the same principle to a judge who is confronted

---

80   bKet.85b; bKet.94a-b. For further discussion of this rule, see text accompanying note 30 in Chapter 6 below.
81   bKet.94b; bGit.14b. This is a Babylonian Baraita; see Epstein *Mevoth Lesifrut Hattannaim* (Jerusalem, 1957) pp. 245-6; Heiger, *Otzar Habrajtot*, vol. 8, p. 151.

with a similar situation.[82] The Baraita clearly juxtaposes the view of the Palestinian Sages and that of the Babylonians. Thus, Samuel's rule is consistent with the view which was generally accepted in Babylon while it conflicts with the view held in Palestine (as shown, *inter alia*, in the Baraita which contradicts Samuel's rule).

The term *shuda dedaynee* occurs seven times in the Bavli,[83] but its precise meaning is never discussed. Apparently, the term was well known in Babylon and did not require any clarification. This is not so in the Yerushalmi, where the term is used only once, and in that instance it is followed by an explanatory remark:

34   When a single parcel of land is claimed by two [contradictory] deeds, Beth Din may decide in favor of whomever it wishes.[84]

The need for an explanation of the term suggests that it was not widely known in Palestine. It is also interesting to note that in this sole instance of its occurrence in the Yerushalmi there are two attempts to show that the rule contradicts a Mishnaic ruling,[85] and hence that it is not valid. The Baraita cited by the Bavli as a source for Samuel's rule is not mentioned in the Yerushalmi.[86]

A further peculiarity in the Yerushalmi is worth mentioning. The Yerushalmi reads *shuhada dedaynee* instead of the Babylonian *shuda dedaynee*. The standard dictionaries, following a Geonic interpretation, derive *shuda* from *shuhada*.[87] However, the conjunction

---

82   See H. Ben-Menahem, "The Judge as an Agent," (Hebrew) *Shenaton Hamishpat Ha-Ivri* (1983) vol. 9-10, pp. 51-71.
83   bKet.85b; bKet.94a-b; bKid.74a; bGit.14b-15a; bB.B.35a; bB.B.62b; bShebu.30a-b.
84   yKet.10:4 (33,4), yKet.10:5 (34,1). See the reading in Rashba on B.B.35b, Ran on Shebu.30b and Meiri on Ket.85b.
85   According to the Yerushalmi, Samuel's rule contradicts a Mishnah, while according to the Bavli the contradiction to Samuel's rule is found in a Baraita. A Mishnah carries more weight than a Baraita as a source of objection to an Amoraic statement. See bGit.27b and bB.M.34a.
86   See also Rif on Ket. *ad loc.* who argues that the notion is not accepted by the Yerushalmi; H. Rajnes, "Shuda Dedaynee" in *Massot Umehqarim* (Jerusalem – New York, 1972) p. 85ff.
87   Aruch, vol. 6, p. 124; vol. 8, p. 30; Levy, *Worterbuch Uber Die Talmudim und Midraschim* (Berlin, 1924) vol. 4, p. 516; J.N. Epstein, *Introduction*

shuhada dedaynee, bribe of the judges, hardly fits the context. Moreover, the conjunction has a strong negative connotation, and it is hard to understand why Samuel would choose such a provocative expression to convey his novel opinion.[88] It is suggested, therefore, that the word has a common etymology with the Arabic *sud*, authority.[89] The conjunction "authority of the judges," which occurs in other Talmudic passages,[90] fits appropriately into the context and accurately expresses the view of Samuel.[91]

If this interpretation is correct, it raises the possibility that the Yerushalmi deliberately substituted *shuhada* for *shuda* in order to express its disapproval of Samuel's innovation by giving it a negative connotation.[92]

B. *The Rule of R. Eliezer b. Jacob: Beth Din May Pronounce Sentences even where Not Warranted by the Halakhah*

This rule is perhaps the most explicit statement found in the Talmud to the effect that a court can deviate from the law and base its

---

to Amoraic Literature, Babylonian and Yerushalmi Talmud (Hebrew) (Tel Aviv, 1962) p. 261; Epstein, *Mavo Lenusach Hamishnah* (Jerusalem, 1948) p. 103, n. 5.

88 For the same reason, it is unlikely that Samuel adopted an existing popular terminology. *Cf.* the objection to the standard interpretation raised by Lazarus Goldschmidt in his commentary on bShebu.30a (note 17) and in his Supplements to Levy *op. cit. supra* note 87, p. 687. Although the term *shohad* is sometimes used in biblical Hebrew in a neutral sense (I Kings 15:19; II Kings 16:8; Proverbs 17:8; 21:14), in the Bavli it always has a negative connotation; see bShab.116b; bJev.63b; bKet.105a-b; bGit.28b; bKer.28b.

89 *Cf.* E. Lane, *Arabic English Lexicon* (London, 1867) Book 1, part 4, 1461. I am indebted to Mr. E. Ovadiah for this suggestion.

90 See bJev.67b (and parallels); bJev.90b (and parallels); bKet.100a (and parallels).

91 See *Caftor Vapherach* by Estori haPerchi (ed. A.M. Luncz) (Jerusalem, 1897) Chapter 12, p. 322. *Shuda dedaynee* is thus the converse of another term, employed also by Samuel, *ulbena dedaynee*, bGit.36b.

92 *Cf.* J.A. Wiesner, *Givat Jerushalim* (Hebrew) (Wien, 1872) p. 53. (Also in *Hashachar*, vol. 2, Wien, 1871, p. 53.) See also S. Lieberman, *Hayerushalmi Kiphshuto* (Jerusalem, 1934) p. 443.

ruling on extra-legal considerations.[93] The scope of power granted to the court according to this Tannaitic rule is not restricted in the Bavli in any significant way. The only limitation which the Bavli imposes on the rule is that the power must not be exercised with the "intention of disregarding the Torah, but in order to safeguard it."[94]

The Yerushalmi, on the other hand, radically limits the scope of this judicial power. Immediately after its *sole* reference to the rule, the Yerushalmi reports the following controversy between two Palestinian Amoraim:

35   How far? R. Lazar b. R. Jose says: as far as hearsay (*zimzum*); R. Jose says: [Conviction] by witnesses [only] but without forewarning (*hatra'a*).[95]

The opening question "how far?" clearly demonstrates the Yerushalmi's assumption that recourse to this judicial device must be restricted. From the views of R. Lazar and R. Jose it is evident that both of them understood the rule as merely authorizing some kind of deviation from the laws of procedure. R. Lazar interprets the rule as allowing the court to convict a person on the basis of hearsay,[96] even

---

93   bSanh. 46a; bJev.90b. For a detailed discussion of this rule, see text accompanying note 2 in Chapter 6.
94   bSanh. *loc. cit.*; bJev. *loc. cit.*; see also Elon, *Jewish Law*, vol. 2, p. 422, n. 94.
95   yHag.2:2 (78,1).
96   On *zimzum* (hearsay), see Lieberman, 5 *Tarbiz* (1933-4) p. 99, and compare bKid.80a, 81a and bSanh.26b. But see also bMeg.25b. A similar restriction of a Tannaitic provision is found in bSanh.81b. The Talmud there discusses mSanh.9:5 which stipulates that if a person commits a murder without witnesses, the court should take him to a prison cell and feed him with bread of adversity and water of affliction. The Talmud, however, understands that the crime was witnessed but that there was some formal defect in the testimony, and hence the offender could not be executed. B. Jackson (*Essays in Jewish Legal History* (Leiden, 1975) 188) maintains that the Mishnaic provision was restricted to procedural defects because the Rabbis were reluctant to apply a penalty contrary to Biblical law, which explicitly requires two witnesses (Num.35:30; Deut.17:6;19:15). However, the Talmudic restriction follows a practical difficulty raised by the Talmud: If there were no witnesses, how do we know who committed the crime? The Babylonian Talmud does not relate the restriction to its reluctance to act against the

though there is no direct evidence that the person actually committed the alleged crime. R. Jose, on the other hand, requires the testimony of witnesses for convicting a person, and the only deviation which he allows on the basis of the rule is the waiver of the normally required forewarning of the criminal.

It follows that the Yerushalmi would not approve of a deviation which created a new crime (the case of the man who had sexual intercourse with his wife in public) or imposed a penalty not prescribed by law (the case of the man who rode a horse on the Sabbath). The deviations referred to by the two Amoraim must be taken not to illustrate, but to exhaust, their respective views. The opening question "how far?" suggests *prima facie* that the Yerushalmi seeks a demarcation line which would separate deviations permitted by the rule from those which are not. However, such an interpretation is untenable, since there is no way of constructing a linear scale according to which one could determine the place of a given deviation in relation to the demarcating principle. One has to conclude that each of the two Amoraim restricted the kinds of permissible deviation by linking the rule to a particular point of procedure, excluding by implication all other forms of deviation. The far-reaching consequence of this observation is that the scope of R. Eliezer b. Jacob's rule is extremely limited in the Yerushalmi. This narrow interpretation limits the original meaning of R. Eliezer b. Jacob, and facilitates reconciliation of his revolutionary notion with the more conservative outlook of the Yerushalmi.

C. *The Invalidity of Erroneous Rulings*

The restrictive attitude of the Yerushalmi towards the notion of judicial power is also revealed in the related issue of the validity of erroneous rulings.

---

law, as is the case in yHag.1:1. It is also worth mentioning that the Yerushalmi in Sanh.9:10 (27,2), which also restricts the Mishnaic ruling to mere procedural defects, does not relate it to the practical difficulty raised by the Bavli and might well be motivated by its reluctance to deviate from the law.

Consistent with its overall attitude that judges have power to rule only on the basis of the law, the Yerushalmi reverses the rule which imposes on everyone an absolute obligation to obey all judicial decisions, even erroneous rulings. In direct opposition to Siphre,[97] and in an explicit attempt to refute the latter's well-known interpretation, the Yerushalmi interprets Deuteronomy 17:11 in the following way:

36 It was taught: Might one think that even if they tell you that right is left and left is right you should listen to them, [therefore] Scripture says "to go right and left," that they will tell you right is right and left is left.[98]

Even if one could reconcile the two contradictory exegeses of Siphre and Yerushalmi by relating each of them to a different addressee,[99] the fact remains that the Yerushalmi holds that only legally correct rulings are binding.[100]

In this context reference should also be made to another discrepancy between the two Talmudim. In attempting to comfort R. Joshua, who was ordered by R. Gamliel to appear before him with "his staff and money" on the day which the former thought to be the Day of Atonement,[101] R. Akiba cites an old Tannaitic exegesis which reads as follows:

37 Scripture says "you" "you" "you" three times,[102] to indicate that "you" [may fix the festivals] even if you err inadvertently, "you" even if "you" err deliberately, "you" even if "you" are misled.[103]

---

97 Siphre ad Deut. (ed. Finkelstein) p. 207.
98 yHor.1:1 (45,4). For further discussion of this interpretation, see text accompanying note 72 in Chapter 6 below.
99 See text accompanying note 87 in Chapter 6 below.
100 The Yerushalmi introduces the Baraita as a source the ignorance of which constitutes decisive proof that the student is not "capable of deciding matters of law." (yHor. *loc.cit.*) The parallel *sugya* in the Bavli (b.Hor.2b) does not present knowledge of this Baraita as a requirement for being "capable of deciding matters of law." It may therefore be inferred that the Bavli did not know the Baraita recorded in the Yerushalmi, or at least did not consider it of great importance. See also *Mare Panim* on yHor. *ad loc.*
101 mR.H.2:9; bR.H.25a.
102 *Otam* (them) in Lev. 23:2; 23:4 and 23:37 is read *atem* (you) for exegetic purposes.
103 bR.H. *loc. cit.*

Although referring to a very specific matter, this interpretation grants the court unlimited power to act on its own discretion, and confers total authority to the ruling regardless of its correctness.[104]

In the Yerushalmi, this far-reaching interpretation has no parallel. According to the Yerushalmi, R. Akiba's interpretation upholds the ruling of the court even if it turns out to be based on false evidence. However, there is a striking absence of any reference to an unqualified power of the court to establish the day of the festivals on the basis of its own discretion.[105]

4.3 Yerushalmi versus Bavli Reconsidered

The previous sections indicated a difference between the Bavli and the Yerushalmi with regard to their respective views of judicial power. Such an analysis would gain support if it could be shown that the distinction is part of a more general difference between the two Talmudim. A relation between general characteristics and background of the two Talmudim and their respective views on judicial power would greatly enhance the argument that the discrepancy discussed in previous sections is indeed systematic rather than accidental. This section attempts to establish such a relation by viewing the Yerushalmi's limited approach to the exercise of judicial power within a broader context and fitting it into a more general frame of reference.

The Yerushalmi's insistence on strict adherence to the law can be regarded partly as an expression of its policy to unify the halakhah by eliminating legal pluralism and partly as a result of its polemical activity against deviant sects in Palestine. The absence of these two factors from the cultural-legal climate of Amoraic Babylon might account for the Bavli's less rigid attitude toward judicial deviation.

Let us first consider the Yerushalmi's desire to unify the halakhah.

---

104 For a narrow interpretation of this exegesis see Lieberman, *Tosefta Kepshutah* on Rosh Hashanah (New York, 1962) p. 1037.

105 yR.H.2:7 (58,2); yR.H.3:1 (58,3). See also yNed.6:8 (40,1). Sifra Emor, parasha 9, has *anousin* instead of *mezidin*. Tosefta R.H. 3:1 has *anousin, mout'in, mezidin,* and *shogegin*. Since the interpretation is based on the triple occurrence of *otam* in Lev.23, there is little doubt that Tosefta attempts to account for both versions, Sifra's and Baraita's.

Despite a few controversial passages,[106] the Palestinian data clearly suggest a strong tendency to unify the halakhah and to eliminate variation from the actual application of the law. This tendency is much less noticeable in the Bavli, which often comments, without objection, that in Babylon the people of a given locale followed the ruling of Rabbi A while those of another area observed the contradictory ruling of Rabbi B.[107] The Bavli also reports that, in Eretz Yisrael, in some cases the inhabitants of certain places followed the ruling of those Rabbis under whose "jurisdiction" they lived, which rulings were contrary to the generally accepted view. However, these traditions are missing from the Yerushalmi. For example, on mShab.19:1, which records R. Eliezer's minority opinion about the kind of preparatory work, if any, one is permitted to do on the Sabbath in order to perform a circumcision, the Bavli reports:

38 "In R. Eliezer's locality they used to cut timber to make charcoal for making iron on the Sabbath. In the locality of R. Jose the Galilean they used to eat the flesh of fowl with milk" [in accordance with the view of R. Jose the Galilean].[108]

The view of R. Jose the Galilean appears in mHul.8:4, Mekhilta, Mishpatim 20, (ed. Horovitz) p. 336, and in Siphre (on Deut.) 104, (ed. Finkelstein) p. 163, but in none of these Tannaitic sources is it related that the view of R. Jose was actually put into practice. Nor is there any Tannaitic or Palestinian verification of the tradition concerning the people in R. Eliezer's locality.

---

106 yBer.8:1 (11,1); yEru.1:4 (19,1).
107 bA.Z.40a; bB.B.153a; bHul.18b and 57a.
108 bShab.130a (and parallels). Another example is bJev.99b (bKet.28b): "For it was taught: no share is given to a slave unless his master is with him, so R. Judah; R. Jose however ruled: The slave may claim that if I am a priest give me for my own sake, and if I am a priest's slave give me for the sake of my master. In the place of R. Judah [men of doubtful status] were raised to the status of priesthood [on the evidence that they received a share of *terumah*]; in the place of R. Jose, however, no one was raised to the status of priesthood [on the evidence of having received a share of *terumah*]." The last paragraph is, so it seems, a late Babylonian addition. The Tosefta in Jev.12:6 knows nothing of these local practices. But see the following note.

It seems that these reports are late Babylonian traditions, perhaps fabricated in order to justify the great variation of the halakhah in Babylon.[109]

It should also be noted that the sequence of bShab.130a has a strong polemical flavor:

> R. Isaac said: there was one town in Palestine where they followed R. Eliezer and died there at the proper time [never prematurely, i.e., they were not punished]. Moreover, the wicked State once promulgated a decree against Israel concerning circumcision, yet did not decree it against that town.[110]

Unlike the pluralistic attitude of the Bavli, the Yerushalmi holds that a Master may not actually practice his individual concept of the law. The quest for strict uniformity in the actual application of the law is well evidenced throughout the Yerushalmi. For example, mBer.1:1 records a tradition according to which R. Gamliel once instructed his sons to recite the *shema* of *arvith* in accordance with his own opinion, against that of the Sages. To this the Yerushalmi raises the following objection:

39 And does R. Gamliel ignore the ruling of the Sages and give a decision according to his view?

In order to support the underlying principle that a Rabbi may not put his view into actual practice against the view of his colleagues, the Yerushalmi cites three examples from which such a conclusion can be drawn.[111] No such objection to R. Gamliel's ruling occurs in the Bavli, which allows the Rabbis a greater degree of freedom and therefore

---

109 One could also argue that the Yerushalmi deliberately suppressed old Tannaitic traditions which were not congruent with later Palestinian developments.
110 See text accompanying note 113 below.
111 yBer.1:1 (3,1). All three examples are related to the Tannaim; two are reported in the Tosefta (Shabbat 12:12; Ohalot 4:2), the third one has no verification in Tannaitic literature. For a different evaluation of this passage see Louis Ginzberg, in his commentary *ad loc.* See also yBez.4:3 (62,3). Liberman in *Hayerushalmi Kipshuto* (p. 19, mavo) goes too far in interpreting the phrase *"achrayhem achreyhem"* (in yBez. *ibid.*) to include even if they should err.

does not feel that the story presents a difficulty.[112]

The third example which the Yerushalmi cites in Berakhot is a striking one for our purpose in view of its parallel in the Bavli. The Mishnah in Shebi.9:1, records a dispute between R. Simeon and the Sages over the question of whether aftergrowths are permitted in the Sabbatical year. The precise view of R. Simeon changes according to variant readings in mShebi.9:1 and bPes.51a, but in any case it is clear that R. Simeon permitted a kind of aftergrowth that was forbidden by the Sages. According to a tradition cited in yBer.,[113] R. Simeon once encountered a certain man collecting aftergrowths in the Sabbatical year; whereupon he condemned the collector for violating the law. When asked by the violator whether it was not so that R. Simeon allowed the collecting of aftergrowths in the Sabbatical year, R. Simeon replied, "But is it not so that my colleagues are in disagreement with me?" The story concludes that R. Simeon cursed the violator and that the curse came true. It is interesting to compare this concluding remark with bShab.130a quoted above, which relates that the inhabitants of a certain town were not punished although they had practiced a minority view of R. Eliezer. Moreover, bPes.51a explicitly relates that R. Simeon did practice in accord with his own view:

40 ... I who saw R. Simeon b. Yohai eating it ...

Of the additional cases[114] cited by the Yerushalmi to illustrate the principle that a Master may not put into practice his own view, one merits special attention. The Mishnah in Shab.5:4 relates that R. Eleazar b. Azariah's cow used to go out on the Sabbath with a thong between its horns, an act which according to the Sages constitutes a violation of the law of Sabbath.[115] The Yerushalmi is troubled by this report, since it implies that a Rabbi had actually put into practice his own view when it was contradicted by that of his colleagues. After an

---

112 The only peculiarity observed by the Bavli is that as the story stands it appears that until that incident the sons of R. Gamliel were not aware of their father's opinion.
113 yBer. *loc. cit.* See also Kohelet Rabba, parasha 10.
114 yDemai 3:3 (23,3); yPes.7:2 (34,2); yA.Z.3:10 (43,2); yShebi.9.4 (39,1).
115 mShab.5:4; mBez.2:8; mEd.3:12. See T. Zahavy, *The Tradition of Eleazar Ben Azariah* (Brown University, 1977) p. 38.

unsuccessful preliminary attempt to argue that R. Eleazar b. Azariah only taught his view but did not practice it, the Yerushalmi asserts that, in spite of what is said in the Mishnah, the controversial cow did not actually belong to R. Eleazar b. Azariah himself but to his wife. Indeed, R. Eleazar b. Azariah took great pains to show repentance for his wife's conduct.[116] Thus the supremacy of the principle of uniformity in the actual application of the law is preserved.

The Bavli, on the other hand, is not troubled at all by the Yerushalmi's problem. True, the Bavli also asserts that the cow did not belong to R. Eleazar b. Azariah. However, unlike the Yerushalmi, the Bavli comes to this conclusion because it finds it too difficult to assume that R. Eleazar b. Azariah, who was known to be a wealthy man, owned only one cow.[117]

In its attempt to enforce conformity, the Yerushalmi employs the somewhat obsolete principle of the rebellious elder, *zaken mamre*. The concept of *zaken mamre* is generally associated with the Sanhedrin, and a rebellious elder is a judge who renders a decision contrary to a ruling issued by the High Court in Jerusalem.[118] Yet it seems that the concept of *zaken mamre*, at least metaphorically, survived long after the Destruction. The term is used by one Amora in the course of a dispute with a colleague over a legal issue. Seeking to compel his opponent to abandon his dissenting view, R. Yossi says to R. Pinchas:

42 Retract your opinion or I shall write [that you are a] *zaken mamre*.[119]

The use of the term in this context indicates that in Palestine the freedom of the Rabbis to advocate dissenting views was limited, and

---

116 yShab.5:4 (7,3); yBez.2:8 (61,4). For the Hebrew sources, see Appendix, no. 41.
117 bShab.54b; bBer.23a. The tendency of both Talmudim regarding deviant behavior can further be seen in their respective attitudes towards Michal's custom to put on *tefilin*. While the Babylonian Talmud reports the episode with no reservations (bErub.96a), the Yerushalmi states that the Sages criticized her deviant behavior (yBer.2:3 (4,3); yErub.10:1 (26,1)).
118 mSanh. 11:2; Sifre ad Deut. (ed Finkelstein) pp. 205-207.
119 yJev.10:4 (11,1); yGit.8:6 (49,3) and see *Ahavat Zion, ad loc.* See also Z. Frankel, *Mevo Hayerushalmi*, p.121b and p.156.

that social pressure was employed to reduce controversies. By contrast, in the Bavli there is no parallel instance of this use of *zaken mamre*. In one passage the Yerushalmi does attribute the term to the Babylonian Amora, Samuel. In a dispute with Rav over the validity of a *takkanah* ascribed to R. Judah Hanasi permitting the eating of gentile oil, Samuel compels Rav to eat gentile oil to show his acceptance of the *takkanah*. "Said Samuel [to Rav]: Eat, or I shall write [that you are a] *zaken mamre*."[120] But it seems most likely that this is a Babylonian incident reported by the Yerushalmi in its own terms. This view is supported by the fact that a similar incident between Rav and Samuel which is recorded in the Bavli makes no reference to *zaken mamre*.[121]

The tendency to unify and centralize the halakhah, which began after the Destruction and of which the banning of R. Eliezer and the incident concerning R. Joshua and the Day of Atonement[122] are the most famous examples, continued well into the Amoraic period. It played a crucial role in shaping and defining the concept of judicial power, and was powerful enough to motivate a distorted account of a certain Tannaitic ruling in the Yerushalmi. The Tannaitic ruling deviated from the halakhah proper in order to preserve the supremacy of the High Court, a principle which in itself was congruent with the policy to unify the law. The Tosefta in Nidah 1:5 records a dispute between R. Eliezer and R. Joshua relating to the laws of *nidah*. On a question pertaining to the ritual state of four classes of women, R. Eliezer holds a lenient view whereas R. Joshua is of a stricter opinion. The Tosefta relates that during the lifetime of R. Eliezer the people followed his ruling, while after his death, R. Joshua reversed the practice so as to agree with his own view.[123] Both Talmudim record a Baraita in which this account is reversed: during the lifetime of R. Eliezer, R. Joshua instructed the people to observe his own ruling, while after the death of R. Eliezer he changed his instruction and ordered the people to follow the ruling of the late R. Eliezer.[124]

---

120 yA.Z.2:8(41,4); yShab.1:4(3,4); see also yTer.10:2 (47,2).
121 bHul.111b; see also bA.Z.36a.
122 bB.M.59b; bBer.19a; yM.K.3:1 (81,4); bR.H.25a. See also mEd.5:6.
123 See Lieberman, *Tosafoth Rishonim* on tNid.1:5.
124 bNid.7b; yNid.1:3 (49,1). For the Hebrew source, see Appendix, nos. 43 and 44. See also Halevy, *Doroth Rishonim* vol. 5, p. 294; Gilat,

Both Talmudim comment on this tradition and attempt to explain the contradictory instructions of R. Joshua. There is, however, a significant difference between the two reports, which correspond to the different manner in which the two Talmudim view strict adherence to the law. From the Bavli's account it appears that although R. Joshua came to recognize the correctness of R. Eliezer's ruling (apparently because it was based on tradition) he nevertheless forbade the people to practice it lest they consequently follow R. Eliezer's view in other matters. R. Joshua would be rendered powerless to counteract this tendency because of R. Eliezer's great reputation and authority. However, once the authority of R. Eliezer diminished because of his death the potential threat disappeared, making restoration of the old rule possible. This account assumes and demonstrates that deviation from the law may occasionally be justified on extra-legal grounds. In order to achieve a political goal, the supremacy of the Beth Din, R. Joshua deviated from a rule which he himself recognized as legally correct.[125]

This account is unacceptable to the Yerushalmi since it asserts that the halakhah proper was not enforced. Therefore the Yerushalmi maintains that R. Joshua's second ruling was due to a change in his legal conception of the rule (a change which both accounts assume to have taken place). This turning point, the Yerushalmi maintains, happened to coincide with the death of R. Eliezer. According to this account, R. Joshua never deviated from the law. Both of his instructions followed the legal position that he held at the time that he issued his orders. This account is extremely odd. The Baraita clearly relates the second instruction of R. Joshua to the death of R. Eliezer, and the argument of an accidental simultaneous occurrence is not very convincing. One gets the impression that the more realistic account presented by the Bavli is being purposely suppressed because it is at variance with the strict adherence to the law demanded by the Yerushalmi.

Mishnato shel R. Eliezer b. Horkenus (Tel Aviv 1968) p. 326; M. Guttman, "Hillelites and Shammaites: A Clarification," *HUCA* (1957) vol. 28, 115 at pp. 119-21.

125 See Gilat, *op. cit. ibid.*

YERUSHALMI VERSUS BAVLI

The Yerushalmi's attitude towards extra-legal considerations as presented in this chapter seems to provide the background for its negative evaluation of Pinchas's act. As related in Numbers 25:7-9, Pinchas acted on an impulse when he killed the Israelite and the Midianite woman without a trial. The Bavli sees it as a noble act commanding great respect and praise.[126] Indeed, Numbers 25:10-14 itself ascribes to Pinchas the deliverance of the Israelites and the arrest of the plague. Nevertheless the Yerushalmi maintains that Pinchas acted against the will of the Sages, who were so displeased that they considered excommunicating him.[127] The Yerushalmi does not specify the negative aspect of Pinchas's act, but it is evident that it considers the execution to have been a transgression against the law.

This survey of the Yerushalmi's hostile attitude towards extra-legal considerations may be concluded by noting that not even once does the Babylonian maxim *dina demalkhuta dina*[128] (the law of the state is the law) occur in the Yerushalmi.[129] The maxim presents some jurisprudential problems which so far have not been dealt with by scholars. It is not clear, for example, whether the rule applies to individuals, judges, or both. It is also not clear whether the rule allows reference to gentile law (power-conferring rule) or prescribes it (duty-imposing rule).[130] Be that as it may, the rule constitutes a channel through which gentile law could penetrate into the halakhah.

Rabbi Herzog maintains that the rejection of the maxim in Palestine was dictated by "national pride." He holds that:

> In Palestine the imperial law was the law of the hateful power which had destroyed Israel and robbed him of his fatherland, while in the Parthian Empire the imperial law was the law of that noble power which had at one time acted as Israel's redeemer ...[131]

---

126 bSanh.82a-b.
127 ySanh.9:7 (27,2). For the Hebrew source see Appendix, no. 45; see also B. Jackson, *Theft in Early Jewish Law* (Oxford, 1972) p. 169.
128 bNed.28a; bGit.10b; bB.K.113a; 113b; bB.B.54b; 55a.
129 See I. Herzog, *The Main Institutions of Jewish Law* (London, 1965) 2d. ed., vol. 1, p. 30. But see also *ibid.* p. 31.
130 See S. Shilo, *Dina DeMalkhuta Dina* (Jerusalem, 1974) and the book review by H. Ben-Menahem in 27 *JJS* (1976) 219.
131 Herzog, *op.cit.* p. 30.

In any event, the rejection of the maxim may be seen as yet another manifestation of the Yerushalmi's overall approach as described above.

As has been noted previously, the Bavli developed a tolerance for legal pluralism. Unlike the Yerushalmi, the Bavli is not disturbed by early Tannaitic traditions which imply that certain Rabbis put into practice their individual views in opposition to the generally accepted rule. Moreover, the Bavli quotes allegedly Tannaitic traditions which demonstrate the diversity of the halakhah in the Tannaitic era, traditions for which no confirmation is to be found in Tannaitic or Palestinian sources. The pluralistic view of the Bavli is clearly manifested in the following passage which is an Amoraic comment (with no parallel in the Yerushalmi) on a Tannaitic exegesis.

Siphre interprets Deut. 14:1, *lo titgodedu*, as "You shall not form separate sects."[132] Finkelstein relates this exegetical interpretation to the growth of separatist sects in Palestine in the early generations of the Tannaim.[133] The Bavli, however, understands this interpretation as referring to the problem of pluralism within the halakhah, and seeks therefore to limit the scope of the prohibition expressed in this Tannaitic interpretation:

46   Abaye [said]: The warning against opposing sects is only applicable to such a case as that of two courts of law in the same town, one of which rules in accordance with the views of Beth Shammai while the other rules in accordance with the views of Beth Hillel. In the case of two courts of law in two different towns [the difference in practice] does not matter ... Rava said to him: The warning against opposing sects is only applicable to such a case as that of one court of law in the same town, half of which rule in accordance with the views of Beth Shammai while the other half rule in accordance with the views of Beth Hillel. In the case, however, of two courts of law in the same town [the difference in practice] does not matter.[134]

---

132   Sifre ad Deut. (Ed. Finkelstein) p. 158.
133   Finkelstein, Sifre *ibid.*, n. 1.
134   bJev.14a. This passage follows a debate on whether a dissenting view of Beth Shammai was actually put into practice by its advocators. The Yerushalmi's view of this matter is unequivocal: This practice was stopped by the *bat kol* (yJev.1:6 (3,2)). The Bavli, on the other hand, does not conceive the *bat kol* as a decisive factor and leaves the issue open for debate.

The Bavli not only tolerates legal pluralism but shows reluctance to limit it.

It seems that one can safely conclude on the basis of the foregoing comparative survey that the two Talmudim convey two distinct and separate notions: While the Yerushalmi rejects any form of legal pluralism and strives to harmonize contradictory accounts, the Bavli accepts legal pluralism as a commonplace to which frequent positive references are made.[135]

The logical connection between a policy to unify the halakhah on the one hand and opposition to judicial deviation on the other is evident. A policy seeking to deny legal pluralism imposes on the judges an absolute obligation to obey the law. Whether a decision opposing the generally accepted rule is based on what the judge believes to be legally correct or on what he perceives as socially or morally desirable is immaterial. The outcome to be avoided is the same: a discrepancy between the generally accepted rule and the decision in a particular case. A judge who deviates from the rule without challenging its legal validity undermines the uniformity of the law as much as his colleague who disputes the legal validity of an accepted rule and therefore does not follow it.

A decentralized legal system, one which allows judges to exercise a great degree of freedom in determining the law and which consequently has variants of the "law," is apt to be more tolerant of judges who deviate from the law. However, the correlation between the structure of a system and its attitude towards judicial deviation is not a simple one. While a centralized legal system is inherently opposed to judicial deviation, the opposite is not necessarily true. One can well conceive of a decentralized legal system which nevertheless requires judges to base their decisions exclusively on legal reasoning.

The remainder of this chapter proposes an historical hypothesis which might account for the conceptual difference between the two Talmudim. This brings us to the second element stated in the beginning of this section. As mentioned, the tendency to unify the halakhah by eliminating legal pluralism was born in Palestine after the Destruction, and it is commonly considered as the Rabbinic response to the religio-national disaster. Another major historical phenomenon, the

---

135 See notes 107-108 above.

rapid spread of Christianity, might also have played an important role in fostering a hostile attitude towards judicial deviation.

The existence in Palestine of separatist sects (of which Christianity became the most powerful) who objected to the teaching of the Rabbis while claiming to be the true interpreters of the Torah, created a situation in which the authority of the halakhah was threatened from within.[136] The Destruction and the religious confusion that followed, and the additional problem of a continuously growing dissident sect, forced the Rabbis to take defensive measures in order to preserve the authority of the halakhah. No doubt, the Rabbis were closely familiar with notions such as those expressed in the Sermon on the Mount. The idea that the halakhah as expounded by the Rabbis was not an exclusive guide for the conduct of one's life, an idea which occurs in the teaching ascribed to Jesus,[137] and which probably had some appeal among the people, could not be ignored by the Rabbis if they were to safeguard the integrity and the absolute authority of the halakhah. In this campaign, the Rabbis employed a variety of means,[138] one of which merits brief consideration. In order to reinforce their views and beliefs on the one hand, and to refute and repudiate that of their opponents on the other, the Rabbis used the dimension of Aggadah. The important role that the Aggadah played in this religio-cultural campaign is commonly taken to explain the existence of a vast body of Aggadah in Palestine in contrast with its relative paucity in Babylon.[139]

In Babylon, the gentiles amongst whom the Jews lived were part of the pagan world and, while it is true that not all Babylonian Jews were as observant as the Rabbis wished them to be, the pagan climate of the outside world did not pose an immediate threat to the integrity

---

136 See O. Irsai, "Jacob of Kfar Niburaia: A Sage Turned Apostate" (Hebrew) *Jerusalem Studies in Jewish Thought*, vol. 2 (2), (1982-3) p.153. On the tendency to eliminate legal pluralism in Palestine, see Elon, *Jewish Law*, vol. 3, pp. 873-875.
137 For example, Matthew, Chapters 15 and 23,
138 See M. Avi-Yonah, *The Jews of Palestine: Political History From the Bar-Kokhba War to the Arab Conquest* (New York, 1976) Chapter 6.
139 See J. Heinemann, *Aggadah and Its Development* (Hebrew) (Jerusalem, 1974) p. 163 ff. and the literature there cited. See also A.J. Heschel, *Theology of Ancient Judaism* (Hebrew) (The Soncino Press, 1962) vol. 1, p. xvi.

of the halakhah. The differences between Babylonian Jews and the native pagans were so great that in spite of some pagan influence on the Jews, the Rabbis did not feel the need to engage in polemics with the pagans. At any rate, it certainly was not as urgent a matter as it was for their colleagues in Palestine.[140]

The Gospels report several incidents in which Jesus and his disciples are engaged in halakhic disputation with the Pharisees.[141] The repeated theme in all these incidents is whether the conduct of Jesus or his disciples in a given situation follows the halakhah. While the Pharisees constantly argue that nothing short of the Rabbinic interpretation of Scripture represents the law, Jesus argues for a new interpretation. In one case Jesus bases his new interpretation on an incident recorded in Samuel according to which David deviated from Biblical law. In the view of Jesus, this reported deviation justifies other types of deviations.[142]

In another case, when the Pharisees accuse his disciples of violating a Rabbinic tradition, Jesus argues that the Rabbinic tradition itself is a transgression against Biblical law.[143] It seems natural for this kind of argumentation to produce discomfort among the Rabbis with early recorded deviations, and to result in attempts to explain them away. It therefore became essential for them to emphasize that only Rabbinic interpretation represents the halakhah and that the halakhah is the sole guide for one's life.[144]

---

140 bPes.56a; bA.Z.4a; see also J. Neusner, "How Much Iranian in Jewish Babylonia," in *Talmudic Judaism in Sasanian Babylonia* (Leiden, 1976) p. 139ff. See also Neusner, *Apharahat and Judaism* (Leiden, 1971).

141 Matthew 12:1-8; 12:9-13; 15:1-10; 19:3-13; Mark 2:18-23; 2:23-28; 3:1-7; 7:1-24; Luke 6:1-12. See also Tertullian, *Adversus Marcionem* (tr. F. Evans, Oxford, 1972) IV, 12, where the siege of Jericho is cited as an example of breaking the law: "The Sabbath was on that occasion broken by Joshua so that this too might be taken as referring to Christ." But see also Y. Baer, "Some Aspects of Judaism as Presented in the Synoptic Gospels" (Hebrew) *Zion*, vol. 31 (1966), p. 117.

142 Matthew 12:1-2 and parallels. See M. Kister, "Plucking of Grain on the Sabbath and the Jewish-Christian Debate," *Jerusalem Studies on Jewish Thought* (Jerusalem, 1983-4) vol. 3 (3), P. 313.

143 *Ibid.* 15:1-10 and parallels. See also J. Parkes, *The Conflict of the Church and the Synagogue* (Philadelphia, 1964) p. 38ff.

144 The foregoing explanation seems to resemble the argument put forward by Rabbi Kook in defending his ruling on the use of legume oil on Pass-

In the history of ideas one often encounters a situation in which the circumstances which gave birth to a certain notion or concept have disappeared, yet the concept itself continues to flourish. This occurs because of an intrinsic dynamic built into the concept, which has its own logic. This is especially the situation in the case of legal and meta-legal concepts, which in the nature of things are dealt with very conservatively.[145] Thus, it is not claimed that one can find a Christian background wherever the Yerushalmi insists on strict adherence to the law. The only point made here is that the Palestinian Amoraim, unlike the Babylonians, faced an overall situation in which strict adherence to the law provided an understandable response to their indigenous problems. In this respect the opposition to judicial deviation found in the Palestinian Talmud is unique. The next chapter seeks to show that sporadic criticisms occurring in the Babylonian Talmud do not culminate in any similar comprehensive opposition to judicial deviation.

---

over. (See text accompanying note 23 in Chapter 1 above). However, while R. Kook was explicit about the halakhic relevance of social conditions, the Talmudic sages did not articulate their scruples. Indeed, the reconstruction of judicial policy in Palestine as offered in this section, does not necessarily entail the claim of conscious deliberations on the part of the Talmudic sages. Social pressures of the kind that were active in Palestine may be very effective even when those involved are unaware of them. See also E. E. Urbach, "The Repentance of the People of Nineveh and the Discussions between Jews and Christians" (Hebrew), *J. N. Epstein Jubilee Volume* (ed. S. Assaf et al., Jerusalem, 1950) p. 118.

145 Silberg, *op. cit.* p. 55.

CHAPTER 5

OPPOSITION TO EXTRA-LEGAL CONSIDERATIONS

Apart from the hostile attitude toward extra-legal considerations sometimes found in the Yerushalmi, the Bavli contains no explicit systematic opposition to the employment of extra-legal considerations in judicial reasoning.

The Babylonian Talmud and some Tannaitic sources, however, do contain passages which imply that objection to the use of extra-legal considerations was occasionally voiced. These passages can be divided into two types:

1. Those containing criticism of judicial decisions which were allegedly decided on the basis of extra-legal considerations;
2. Those containing principles and statements bearing upon the problem of extra-legal considerations which imply opposition to extra-legal considerations.

Accordingly, these two groups will be examined to determine whether the opposition they express is sufficient to rebut the thesis that Talmudic law recognizes and accepts the concept of extra-legal considerations in judicial decision-making.

5.1 Criticism of Judicial Decisions Which Were Allegedly Based on Extra-Legal Considerations

The recognition that judges occasionally resort to extra-legal considerations is essential for a proper evaluation of judicial decisions, for any criticism of a judicial decision which relied upon extra-legal considerations will be utterly beside the point if it merely constitutes an argument that legal precedent required a different ruling. Rather, a reviewer dissatisfied with such a decision might argue that judges ought never to rule on the basis of extra-legal considerations, or that the particular case at hand does not constitute an appropriate situation for the employment of extra-legal considerations.

In the Babylonian Talmud there are numerous instances of criticism of judicial decisions based upon a court's alleged oversight of legal principles. In fact, such criticism constitutes the basis of Talmudic discussion. Criticism of decisions on the ground that they were based on extra-legal considerations, however, is rare: there are only a few such cases in the entire Babylonian Talmud. In view of the considerable number of judicial decisions based on extra-legal considerations, the rarity of this type of criticism is significant, suggesting that recourse to extra-legal considerations was generally acceptable.

In this context, a certain decision of R. Nahman to which Rava objected on the ground that the law dictated a different ruling is noteworthy.[1] When Rava realized that R. Nahman had based his decision on extra-legal considerations, he withdrew his complaint and no further objection is reported. On another occasion where R. Nahman was thought to have ruled contrary to the law, R. Huna b. Hyya, who was present in the courtroom, asked R. Nahman whether his decision was rendered in accordance with the law. Later, he explained that his question referred to the possibility of deriving a legal principle from R. Nahman's decision. Had R. Nahman ruled contrary to the law, R. Huna would have concluded that a legal precedent could not be derived from the ruling; however, there was no objection to the ruling on the ground that it had been decided on the basis of extra-legal considerations.[2] These cases will be discussed below in greater detail.

The following examples of criticism of a judicial decision should therefore be viewed in the light of this general background.

A. *The Case of the False Witness*

The Tosefta records the following incident:[3]

---

[1] bB.K.96b.
[2] bB.K.116b.
[3] tSanh.6:6; ySanh.6:3 (23, 2); bMak.5b; bHag.16b; Midrash Tannaim (ed. Hoffman) p. 117; Yalkut Shimoni on Ex.23:7.

OPPOSITION TO EXTRA-LEGAL CONSIDERATIONS 101

47 Said R. Judah b. Tabbai: May I see consolation[4] if I did not put to death a false witness, in order to uproot from the heart of the Boethusians [their false opinion]; for they would say, [the false witness is not put to death] unless the accused has [first] been put to death. Said R. Simeon b. Shetah to him: May I see consolation if you have not shed innocent blood, for the Torah said "On the testimony of two or three witnesses the accused will be put to death."[5] Just as there must be two witnesses so also the false witnesses [cannot be punished unless] both [are punished].

The Mekhilta records the same story in a different version:[6]

48 Once Simeon b. Shetah sentenced to death a false witness (*zomem*). Said R. Judah b. Tabbai to him: May I see consolation if you did not shed innocent blood, for the Torah said that you may sentence [a murderer] to death on the evidence of witnesses, and [also] you may sentence false witnesses to death on the basis of their refutation. Just as there must be two witnesses giving evidence, so also there must be two against whom refutation evidence is established.

The Mekhilta differs from the Tosefta and parallels in two respects. First, it reverses the roles of the participants, ascribing the decision to execute the false witness to R. Simeon b. Shetah and the opposition to it to R. Judah b. Tabbai.[7] Second, it omits the reasoning which follows the decision ("in order to uproot from the heart of the Boethusians . . .").

The contradiction between these two traditions provoked a wide range of comments and suggestions as to how it arose.[8] However, the

---

4   *Er'eh benekhama.* See tSanh.8:3; tKet.5:10; Mekhilta (ed. Horovitz) p. 171: bPes.54b; hTan.11a; Luke 2:25; Tosafoth on bHag.16b; Aruch, q.v. *nekhama*; J. Levy, *Worterbuch Uber die Talmudim und Midraschim* (Berlin, 1924) vol. 3, p. 370, Falk, *Introduction to Jewish Law* (Hebrew) (Tel Aviv, 1971) vol. 2, p. 323, n.4.
5   Deut. 17:6.
6   Mekhilta (ed. Horovitz) p. 327.
7   But *cf.* Yalkut Shimeoni *loc. cit.*
8   Geiger, *Urschrift und Uebrsetzungen der Bibel* (Breslau, 1857) pp. 140-1; Weiss, *Dor Dor Vedorshav* (Wilna, 1904) vol. 1, pp. 130-2; L. Finkelstein, *The Pharisees* (sec. ed., Philadelphia, 1962) vol. 2, p. 696; C. Chernowitz, *Toledoth Hahlakha* (New York, 1936) vol. 2, p. 330; Z. Zeitlin, *Hazedokim Vehaperushim* (New York, 1936) p. 30; J. Neusner, "By the Testimony of two Witnesses in the Damascus Document and in Pharisic-Rabbinic Law," 8 *Revue de Qumran* (1972) p. 197;

various attempts to reconstruct the historical truth are all unsatisfactory, since the historical evidence is simply inconclusive. The question whether it was R. Simeon b. Shetah or R. Judah b. Tabbai who executed the false witness,[9] or whether the explanation dated from the decision or was added later (original reasoning or ascribed reasoning) need not occupy us here. Historical reconstruction is only secondary to our immediate concern, which is the understanding of the tradition that has been transmitted to us. Modern scholars, in attempting to reconstruct events as they actually took place, fail to give sufficient attention to the preserved tradition. Thus, by labelling the reasoning in the Tosefta as a later addition, scholars feel free to ignore it. But it should be remembered that the reasoning reflects the thinking of the Rabbis at quite an early stage and thus requires close examination. Perhaps we cannot say much about the historical Simeon b. Shetah, but surely we can portray the thinking of the Rabbis by analyzing the ideas and views ascribed by them to Simeon b. Shetah and to other authorities. Accordingly, let us examine the case of the false witness as it has been preserved and transmitted to us.

R. Judah b. Tabbai is said to have executed a false witness contrary to the legal rule accepted by himself, in order to uproot, by this public example, a contradictory opinion of the Sadducees. Their opinion was that false witnesses were not put to death unless the accused had already been executed as a result of the false testimony. There is no doubt that as the story stands R. Judah did not err in the law, but deliberately violated it.[10] He was so determined to demonstrate that, contrary to the Sadducees' view, it was lawful to execute false witnesses before the accused was himself put to death, that he did so even

---

G. Alon, *Mehqarim Betoldot Yisrael* (Tel Aviv, 1957) vol. 1, p. 94; Falk, *op. cit.*, vol. 1, p. 110. But compare with *ibid.* vol. 2, p. 162; B. Lifshitz, "On Six Double Meaning Words or Phrases," (Hebrew) 51 *Tarbiz* (1982) p. 399 at p. 408.

9   Ascertaining the identity of this historical personality by comparing the incident with similar stories is by no means reliable. See Derenburg, *Essai sur l'Histoire et la Geographic de la Palestine* (Paris, 1867) p. 69, n.1.

10 When the claim is made that a judge has erred, the sources do not refrain from stating it explicitly; *cf.* mSanh.7:2 and the Talmudic discussion thereon (bSanh.52b)

when he had refutation evidence against only a single false witness, a circumstance where no legal execution should have taken place. R. Simeon b. Shetah is reported to have objected to the ruling of R. Judah b. Tabbai. The opposition to the ruling is also indicated by the next remark in the Tosefta and parallels:

> At that moment R. Judah b. Tabbai took upon himself not to rule except according to R. Simeon b. Shetah.[11]

The crucial question, of course, is whether this objection is an opposition to the general principle that judicial decisions can be based on extra-legal considerations or is merely an objection to the application of the principle to the particular case under consideration.

The author of *Hazon Yehezkel* is of the opinion that the latter position is correct. He believes that there was another disagreement between the Pharisees and the Sadducees about whether refutation evidence had to be established against both witnesses before execution could take place.[12] According to *Hazon Yehezkel*, the Sadducees maintained that if refutation testimony had been established against one witness only then that witness was liable to be executed even though the second witness might be set free. This view is also ascribed to the Sadducees by Weiss.[13] On the other hand, the Pharisees maintained that refutation testimony had to be established against both witnesses before execution of either of them could take place. Accordingly, the author of *Hazon Yehezkel* argues that Simeon b. Shetah opposed the ruling of R. Judah b. Tabbai on the ground that although it might uproot one false opinion of the Sadducees it would nevertheless support another. Namely, the view that a false witness is put to death upon refutation evidence being established against him alone, whereas

---

11 tSanh.6.6; see also bMak *loc. cit.*

12 Y. Abramski, *Hazon Yehezkel* on Tosefta Sanhedrin (Jerusalem, 1964) *ad loc.* Compare with Z. Chajes, *Torat Hanevim* (Jerusalem, 1958) p. 32.

13 Weiss, *op. cit.* p. 132. Weiss bases his argument on Deuteronomy 19:18, which uses the singular form *ed*. The Sadducees, as is well known, did not endorse the thirteen hermeneutical rules by which the Pharisees interpreted Scripture. Hence, argues Weiss, the Sadducees would not require (as did the Pharisees contrary to the plain meaning of Scripture) that both witnesses be executed. This argument, however, oversimplifies the controversy between the two schools.

according to the law, as understood by the Pharisees, the single false witness ought not to be executed.

This is an attractive argument. However, the problem with it is that it is historically unfounded. There is no independent evidence to verify that there was indeed such a controversy between the two parties.

D. Victor explains the opposition of R. Simeon b. Shetah in terms of the notion of *lehotzi melibam shel Zedokim*.[14] He surveys all the passages in which the term is used, and argues that only in this one was the halakhah pushed aside in order to uproot a false opinion from the heart of the Sadducees. As a rule the Rabbis, in taking issue with their opponents' views, would choose between two possibilities which were both sanctioned by the law.[15] Concluding that an indispensable element of the concept is that the halakhah should not be transgressed in the process of demonstrating the error of the Sadducees, Victor holds that because R. Judah b. Tabbai did violate the halakhah in this particular case, he was opposed by R. Simeon b. Shetah.

But if that were the case, the main criticism of R. Simeon b. Shetah is missing. All the sources which record the incident emphasize the shedding of innocent blood and not the mere fact of violating the halakhah.

Moreover, contrary to Victor's view, it seems that it was the Sages' policy to depart from the law in order to stress and strengthen their views on matters subject to public debate and opposition. The following example does not mention the Sadducees but it undoubtedly falls into this category. It is related in connection with a legal problem disputed between R. Eliezer and R. Joshua concerning the laws of *nidah* that although R. Joshua eventually accepted the opinion of R. Eliezer,[16] he ordered the people not to act in accordance with it.

> 49 Throughout the lifetime of R. Eliezer the people acted in accordance with the ruling of R. Joshua, but after the death of R. Eliezer, R. Joshua rein-

---

14 D. Victor, "Extra Legal Decisions of Beth Din," *Petach, A Journal of Thought and Reflection*, College of Jewish Studies, Vol. 2 (1975) pp. 19-24.
15 See mPara 3:3 and parallels; bYoma 53a.
16 mNid.1:3. See Albeck, *Shisha Sidre Mishnah*, (Jerusalem, 1952-8) *ad loc.*

troduced the earlier practice. Why did he not follow R. Eliezer during his lifetime? Because R. Eliezer was a shamuti [excommunicated (Rashi) or a *Shamaite* (R. Tam)] and he felt that if they would act in agreement with his ruling in this matter they would act in agreement with his ruling in other matters also, and that out of respect for R. Eliezer no one could interfere with him; but after his death when people could well be interfered with, he reintroduced the original ruling [i.e., R. Eliezer's ruling].[17]

The Babylonian Talmud interprets R. Joshua's instruction not to act according to the law (R. Eliezer's ruling) as a part of his political campaign against the view of R. Eliezer.[18]

Thus, in actual practice there were incidents of deviation from the law in order to uproot dissident opinions.[19] It seems, therefore, that in this respect the decision of R. Judah b. Tabbai accorded with the prevailing political theory of the Rabbis.[20]

In principle, I would follow the view of *Hazon Yehezkel* that the objection to the ruling does not imply general opposition to the principle of extra-legal considerations. It seems to me, however, that the objection to the ruling originated in the fact that human life was involved. The charge against R. Judah b. Tabbai is repeated in every record of the incident. Moreover, it seems that the objection originally included only this complaint. The additional remark in the text proof

---

17   bNid.7b and parallels. For a full discussion of this passage, see the text commencing with note 122 in Chapter 4.
18   Following one view rather than the other had practical consequences. If, for example, a woman who was considered ritually clean by R. Eliezer but ritually unclean by R. Joshua touched *toharoth*, according to the latter the *toharoth* became unclean and the woman was responsible for the damage caused by her touch (mGit.5:4). R. Joshua would have obliged such a woman to pay for the *toharoth* even though according to the halakhah she should have been exempt.
19   An experimental refutation of an halakhic opinion is reported in bHul.57b: "It was said of R. Simeon b. Halafta that he was an experimenter in all things. He once made an experiment to uproot from the heart of R. Judah . . ." Note the common terminology and names here and in tSanh.6:6.
20   See also tR.H.1:15 and bR.H.22b, and Rashi thereon.

paragraph, "For the Torah said," appears to be an editorial insertion.[21] As was pointed out above, the Mekhilta omits the explanation "to uproot from the heart of the Sadducees," probably because of hostility toward the employment of extra-legal considerations.[22] An explanation for R. Judah's ruling had to be provided, and was supplied in an indirect way in the reply of R. Simeon b. Shetah. By adding the "For the Torah said" paragraph it is implied that R. Judah b. Tabbai erred in the application of the law, a most unlikely possibility. The Tosefta which records the explanation could indeed have omitted the "for the Torah" paragraph, but it was already influenced by the Mekhilta. The original objection, however, is preserved in the Yerushalmi which records the reply of R. Simeon b. Shetah without the text proof paragraph:

50   May I see consolation if it is not related to you as if you shed innocent blood.[23]

The "to uproot from the heart of the Sadducees" argument must be distinguished from a similar argument often employed by the Rabbis, that of "because the time so required." On the basis of the few cases in which the two concepts occur it is hard to make a sound generalization. It appears, however, that while the former refers to an ideological dispute about the correct interpretation of the halakhah, the latter was invoked to justify deviation from the law on the occasion of widespread moral corruption in the community.[24] (Moreover, as discussed in Chapter 6, it was sanctioned by a power-conferring rule and was thus crystallized into the law). Only in the latter case did the Rabbis approve of capital punishment even when not provided for by law. This distinction explains why some sources cite with approval the various incidents in which people were sentenced to death contrary to the law, while the execution of the false witness is sharply

---

21   Note the variant reading of this paragraph, which also indicates a later insertion.
22   See text accompanying note 6 above.
23   ySanh.6:3 (23, 2).
24   See bSanh.46a and parallels. See also J. Ginzberg, *Mishpatim Leisrael*, (Jerusalem, 1956) p. 220; E. Quint and N.S. Hecht, *Jewish Jurisprudence: Its Sources and Modern Applications* (New York, 1980) Vol. 1, pp. 172-178.

OPPOSITION TO EXTRA-LEGAL CONSIDERATIONS 107

criticized. The Rabbis approved of capital punishment, even if contrary to the law, where the moral state of society was in actual danger, but did not feel themselves entitled to resort to the extreme measure of execution merely to reinforce and publicize their view in a contemporary cultural-halakhic dispute.

It follows, then, that the objection to the ruling of R. Judah b. Tabbai was based on the fact that capital punishment had been carried out contrary to the law in an ideological dispute. No reference was made to the principle that judges should be remote from public discussions and should base their decisions exclusively on legal material. It seems, indeed, that such a principle was not endorsed by the Rabbis.

B. *The Case of the Rebellious Wife*

51 R. Zebid's daughter-in-law rebelled (against her husband), and she had in her possession a silk. Amemar, Mar Zutra and R. Ashi were sitting together and R. Gamda sat beside them.[25] And in the course of the session they ruled [if a wife] rebels she forfeits her worn-out clothing that may still be in existence. Said R. Gamda to them: Is it because R. Zebid is a great man that you flatter him? Surely R. Kahana stated that Rava had only raised this question but had not solved it.[26]

The legal issue involved in this case is whether, as a measure of punishment, a wife who rebelled against her husband[27] forfeited her worn clothes (clothes which she had brought with her when she married and which were appraised and entered in her ketubah). The court ruled that the rebellious wife lost her worn clothes and ordered

---

25 On the term *yativ* see Tosafot on bA.Z.63b; D.M. Goodblatt, *Rabbinic Instruction in Sasanian Babylonia* (Leiden, 1975) p. 221ff.
26 bKet. 63b.
27 "The wife is regarded as a *moredet*, rebellious wife, when she persistently refuses to cohabit with her husband (bKet. 63a-b) . The *moredet* falls into one of two categories: first, that of a wife who refuses to cohabit with her husband because of anger or a quarrel; second, that of a wife who refuses to cohabit with her husband because she cannot bring herself to have sexual relations with him." (*Judaica* vol. 8, p. 1122). Traditional scholars differ as to which of these categories R. Zebid's daughter-in-law belonged to. See Rashi and Rabenu Nissim *ad loc*. However, the precise nature of her rebellion is of no interest here.

R. Zebid's daughter-in-law to return to her husband a certain silk that was in her possession. R. Gamda criticized this decision, arguing that the relevant halakhah has not been decided either way and hence, according to a well-established principle that no one can claim money on the basis of an undecided law,[28] the silk ought to be left in the possession of the wife. In his objection to the ruling, R. Gamda implies that the court deliberately violated the foregoing principle because R. Zebid was a "great man."[29]

It is true that the court did not state this as a ground for its decision. However, since R. Gamda was present at the trial and was addressing the judges, it is unlikely that he would have imputed such conduct to the court, an imputation tantamount to an accusation of partiality, had he not had sufficient grounds for doing so.[30] For the

---

28 "The onus of proof is on the claimant," bB.K.46a. See also Sifre ad Deut. (ed. Finkelstein) p. 27 and see *ibid.*, n. 3. Though an explicit reference to the maxim occurs in Rabbinic sources (Tannaitic and Amoraic) only with regard to a factual doubt as distinct from a legal doubt, the Amoraim followed the maxim in the latter case as well. See bB.K.99b; bB.M.102b; bB.B.32b; Tosafot on bB.B.62b; Gulak, *Law of Obligation and its Guaranties* (Hebrew) (Jerusalem, 1939) p. 115; *ET* vol. 9, p. 451.

29 *Gavra rabba.* I use this term throughout although the sources also refer to *zurba merabanan* and *adam hashuv.* Neusner (*History of the Jews in Babylonia* (Leiden, 1968) vol. 3, p. 82) suggests that "*gavra rabba* is a technical term meaning that the person had achieved mastery in reasoning about rabbinical traditions." The term occurs in the Talmud more than 38 times; in more than 25 passages there is reference to *adam hashuv* and there are more than 38 references to *zurba merabanan.* I could not detect any regularity in these terms; the Talmud uses the terms interchangeably. See also "*zurba merabanan,*" B. Mormelschtein, *Abhandlungen zur Erinnerung an H.P. Chajes,* (Wien, 1933) pp. 223-230; W. Bacher, *Tradition und Tradenten,* (Leipzig, 1914) p. 618. But see also S. Berman, "Adam Hashub: New Light on the History of Babylonian Amoraic Academies," *Dine Israel,* xiii -xiv (1986-88) p. 123, and Z. Steinfeld, "Adam Hashub Shani," (Hebrew) *ibid.* p. 193.

30 Compare the following Palestinian case from bKet.84b and note that the term "flattery" appears in both cases: "The people of the Nasi's household once seized in an alley a bondwoman belonging to orphans. At a session held by R. Abbahu, R. Hanina b. Papi, R. Isaac Nappaha, and in whose presence sat also R. Abba, they were told: Your seizure is quite lawful. Said R. Abba to them: Is it because these people are of the Nasi's household that you are flattering them? Surely when certain

OPPOSITION TO EXTRA-LEGAL CONSIDERATIONS 109

same reason, the explanation given by Shita Mekubezet,[31] that the court maintained that the law with respect to this issue had in fact been decided, is not satisfactory. The passage quoted above continues as follows:

> 51 Another version: In the course of their session they ruled: [if a wife] rebels she does not forfeit her worn-out clothes that may still be in existence. Said R. Gamda to them: Is it because R. Zebid is a great man [who would humbly accept the ruling] that you turn the law against him? Surely R. Kahana stated that Rava had only raised this question but had not solved it?[32]

As the Tosafoth (*ad loc.*) correctly observes, R. Gamda's complaint would have been groundless if the court had ruled that the wife should keep the silk in her possession, since this ruling would have accorded with the principle that no claim can be made on the basis of an undecided law. Moreover R. Zebid himself was not a party to the case, and the court could not rely upon his modesty as a guarantee that his son (who was the affected party) would not appeal the ruling.

Kaplan has pointed out that "this passage (i.e., the two versions) contains two contradictory accounts of a trial at which R. Ashi sat as a judge; evidently it was not edited by R. Ashi."[33] Indeed, it seems that the second version was inserted in order to counter the impression left by the first version that the court had been partial and had ruled in favor of R. Zebid. In particular it should be noted that there is no indication in the first version that the court had reversed its ruling; the usual term denoting a reversal of a ruling, *savar*, is not used here. A. Weiss provides other examples in the Talmud where another version is added in order to counter an impression made by the first account.[34]

---

judges gave a decision in agreement with R. Tarfon (i.e., according to your ruling) Resh Lakish reversed their ruling."
31 On bKet. *ad loc.*
32 This argument is clearly inapplicable to the former account, in which R. Zebid's son benefited from his father's favored position.
33 J. Kaplan, *The Redaction of the Babylonian Talmud* (New York, 1933) p. 103.
34 A. Weiss, *The Talmud in its Development* (Hebrew) (New York, 1954) pp. 221, 238, 240. See also L. Jacobs, "How much of the Babylonian Talmud is Pseudepigraphic?" 28 *JJS* (1977) 46.

The reasoning attributed to the court in the first account squares with a tendency of Babylonian Jewish courts to differentiate between a great man and an ordinary person in the application of the law. According to a Talmudic principle, the law with regard to a great man sometimes differs in certain respects from the general rule regulating the normal state of affairs. Thus, for example, the forms of acquisition of certain kinds of movable property differ in the case of a great man from those appropriate to ordinary people.[35] Similarly, a litigant is allowed to refresh the memory of a great man who testifies on his behalf, but not when the witness is an ordinary person.[36] The courts have expanded this principle, and various cases are recorded in which judges based their decision on the fact that one of the litigants was a great man.[37] Decisions are also reported in which judges deviated from the law on the same ground.[38] Rava, one of the judges most active in introducing this policy,[39] said of himself:

> May I be rewarded on the ground that when a disciple came before me in a lawsuit, I did not lay my head upon my pillow before I had sought points in his favor.[40]

---

35 bB.M.9b.
36 bKet.20a-b. For more examples, see: bShab. 139b; bM.K.11b; bJev.121a; bB.B.22a; 168a; 174b; *ET* (Hebrew) vol. 1, p. 175; E. Urbach, *The Sages: Their Concepts and Beliefs* (tr. I. Abrahams) (Jerusalem, 1975) pp. 626-627.
37 bB.K.59b; bB.M.68b; bB.B.144a; bShab.121b.
38 bPes.52a; bNaz.59a.
39 On this policy, see bNed.62a-b; bShebu.30b; bM.K.17a; bB.B.22a; bShab.119a. The first reference to the privileges of a "great man" occurs in Amoraic sources. The closest Tannaitic counterpart to "great man" is *haver*, but there is a great difference between the two concepts; the status of *haver* was relevant mainly to the laws of purity. (See *ET*. vol. 12, p. 502). The only instance in Tannaitic literature which implies a different standard for a "great man" occurs in mTan.3:8 (and parallels) in the case of Honi. R. Simeon b. Shetah sent to him [saying]: "If you were not Honi, I should have pronounced a ban against you . . . ." See also the story about Thaddeus of Rome in bBer.19a and bPes.53b. But these can hardly be considered judicial cases. See Alon, *Toledot Hayehudim beEretz Yisrael* (Tel Aviv, 1967) vol. 1, p. 124.
40 bShab.119a.

In one case Rava permitted two great men to settle and trade in a town though it was not their place of residence, contrary to the law regulating trade monopolies,[41] reasoning that as they were Rabbis, they would be disturbed in their studies if they had to return to their own town.

In view of all these sources, how should R. Gamda's objection be assessed? Here we are again faced with the question of whether the objection expresses general opposition to extra-legal considerations or disagreement with a specific argument.[42]

The principle stated above, that when applied to a great man the law may differ from the general rule, was attacked on various occasions. As opposed to Rava's dictum, Mar b. R. Ashi declared, "I am unfit to judge in a scholar's lawsuit because he is as dear to me as myself and a man cannot see anything to his own disadvantage."[43] According to Mar b. R. Ashi a great man ought to be treated exactly as an ordinary person, and being aware of the fact that he would favor a great man he refrained from sitting in a trial in which a great man was involved.

R. Ashi's pronouncement to the effect that a debtor may demand the creditor's oath (verifying that a bond is valid) only if the creditor is not a great man, was objected to by R. Yemar on the ground that scholars should not be favored. In R. Yemar's own words, "May a Rabbinic scholar strip men of their cloaks?"[44]

Similarly, various decisions are reported in which great men were punished as ordinary people, though there was some reluctance to do so.[45] Thus it appears that alongside the tendency to favor a great man, opposition to this attitude was developing. R. Gamda's objection must be viewed in light of this development. The "privilege" of a great man is referred to by R. Gamda as "flattery," a term with clear negative connotations.[46] The same term occurs in other sources which

---

41 bB.B.22a. See text accompanying note 20 in Chapter 1 above.
42 The same question applies to the passage refe note 30 above.
43 bShab.119a.
44 bShebu.41a.
45 bM.K.17a; bPes.52a.
46 Sifre ad Num. 35:33; bSot.41b; bKid.49b.

voice opposition to the policy of favoring a great man.[47]

The objection to the ruling, then, is not an expression of opposition to the general principle that judges may occasionally have recourse to extra-legal considerations. Rather, it refers to a general policy of Talmudic judges of differentiating between great men and ordinary people.

C. *The Case of the Notorious Robber*

52 A certain man who misappropriated a pair of oxen from his fellow went and did some ploughing with them and also sowed with them some seeds, and at last returned them to their owner. When the case came before R. Nahman he said [to the sheriffs of the court]: Go forth and appraise the increment. But Rava said to him: Were only the oxen instrumental in the increment, and did the land contribute nothing to the increment? He [R. Nahman] replied: Did I ever order payment of the full increment? I surely meant only half of it. He [Rava], however rejoined: Be that as it may, since the oxen were misappropriated they merely have to be returned intact, as we have indeed learnt: "All robbers have to pay in accordance with [the value] at the time of robbery." [Why then pay for any work done with them?] He [R. Nahman] replied: Did I not say to you that when I am sitting in judgment you should not make any suggestions to me, for Huna our colleague said with regard to me that I and King Shapur are brothers in respect to civil law? That man [who misappropriated the pair of oxen] is a notorious robber and I want to penalize him.[48]

Rava argues that the legal rule governing this case is the one stipulated in mB.K.9:1: "All thieves make restitution according to the value at the time of theft." Since the robber had returned the stolen oxen, he should have been ordered to pay only an amount representing the depreciation in value between the time of the oxen's theft and the time of their return. R. Nahman did not follow this rule; instead he assessed the liability of the robber on the basis of the benefit he had derived from the stolen oxen.[49] For our purposes, the crucial

---

47 bM.K.17a; bShebu.30a-b; bKid.70b; bKet.84b.
48 bB.K.96b. According to Ms.M. the word *atika*, notorious, is missing.
49 Jackson, *Theft in Early Jewish Law* (Oxford, 1972) p. 202 points to an earlier Shamaite attitude (Sifra Hova, Par. 13:13) to that effect, but con-

point is that after R. Nahman's initial attempt to justify his decision on legal grounds failed, he acknowledged that his ruling was in fact based on the extra-legal consideration of a desire to penalize a notorious robber. This declaration satisfies Rava and the discussion ends.[50] It appears that Rava objected to R. Nahman's initial presentation of his ruling as being based on the law when in fact it was not. By contrast, Rava had no quarrel with R. Nahman when he declared that his ruling was motivated by extra-legal considerations. This implies that Rava also, and not only R. Nahman, recognized that judicial resort to extra-legal considerations was acceptable.

R. Nahman's reference to King Shapur is not very clear. According to one Geonic interpretation, R. Nahman equates his ruling with those of the gentile ruler King Shapur in the following respect: just as decrees and rulings of the gentile ruler are binding from a halakhic point of view (because of Samuel's rule that the law of the state is law even though it is not based on halakhah), so too his own ruling should be valid even though it is not derived from accepted halakhic sources.[51] The intelligibility of this interpretation stems from the fact that it provides the ground from which R. Nahman derived his power to rule by extra-halakhic reasoning through equating this power to that of a gentile ruler.

D. *The Case of the Informer*

53 A certain person showed [to robbers] a heap of wheat that belonged to the Exilarch. He was brought before R. Nahman and ordered by

---

cedes that R. Nahman justified his ruling on "policy grounds" rather than on the law.

50 *Cf.* A.I. Kook, *Mishpat Kohain* (Jerusalem, 1937) section 143, p. 318. For a detailed discussion of the problem of the relation between R. Nahman's ruling and the legal maxim *ein danin dine kennassot bebavel*, see J. Ginzberg, *Mishpatim Leisrael* (Jerusalem, 1956) pp. 80-85. See also M.D. Judilovitz, *Pumbedita* (Jerusalem, 1938), Appendix 9, p. 136.

51 *Otzar Hageonim* (ed. B. Lewin) on B.K. (Jerusalem, 1943) p. 155. This Geonic interpretation escaped the otherwise careful study of S. Shilo, *Dina De-Malkhuta Dina* (The Law of the State is Law) (Hebrew) (Jerusalem, 1974). Rashi, following bB.B.115b, equates King Shapur with the Amora Samuel. See also J. Neusner, *A History of the Jews in Babylonia* vol. 3, (Leiden, 1968) p. 302.

R. Nahman to pay. R. Yoseph happened to be sitting in front of R. Nahman. R. Huna b. Hiyya said to R. Nahman: Is this a law or a fine (*dina* or *kenasa*)? He replied: This is the ruling in our Mishnah as we have learnt it: If it was caused through the robber himself he would have to provide him with another field, which we interpreted to refer to a case where he showed [the field to robbers]. After R. Nahman had gone, R. Yoseph said to R. Huna b. Hiyya: what difference does it make whether it is *dina* or *kenasa*? He replied: If it is *dina* we may derive other cases from it, whereas if it is *kenasa* we would be unable to derive other cases from it.[52]

The act of the *mosser*, one who provides the gentile authority with information about the property of others and thus causes its confiscation or misappropriation, is classified in Talmudic law as "indirect damage," the technical term for which is *garme*.[53] The legal duty of one who inflicts indirect damages to compensate the injured party is derived from an injunction of the Sages; Biblical law only imposes a liability for direct damages.[54]

A legal liability which is not derived from Biblical law but which is based on Rabbinic legislation, *takkanah*, is sometimes referred to as *kenas, kenasa* or *kenas hahamim*. Thus one meaning of *kenas* is "established rule."[55] However, *kenas* sometimes denotes a punishment inflicted on an offender in a particular case which is not derived from the law. The second meaning, then, is an *ad hoc* fine. This is the sense in which *kenasa* was used in the notorious robber case.[56]

In the informer case a certain man caused the confiscation of a heap of wheat by exposing it to a gentile authority. The case was also brought before R. Nahman, who ordered the informer to compensate the injured party for the lost wheat. His decision was apparently delivered without citing the reasons upon which it was based. A disciple present in the courtroom inquired whether the decision was based on *dina* or *kenasa*, to which R. Nahman replied "This is the ruling of our

---

52 bB.K.116b. See also bB.K.117a.
53 For an analytical examination of the concept of *garme*, see E. Berkowitz, "The Clarification of the Concepts of Grame and Garme," *Proceedings of the Fifth World Congress of Jewish Studies* (Jerusalem, 1972) vol. 3, p. 51; *ET* vol. 6, p. 461; *Judaica* vol. 7, p. 430.
54 See *ET ibid.*, pp. 466-7.
55 bB.K.27b; bGit.44a; 53a; bJev.118b; bB.B.94a; yB.K.10:6 (7, 3); yGit.5:5 (47, 1).
56 bB.K.96b; see also bHul.132b.

OPPOSITION TO EXTRA-LEGAL CONSIDERATIONS   115

Mishnah, etc."[57] R. Nahman does not specify on which of the two alternatives his decision is based, but should be understood to say that he based his decision on *dina*, the source of which is the Mishnah.[58] The correctness of this interpretation will become clear shortly.

After R. Nahman had left the courtroom another dialogue took place. R. Yoseph, who had not dared to intervene in the discussion in R. Nahman's presence,[59] now asked R. Huna b. Hiyya: What difference does it make whether the ruling is based on *dina* or on *kenasa*? He received this reply: if it is *dina* we may derive other cases from it whereas if it is *kenasa* we are unable to derive other cases from it.

This answer is ambiguous and can be understood in at least two different ways:

a. If R. Nahman ruled on the basis of *dina*, then this case constitutes a precedent and other similar cases must be treated alike; but if R. Nahman ruled on the basis of *kenasa* it does not constitute a precedent, since the decision is based on an *ad hoc* consideration.

b. If R. Nahman ruled on the basis of *dina* we may derive other cases of *garme* from it by means of analogy, but if R. Nahman ruled on the basis of *kenasa* we may not derive other cases of *garme* from it, since it is possible that the Rabbis imposed a fine in this case only; nevertheless, this case constitutes a precedent and similar cases must be treated alike.

This ambiguity stems from the dual meaning of *kenasa*. If R. Huna b. Hiyya used the term *kenasa* in the sense of "established rule," it follows that the second choice is the correct one. If, however, he used the term to mean "*ad hoc* fine," we would have to conclude that the first choice is correct. It should be noted, however, that the fact that a certain legal liability is referred to in the Mishnah does not indicate that it falls under *dina* as opposed to *kenas hahamim*. The Mishnah does contain references to *kenasa* (in its first sense) or, at least, so it was understood by the Amoraim. For example, mGittin 5:4 rules: one who renders unclean (another's foodstuffs) or mixes (*terumah* with

---

57   bB.K. *loc. cit.*
58   This interpretation is also suggested by Ramban, Rashba, and other commentators. See I.H. Daiches, *Netivot Yerushalaim* on B.K. 10:6 (Vilna, 1880).
59   Compare R. Nahman's reaction to Rava's objection at bB.K.96b, discussed in the preceding section.

them) or makes a libation (with his wine), if inadvertently he is free from liability, but if deliberately he is liable (to compensate him).

The imposition of liability in the Mishnah is under *kenasa* (established rule), since according to *dina* one is not liable for damage caused by oneself if that damage is not observable.[60] Whether this interpretation of the Mishnah is historically accurate is not so important. What is important to note here is that the Mishnah was so understood by the Amoraim.[61] The Mishnah imposes a fine on anyone who commits one of the acts described in the Mishnah, if the act was deliberate. This interpretation shows that *kenasa* (established rule) may well occur in the Mishnah as understood by the Amoraim.[62]

Let us now return to our dilemma. R. Nahman, it may be recalled, in answering the question "*dina* or *kenasa*," replied, "It is the ruling of our Mishnah, etc." As just shown, the fact that a certain liability is referred to in the Mishnah does not exclude the possibility that it is *kenas hahamim*. Thus, if R. Huna b. Hiyya used the term *kenasa* in its first sense, R. Nahman's reply is unsatisfactory, since it does not advance our knowledge as to the nature of the liability. In order to attribute any significance to the dialogue between the Master and his disciple we must conclude that the term was used in its second sense. Thus, by citing the Mishnah as the source for his ruling, R. Nahman indicated that his decision was not based on *ad hoc* grounds and could serve as a precedent.

Two arguments may be advanced against this conclusion. The first is as follows. Immediately after the dialogue between R. Huna b. Hiyya and R. Yoseph the following question is raised: "But what is your ground for saying that from *kenasa* we cannot derive any other cases?" From the structure of the passage it is clear here that the Talmud refers to *kenasa* in its first sense. This appears to refute the conclusion that R. Huna used the term in its second sense.

However, the continuation is an additional note and is not an integral part of the dialogue between R. Huna b. Hiyya and R. Yoseph.[63]

---

60 bGit.53a; *ET*, vol. 8, p. 702.
61 bGit. *ibid.*
62 For other examples, see bB.B.94a and yB.K.10:6 (7, 3).
63 In spite of the fact that in Ms. Hamburg the pronouns "He said to him" appear and create the impression that the dialogue continues, see *Dik.Sof. ad loc.*

OPPOSITION TO EXTRA-LEGAL CONSIDERATIONS 117

The question is introduced by the technical term *umena timra*. This term occurs 47 times in the Talmud[64] and in all the cases it has a technical meaning: it is used when an authoritative source is sought, generally a Tannaitic dictum but sometimes a Biblical verse. The employment of this technical term indicates the introduction of a separate unit. In fact, the passage added here was taken from bGittin.[65] It follows that one cannot deduce from the added passage the sense in which R. Huna b. Hiyya used the term.

The second argument that may be raised against the conclusion is as follows. R. Johanan, the Palestinian Amora, comments on the Mishnah referred to by R. Nahman by stating that the liability imposed by it falls under *kenas hahamim*. This interpretation occurs only in the Yerushalmi.[66] One could argue that, assuming that R. Huna b. Hiyya was aware of the Palestinian interpretation, R. Nahman, in referring to the Mishnah, intended to imply that his decision was based on *kenas hahamim*. This account of R. Nahman's reply, however, reads into the text what is simply not there. The laconic style of R. Nahman does not carry with it any reference to R. Johanan's interpretation. In fact it has been suggested that on this issue the two Talmudim contradict each other.[67]

Having established that the term of *kenasa* in the informer dialogue refers to an *ad hoc* fine, we can conclude that there was no objection to its implementation. By implication, the passage demonstrates that recourse to extra-legal considerations was acceptable.

From the four cases discussed above, it is clear that the Talmud did not object to extra-legal considerations as such; it did, however, debate the validity of extra-legal considerations when capital punish-

---

64 According to *Otzar Leshon Hatalmud* (ed. C.J. Kasowski, Jerusalem, 1954)
65 bGit.53a. The two *sugyot*, the present one and that of Git., are in fact contradictory. See Tosafoth on bMen.58b and *Shita Mekubezet* on bB.K. *ad loc.*
66 yB.K.10:6 (7, 3).
67 *Cf. Netivoth Yerushalmi* on yB.K. *ad loc.* This however need not be the case. The proposition that R. Nahman implied that his ruling was based on *dina* as opposed to *kenasa* in its second meaning does not necessarily contradict R. Johanan's interpretation. The juxtaposition of *dina* and *kenasa* (second meaning) does not exclude the possibility that *dina* is in fact derived from *kenas hahamim*.

ment was involved and when it was employed for the benefit of a great man. It can also be stated with some confidence that the precedential value of rulings based on extra-legal considerations was regarded as limited.

5.2 Principles and Statements Which Imply Opposition to Extra-Legal Considerations

A. *The Midreshei Halakhah*

The Midreshei Halakhah contain some material which suggests a hostile attitude towards the employment of extra-legal considerations in judicial decisions. The material is not extensive and the opposition is not explicit. Nevertheless it seems appropriate to examine whether this material can further our understanding of the concept of extra-legal considerations in Talmudic law. The sources examined include Mekhilta D'Rabbi Ishmael, Mekhilta D'Rabbi Simeon b. Johai, Sifra, Sifre (On Num. & Deut.), Sifre Zuta, and Midrash Tannaim (Melamed).

The dicta in the Midreshei Halakhah which imply opposition to extra-legal considerations are as follows:

1. Mekhilta Mishpatim (ed. Horovitz) p. 323:

54 *Neither shalt thou favor a poor man in his cause* (Ex. 23:3). Why is this said? Because of this: It says *Thou shalt not respect the person of the poor nor favor the person of the mighty* (Lev. 19:15). From this I know only these prohibitions in their exact form. But how about reversing them? It therefore says here *Neither shalt thou favor a poor man in his cause.*

2. Mekhilta Mishpatim (ed. Horovitz) p. 326:

55 *Thou shalt not pervert the judgment of the needy in his cause* (Ex. 23:6). Because it says *Neither shalt thou favor a poor man in his cause* (Ex. 23:3) from which I know only about the poor. But how about the needy poor? It says here *thou shalt not pervert the judgment of the needy in his cause.* If you have in a trial before you a wicked man and a pious man, do not say that since this man is wicked, I will turn judgment against him. It is with reference to this that it is said *thou shalt not pervert the judgment of the needy in his cause,* of one who is poor in good deeds.

3. Mekhilta D'Rabbi Simeon (Melamed) p. 214:

56 *Neither shalt thou favor a poor man* (Ex. 23:3). Can it mean that one should not favor the poor in charity? For this it is said: *in his cause* that he shall not favor the poor in his cause; that you shall not say this man is poor, this man is of a respectable family, I will pronounce judgment in his favor and he will then be able to maintain himself honestly. For this it is said *neither shalt thou favor a poor man in his cause* and further on it is said *thou shalt not respect the person of the poor* (Lev. 19:15).

4. Mekhilta D'Rabbi Simeon (Melamed) p. 215:

57 *Thou shalt not pervert the judgment of the needy* (Ex. 23:6) Why do I need this? Has it not been stated already *thou shalt not pervert judgment* (Deut. 16:19) either in favor of the poor or in favor of the rich? Why does it say *thou shalt not pervert judgment of the needy*? This is to include the case of a man who is poor in good deeds. For you should not say that since he is a wicked man he must be lying and this one must be telling the truth, and I will pervert the judgment against him. For this it is said *thou shalt not pervert judgment of the needy*.

5. Sifra Kedoshim 4:

58 *Thou shalt not respect the person of the poor* (Lev. 19:15). You shall not say that he is a poor man, and since this rich man and I are under an obligation to support him I will pronounce judgment in his favor and he will then be able to maintain himself honestly.

6. Sifra Kedoshim 4:

59 *Nor shalt thou favor the person of the mighty* (Lev. 19:15). You shall not say that since he is rich and is a respectable man, I will not put him to shame and see his shamefulness.[68]

7. Sifre Num. (ed. Horovitz) p. 222:

60 *So thou shalt not pollute the land* (Num. 35:33). This is a warning to the flatterers. (See Ramban on Num. *ad loc.*)

---

[68] This follows the text of Sifra ed. Weiss (Wien, 1862). No critical edition of Sifra is as yet available. On this passage, however, see *Sifra Codex Assemani* LXVI (L. Finkelstein, ed. New York, 1956) Introduction (Hebrew) p. 34.

8. Sifre Deut. (ed. Finkelstein) p. 28:

61 *Thou shalt hear the small and the great alike* (Deut. 1:17). Lest you will say that he is poor and since this rich man is under an obligation to maintain him, I will pronounce judgment in his favor and he will then be able to maintain himself honestly. For this it is said *thou shalt hear the small and the great alike*.

9. Sifre Deut. ibid:

62 Another interpretation: *Thou shalt hear the small and the great alike*. Lest you will say how can I discredit the reputation of this rich man because of one *denar*? I will pronounce judgment in his favor, and when he leaves the courtroom I will say to him: Give it him since you are liable. For this it is said *thou shalt hear the small and the great alike*.

10. Sifre Deut. (ed. Finkelstein) p. 198:

63 *Thou shalt not pervert judgment* (Deut. 16:19). You shall not say so-and-so is a nice man, so-and-so is a relative of mine. *Thou shalt not show partiality* (Deut. ibid.). You shall not say so-and-so is poor, so-and-so is rich.

The Midreshei Halakhah anticipate three instances in which a judge might be tempted to deviate from legal standards because of extra-legal considerations:
    a. Rich man v. poor man (Do not favor the poor).
    b. Rich man v. poor man (Do not favor the rich).
    c. Pious man v. wicked man (Do not favor the pious).

The considerations which are envisaged by the Midreshei Halakhah as likely to lead the judge to deviate from the law in such cases are stated precisely: to enable the poor man to maintain himself honestly; to preserve the good reputation of a great man; and to make plain one's hostility to the wicked. (Exegesis 4 envisages a somewhat different consideration: the wickedness of a litigant is conclusive evidence that he is lying).

These considerations, which are unacceptable to the Midreshei Halakhah, are individual considerations, involving the status, economic position or past behavior of one or both of the litigants.[69] In employing these considerations, the judge aims at arriving at a fairer

---

69 See Chapter 1, section 1.5, above.

and a more just solution to the dispute than would otherwise have been reached. The fact that a judge aims at a just solution does not, of course, ensure that justice is really being done. Nevertheless, it seems appropriate to distinguish this set of considerations from the case of the partial judge who deviates from the law on the basis of bias or prejudice. In the latter case the judge does not aim at arriving at a better solution from a moral point of view. This type of deviation from the law might be the result of favoring one of the litigants for personal reasons or discriminating against someone on the basis of their gender, race, or ethnic group.[70]

It might well be that, as no clear distinction is made between the two categories, the former is as unacceptable to the Midreshei Halakhah as the latter. But this does not weaken the conceptual distinction between the two, which is based on the motive of the judge. For reference purposes the former category is denoted as "positive considerations" and the latter as "negative considerations." Exegeses 2, 3, 5, 6, 8, and 9 clearly refer to "positive considerations," while exegesis 10 clearly refers to a "negative consideration."

If Rabbinic sources tend to convey their ideas not by means of abstract principles but by using concrete cases to illustrate the ideas without articulating the ideas themselves, then specific cases dealt with in Rabbinic sources should be taken as illustrations of a more general principle.[71] The relevant principle which can be derived from the above quotations is that individual extra-legal considerations should not figure in judicial reasoning.

That Rabbinic sources convey principles by means of casuistic argumentation is not disputed. However, even if we hold that the applicability of the exegesis is restricted to the cases actually referred to in it, a difficulty would nevertheless arise. The Talmud records various cases which were decided or were alleged to have been decided on the basis of extra-legal considerations, in violation of the exegeses quoted above. To recall but a few: the case of the sons of Rokhel,[72]

---

[70] See E. Green, *Judicial Attitude in Sentencing* (London, 1961) ch. 4; A.K. Bottomley, *Decisions in the Penal Process* (London, 1973) ch. 4, p. 148.

[71] See B. Jackson, *Essays in Jewish and Comparative Legal History* (Leiden, 1975) pp. 16-17.

[72] mB.B.9:7.

in violation of exegesis 2; the case of the porters,[73] in violation of exegesis 5; and the case of R. Zebid's daughter-in-law,[74] in violation of exegesis 6. Must we therefore conclude that there is a contradiction between the various Rabbinic sources? Is there any significance in the fact that the Midreshei Halakhah concur with the Yerushalmi and not with the Babylonian Talmud?

The student of the exegeses quoted above encounters a striking phenomenon: all are reported anonymously. In his *Prolegomena to Tannaitic Literature* (p. 513), Epstein suggests that anonymous exegesis is of very early origin. If he is correct, then the above exegesis is a reflection of the thinking of early scholars. Urbach has demonstrated that early exegesis was the product of work done by the *Soferim*.[75] "The latter are not to be identified with the Sages and certainly not with the Great Synod ... an examination of the sources clearly indicates that the status of the *Soferim* was inferior to that occupied by the elders and the Sages." Unfortunately, we lack conclusive evidence identifying the authors of the above exegeses as the *Soferim*; a precise identification for such an early period remains a matter for speculation. But it does seem plausible that the above exegeses originated in expositorial (non-practical) circles.

It is reasonable to assume that not all Rabbinic academies were alike. If we suppose that the above exegesis is the work of scholars who were not engaged in applying the law but only in the exposition of Scripture, then we can understand why they insisted upon strict enforcement of the law. The occasional need to deviate from the law makes itself apparent only to professional lawyers and to those administering the law, people who are required to make concrete choices between competing considerations. The exegete, remote from daily life, can allow himself to be an extremist; he can insist on employing only legal standards and on ignoring other considerations.

There is another good reason to assume that the above exegeses originated in expositorial circles and were not endorsed by the Sages. Curiously enough, these well-known dicta are not mentioned even once in the Babylonian Talmud. There is one indirect reference to

---

73   bB.M.83a.
74   bKet.63b.
75   E.E. Urbach, "The Derasha as a Basis of the Halakhah and the Problem of Soferim," 27 *Tarbiz* (1957-8) pp. 166-182.

exegesis 5 in a saying attributed to Resh Lakish. However, this saying appears in bHullin (134a) in a passage dealing with the priestly dues, and reference is made to the exegesis only incidentally. According to a well-established Talmudic principle, great importance is attached to the context in which a saying occurs.[76] The *locus classicus* of dicta concerning the duties of the judge is b.Sanhedrin, b.Shebuoth or b. Ketuboth; but in none of them does that saying, or any of the above exegeses, occur. Had the exegeses been accepted, it would have been appropriate to refer to them in these Gemarot. The omission of any reference to the above exegeses is even more significant in view of the fact that the Talmud frequently warns judges against employing negative considerations.[77] Taken together with the fact that various cases which were decided in violation of these dicta are reported, we must conclude that the Babylonian Talmud did not endorse the philosophy embodied in these dicta. Though the Midreshei Halakhah have obtained normative status, they contain what is evidently old material which was not recognized as binding.[78]

The apparent contradiction between the Midreshei Halakhah and the Babylonian Talmud should be regarded as a dichotomy rather than a contradiction, analogous to the duality of Aggadah and Halakhah. The early exegeses can be regarded as serving a purpose other than the formation and articulation of legal standards. The objection to the employment of extra-legal considerations embodied in the Midreshei Halakhah should be regarded as an expression of an ideal goal, the practical weight of which should not be overestimated. Ideal goals serve as directive principles. They guide but do not bind those to whom they are addressed, and they indicate certain tendencies without excluding dissenting opinions.[79]

---

76 bSanh.34b; bB.K.102a; bA.Z.7a; bBer.27a; bKid.54b; bBekh.26a.
77 bKet.105a-b; bShebu.30a; bSanh.36b. See also M. Beer, *The Babylonian Amoraim* (Hebrew) (Bar Ilan University 1974) pp. 267-268. But see bSanh.6b; yPea4:8 (18, 3) and compare with bSanh.36a and ySanh.4:9 (22, 2).
78 On the distinction between non-binding and binding norms, and the transformation of the former into the latter, see B. Jackson, "From Dharma to Law," 23 *AJCL* (1975) p. 490, n.2.
79 See the previous note. It is also possible that the main objection of the Midreshei Halakhah is to present a judicial decision as if it is based on halakhic considerations when in fact it is not. Under this account the

On the other hand, the opposition to extra-legal considerations recorded in the Yerushalmi, which was discussed in Chapter 4, comes from those responsible for the application of the law. Accordingly, such opposition indicates the legal practice through the eyes of the Yerushalmi. There is no evidence that the Yerushalmi's attitude was inspired by the Midreshei Halakhah. Rather, it developed independently.

B. *Let the Law Cut through the Mountain*

Though not directly quoted in connection with extra-legal considerations, this maxim has a bearing on the problem of solving disputes on the basis of extra-legal considerations. It occurs only twice in Rabbinic sources: in Tosefta Sanhedrin 1:2 and parallels;[80] and in b.Jevamoth 92a.[81]

Tosefta Sanhedrin 1:2-3 records a debate on the question of whether compromise by an arbitrator is preferable to the ordinary judicial process:[82]

---

objection is more procedural than substantive. See bSanh.6a. For a similar reasoning, see also A.I. Kook, *Mishpat Kohain* (Jerusalem 1937) p. 318.

80 ySanh.1:1 (18, 2); bSanh.6b; Midrash Hagadol ad Deut. 1:17; Yalkut ad Ps. 10. The biblical verse, *"Ein hokhmah v'ein tevunah v'ein ezah leneged Hashem"* (Proverbs 21:30), is quoted (bBer.19b) to express the idea of fixing the halakhah in general terms (as opposed to stating the law in a given factual situation) on exclusively legal grounds without paying attention to contextual considerations.

81 In bJev.92a, R. Eliezer discusses the, by then theoretical, question of whether a married woman who had remarried with the explicit permission of a court under the false impression that her first husband was dead, ought to bring a sin-offering. R. Eliezer says: "Let the law cut through the mountain and let her bring a fat sin-offering." Here the maxim is used figuratively to denote that careful examination of the case reveals that though the woman acted on the decision of the court, she ought to bring a sin-offering since the decision was based on a witness's error and not on a legal oversight of the court. Compare this application of the maxim with bSanh.97b; bB.K.39a; 53a; bB.M.117b.

82 For the historical background of this debate, see Sifre (ed. Finkelstein) p. 29, n.5; 5 *Judaica*, p. 857.

64   R. Eliezer b. Rabbi Jose the Galilean says: Whoever compromises offends ... but let the law cut through the mountain;[83] for thus Moses used to say: Let the law cut through the mountain ...

One of the most important differences between resolution of a dispute by means of an arbitrated compromise and resolution by means of the ordinary judicial process is that the arbitrator is not restricted to a specific set of considerations. He may therefore base his decision on extra-legal considerations. As expressed in the maxim, the objection to compromise is not based on the fact that justice is being done outside the framework of the court, but rather on the fact that it is not being done as a result of strict application of the law. Thus, by implication, the maxim rejects the possibility of solving disputes on the basis of extra-legal considerations.

If the maxim represents the prevailing view, one would have to conclude that extra-legal considerations are not authorized by the Talmud. Thus, Dembitz writes, "The Gemara quotes approvingly the saying, Let the judgment pierce the mount."[84]

---

83   Although there is general consent among scholars about the meaning of the maxim, it is not clear what the metaphor stands for. See Aruch s.v. *kav*; Maharsha on Sanhedrin 6b; *Hasdei David* on tSanh.1:2; *Hazon Yehezkel* on tSanh.1:2; B. Cohen, *Jewish and Roman Law* (New York, 1966) vol. 2, p. 670; Z. Falk, *Introduction to Jewish Law* (Leiden, 1972) vol. 1, p. 21. As yet no satisfactory account of the origin of the metaphor has been given. I would like to suggest the following: The juxtaposition of Moses and Aaron as each representing a different attitude calls to mind a historical event about which they differed, namely, the incident of the golden calf (Ex. 32). Unlike the unyielding response of Moses, Aaron's reaction to the sin committed by the Israelites, as interpreted by the Rabbis, was moderate and cautious. (See L. Smolar & M. Aberbach, "The Golden Calf Episode in Postbiblic Literature," 39 *HUCA* (1969) p. 91, at p. 109). Moses, on descending the Mount, ordered the killing of all those who had committed the crime of idolatry (Ex. 32:27). Thus, the law was strictly enforced by Moses in that incident. That this explanation is plausible can be seen from the fact that the Talmud cites a view according to which the verse in Psalms 10:3 (according to Rashi, or Malachi 2:6 according to the Tosafoth) which occurs in the Tosefta refers to the golden calf, see bSanh.7a. For a different account of the origin of the metaphor, see mEr.5:4; tEr.6:13 (bEr.58a).

84   *Jewish Encyclopedia* vol. 10, p. 206 (see also *ibid.* vol. 8, p. 383). Dembitz equates the maxim with the Latin *fiat justitia ruat coelum*. B. Cohen, *op. cit. ibid.* rejects Dembitz's equation.

But is this conclusion correct? It is possible to show that it is not, since opposition to the maxim can be found in the Tosefta itself. R. Eliezer's view is only one of several recorded in the Tosefta. Following R. Eliezer's statement it is related that R. Joshua b. Korhah held a directly opposite view, and subsequently the halakhah is decided according to him.[85]

Moreover, there is a clear indication that the compiler of the Tosefta rejected the policy embedded in the maxim and felt a need to express his opposition immediately after the maxim. The Tosefta continues in a highly unusual fashion with the following comment:

> ... but Aaron loved peace and pursued peace and made peace between man and his fellow as it is written ...[86]

This comment cannot be part of R. Eliezer's original dictum, since the behavior of Aaron referred to in the comment contradicts R. Eliezer's principle. As opposed to the strict enforcement of the law required by R. Eliezer, Aaron attempted to make peace by means of compromise.[87] It must therefore be an addition inserted by the compiler of the Tosefta to counterbalance R. Eliezer's view by expressing a directly opposite opinion.

The following consideration provides further support for the claim that the comment is an insertion. The extreme views of R. Eliezer and R. Joshua are reported at the beginning and at the end of the Tosefta, respectively. Each contains the following elements:

1. R. Eliezer says	1. R. Joshua says
2. He who compromises offends	2. It is a precept to compromise.
3. For it is written	3. For it is written
4. And thus Moses used to say	4. And thus David used to say

We see that each element in R. Eliezer's dictum has a counterpart in R. Joshua's. However, the comment "but Aaron loved ..." has no

---

85   bSanh.6b.
86   Cf. mAv.1:12.
87   A direct reference to this contradiction is to be found in *Sefer Even Haezer* (Prague, 1610) p. 114, by R. Eliezer b. Nathan of Mintz (c.1090 – c.1170). His solution is that the maxim refers to the previous opinion cited in the Tosefta. See also Tosafoth on Sanh. *ad loc.*

OPPOSITION TO EXTRA-LEGAL CONSIDERATIONS 127

counterpart in R. Joshua's dictum. This suggests that it is not part of the original tradition. It should also be noted that the conjunction "but" is used to mark the changing point. This conjunction is employed in a disjunctive manner to denote opposition between what precedes and follows it. In the light of the fact that a view opposed to that of R. Eliezer is cited at the end of Tosefta, the interjection of the compiler's own opinion shows how strongly he opposed the maxim.[88]

Later sources also demonstrate that there was hostility to the policy embodied in the maxim. In the famous story of Kamza and Bar Kamza we read that Kamza, after being offended by the Rabbis, sought vengeance by provoking the Romans against the Jews:

> He went and said to the Emperor: The Jews are rebelling against you. The Emperor said: How can I tell? He said to him: Send them an offering and see whether they will offer it. So he sent with him a fine calf. While on the way he made a blemish on its upper lip ... The Rabbis were inclined to offer it in order not to offend the Romans. Said R. Zechariah b. Abkulas to them: People will say that blemished animals may be offered on the altar. Then the Rabbis proposed to kill Bar Kamza so that he should not go and inform against them. Said R. Zechariah: People will say that one who makes a blemish on consecrated animals is put to death.[89]

The continuity of the story is broken at this point in order to insert a remark which reveals the hostile attitude of the compiler towards R. Zechariah, who is represented here as an extreme advocate of the "Let the law cut through the mountain" policy:

> Said R. Johanan: The humility[90] of R. Zechariah destroyed our House, burnt our Temple and exiled us from the land.

---

88 See Ben Jehuda's *Dictionary*, vol. 1, p. 27; see bBez.16a and Neusner, *The Rabbinic Tradition about the Pharisees before 70*, (Leiden, 1971) vol. 1, p. 325.
89 bGit.56a.
90 On "humility," see D. Rokeah, "Zechariah ben Avkules: Humility or Zealotry?," *Zion*, volume 53, p. 53, and D. R. Schwartz, "More on Zechariah ben Avkules: Humility or Zealotry?," *ibid.* p. 311.

There can hardly be a stronger condemnation of the policy expressed by the maxim than holding its proponent responsible for the destruction of the Temple.

Objection to the policy is also raised in more general terms by the same R. Johanan in bB.M.30b:

> Said R. Johanan: Jerusalem was destroyed only because they gave judgments therein in accordance with Biblical Law. Were they then to have judgments in accordance with untrained arbitrators? But say thus: Because they based their judgments strictly upon Biblical law and did not go beyond the requirements of the law.[91]

This analysis demonstrates that the maxim does not represent the general Talmudic attitude to extra-legal considerations. This, of course, does not show that the Talmud endorses the view that judicial decisions can be based on extra-legal considerations. However, it does remove an objection that could have been raised against this position.

C. *No Pity is to be Shown in a Matter of Law*

The last Tannaitic passage to be examined for possible opposition to extra-legal considerations is as follows:

> 65 If a man died and left a wife, a creditor and heirs and he also had a deposit or a loan in the hands of others: R. Tarfon says it shall be given to the one who is under the greatest disadvantage; R. Akiba says no pity is to be shown in a matter of law; rather it shall be given to the heirs...[92]

The legal principle generally applicable is that ownership passes automatically from the deceased to his heirs, and that movable property of fatherless children cannot be reached by the father's credi-

---

[91] See Sifre ad Deut. (Finkelstein) p. 165; ySanh.1:1 (18, 1); bB.M.88a. The Yerushalmi's omission of this view, ascribed to a leading Palestinian authority, is significant. It is consistent with the Yerushalmi's opposition to extra-legal considerations, as discussed in Chapter 4 above.

[92] mKet.9:2; see also mKet.9:3.

tors.⁹³ In the case contemplated by the Mishnah, however, the goods were not yet in the possession of the heirs. Hence the question arises whether the principle is to be applied here as well. R. Tarfon is of the opinion that in this case the legal principle gives way to a moral consideration, namely, the duty to assist the person who is at the greatest disadvantage, *koshel*.⁹⁴

In spite of Amoraic (and late Tannaitic) attempts to construe *koshel* as a technical term referring to a particular category,⁹⁵ it seems that R. Tarfon's original view was that the determination of who is under the greatest disadvantage may vary according to the circumstances of the case and ought to be subject to the judge's discretion. This interpretation of R. Tarfon's view is based on the simple argument that had R. Tarfon meant to refer to a particular class of people he would not have failed to specify it. Moreover, the variety of Tannaitic as well as Amoraic interpretations of R. Tarfon's view suggests that there was no specific tradition on *koshel*. In addition, R. Akiba's objection (see below) can be understood only if his opponent referred the matter to the judges' discretion, thereby making the legal rule variable.

The judge, according to R. Tarfon, should use his discretion and allocate the goods to whomever he sees fit. However, his decision must be based on a moral consideration, namely the relative economic/bargaining⁹⁶ position of the "successful claimant" in relation to the others.

As it emerges from the Yerushalmi,⁹⁷ the judge must take into account a complicated set of considerations:

---

93   bKet.92a; Yaron, *Gifts in Contemplation of Death in Jewish and Roman Law* (Oxford, 1960) p. 131.
94   The word is taken from Job 4:4. Aruch, s.v. *koshel* derives it from Ps. 105:37. It is interesting to note that, in tBek.2:7-8, R. Akiba uses the word *koshel* in a controversy between himelf and R. Tarfon. See also mBek.2:8, and Albeck, *Shisha Sidre Mishnah* (Tel Aviv, 1952-8) *ad loc.*
95   bKet.84a; yKet.9.2 (33, 1). These Palestinian attempts may stem from the Palestinian policy of eliminating extra-legal considerations from judicial decisions, as discussed in Chapter 4 above.
96   Depending on the various interpretations of *koshel* in the Talmudim.
97   yKet.9:2 (33, 1).

66 R. Jose bar Haninah says it [R. Tarfon's statement] refers to the [claimant who is] weakest in his evidence. For example, [if one lent] before witnesses and [the other] lent with a written document, then it should be given to the one who lent with witnesses. R. Johanan says it [refers to] the one who is physically weakest [and who thereby has difficulty in pursuing his claim] ... R. Aha says it [refers to] a poor person who is also weak.

According to one Amoraic interpretation, *koshel* refers to the one who is physically less fit than the others. The Yerushalmi raises the objection that if the *koshel* (i.e., the physically less fit) were the richest amongst all the claimants, then it would be unjustified to favor him. Hence the criterion is modified to the effect that the favored one must be physically less fit and also the poorest. Likewise, the interpretation of *koshel* given by R. Binyamin in the Babylonian Talmud has to be understood as containing a twofold criterion: greatest disadvantage with respect to proof, and righteousness.[98]

R. Tarfon, in allowing the judge to use his discretion and to take into account varying personal considerations, is prepared to sacrifice certainty in the law and clarity of its rules for the sake of fairness. R. Akiba endorses the opposite position: "No pity," he holds, "should be shown in a matter of law."[99]

For our purposes it is important to evaluate the significance of R. Akiba's objection, especially in view of the fact that the halakhah has been fixed according to him.[100] Determination of the halakhah according to R. Akiba is based on a technical rule, which, in general terms,

---

98 bKet.84a. This interpretation contradicts that of Rashi (followed also by the Soncino edition). *Kasher* here seems to have the same meaning as in Mekhilta (ed. Horovitz) p. 326, *rasha vekasher omedim lefanekh*. The requisite *vekasher* seems to be an additional requirement probably imposed to meet an objection similar to that raised by the Yerushalmi, but here it has been integrated into the original view of R. Binyamin. *Shita Mekubezet* (*ad loc.*) records an altogether different version.

99 See also Midrash Mishle on Prov. 22:22. On *din*, see B. Cohen *op. cit.* vol. 1, p. 52, n. 142.

100 bKet.84b. A Palestinian case in which a decision based on R. Tarfon's view was reversed is recorded in the Babylonian Talmud (*loc. cit.*) and in a more detailed form in the Yerushalmi (*loc. cit.*) This case may provide further evidence of the hostile Palestinian attitude to extra-legal considerations.

determines the halakhah in disputes between R. Akiba and his colleagues; it does not express a policy regarding the problem under consideration nor an evaluation of the issue concerned. It follows that one cannot argue that the fixing of the halakhah according to R. Akiba reflects an opposition to extra-legal considerations. In addition, the Talmud cites an opinion saying that the view of R. Akiba is not binding, but merely preferable.[101]

As to R. Akiba's objection itself, it is important to remember that a general legal norm and not a particular judicial decision is at stake here. R. Akiba objects to R. Tarfon's intention to make the legal rules flexible. He insists on formal reasoning which enables legal rules to be well defined and predictable.[102] Moreover, there is evidence that R. Akiba's objection is not categorical. In the actual application of the law, R. Akiba does not dismiss moral considerations.[103]

D. *Mistakes in the Law and Extra-Legal Considerations*

Talmudic law contains various provisions designed to regulate the case of the errant judge who hands down an erroneous decision not in accordance with the law. The sources distinguish between several types of judges and several types of errors. Consequently, different regulations are provided for each situation.

According to the usage of the term in this book, a decision based on extra-legal considerations is one in which the ruling does not accord with the requirements of the law. If a legal error in a judicial decision is defined in terms of an inconsistency between the decision reached and that which would have resulted from strict adherence to the law, then we are immediately faced with the following question. What bearing do the provisions specified in the Talmud for the case of the errant judge have on the problem of extra-legal considerations in judicial decisions?

The following survey examines the different types of legal errors in judicial decisions discussed in the Talmud, but does not touch

---

[101] bKet. *ibid*. On the significance of *matin*, see *Otzar Hageonim* on Berakoth (ed. B. Lewin, Haifa, 1928) Appendix p. 41.
[102] See Alon, *op. cit. supra* note 39, vol. 1, p. 333.
[103] See mMak.1:10. See also A.I. Kook's letter published in *Pri HaAretz*, vol. 4 (1982) p. 20.

upon the classification of judges.[104]

In the Mishnah we find two statements which the Talmud views as apparently contradicting each other:

1. mSanh. 4:1 reads:

67 In monetary cases they may reverse a decision either [from conviction] to acquittal or [from acquittal] to conviction;[105] but in capital cases they may reverse a decision [from conviction] to acquittal but not [from acquittal] to conviction.

2. mBekh. 4:4 reads:

68 If he judged a matter of law and declared exempt him that was culpable or declared culpable him that was exempt, or declared unclean what was clean or declared clean what was unclean, his decision stands but he has to make reparation out of his own property. But if he was an expert for the court, he is absolved from making reparation.[106]

As pointed out by the Talmud,[107] the contradiction between these two statements is that according to mSanh. 4:1 an erroneous ruling may be reversed whereas according to mBekh. 4:4 such a ruling

---

104 The discussion is further confined to legal errors as distinguished from factual errors. See, for example, mJev.10:2; mKet.11:5. Chapter 1 in Tractate Horayoth deals with erroneous decisions of the High Court in Jerusalem. The types of decision envisaged in this tractate, however, involve ritual matters and not a decision resolving a controversy between two parties. Hence, they do not involve a judicial decision in the true sense. The theme of the tractate is pronouncements affecting the whole community, made by the High Court in its capacity as a legislative body. See mHor.1:3-5.

105 That is to say, either in his favor or to his detriment.

106 *Cf.* tSanh.1:4-5; bSanh.6a; Jacob Mann, "Sefer Hama'asim Libnei Eretz Yisrael (Book of Palestinian Halakhic Practice)," *Tarbiz*, vol. 1 (3), p. 1,10. Compare this ruling with Laws of Hammurabi, section 5, *The Babylonian Laws*, G.R. Driver and J.C. Miles (Oxford, 1968) vol. 1, pp. 68-80. For Babylonian influence on Mishnaic Law, see S. Friedman, "The Case of the Woman With Two Husbands in Talmudic and Ancient Near Eastern Law," *Shenaton Ha-Mishpat Ha-Ivri*, vol. 2 (Jerusalem, 1975) p. 360.

107 bSanh.33a.

remains valid although in certain circumstances the judge may have to compensate the injured party.

It is possible that originally mSanh. 4:1 envisaged a case in which relevant material, unknown at the time of the trial, came to light after the decision had been delivered,[108] whereas mBekh. 4:4 deals with judicial errors. If so, in order to reopen a trial there must be new material available concerning the issue at hand (mSanh.), but a legal oversight on the part of the court does not affect the validity of the decision (mBekh.).[109] The Talmud, however, takes mSanh. 4:1 to refer to a reopening of a trial on the grounds of a judicial error, and hence the apparent contradiction arises between it and mBekh. 4:4.

One Talmudic attempt to reconcile the contradiction involves a distinction between the nature of the judicial errors referred to in the two cases. The Talmud cites an Amoraic saying attributed to R. Assi which reads as follows:

69 If he erred in a law cited in the Mishnah (*toeh bidevar mishnah*) the decision is reversed;[110] if he erred in the weighing of opinions (*toeh beshikul ha'da't*) the decision may not be reversed.[111]

Thus, it is argued, mSanh. 4:1 deals with the former situation whereas mBekh. 4:4 deals with the latter case.

Whether this distinction was invented *ad hoc* to reconcile the two statements or was only invoked here is not too important. Its frequent occurrence throughout the Talmud attests to the fact that the distinc-

---

108 This is in fact the teaching of mSanh.3:8 (tSanh.6:4). mSanh.4:1 repeats some of the rules already stated in previous Mishnayoth; *cf.* mSanh.1:1.
109 That this is a plausible reconciliation of the apparent contradiction can be shown from Mekhilta, (ed. Horovitz) pp. 327-28, which is a more detailed form of the first part of mSanh.4:1. Mekhilta clearly implies new material as a ground for reopening the trial. It stands to reason that the first part of the Mishnah (monetary cases) foresees the situation forseen in the second part of mSanh.4:1.
110 The Hebrew term is *hozer*. The ruling here is to be distinguished from the ruling in mSanh.4:1 which has *mahazirin*. The difference between these two terms corresponds to that between void and voidable. The different terminology, however, is not followed in yKet.9:2 (33, 1).
111 bSanh.33a, and see the following note. For a Roman parallel, see J.M. Kelly, *Roman Litigation* (Oxford, 1966) ch. 5.

tion is deeply rooted.[112] In any event, it is instructive to examine whether the distinction can throw light on the problem of extra-legal considerations.

Dating the maxim is an important element in the attempt to fix its meaning. In Tannaitic sources the term mishnah,[113] which is referred to in the maxim, has a meaning different from that associated with it later in the Amoraic period. In Tannaitic sources the term mishnah refers to the Oral Law in general,[114] whereas in Amoraic sources the same term denotes the corpus of R. Judah Hanasi.[115]

Gulak wants to infer from the "clear classical Hebrew style" of the maxim that it was of a Tannaitic origin. It seems to me that Gulak's assertion is questionable. The Yerushalmi records a dispute between R. Johanan and Resh Lakish about whether both types of errors mentioned above are alike in their legal consequences.[116] While the tradition in the Yerushalmi attests to the fact that the maxim was known at least one generation before R. Assi,[117] it also implies that the maxim was not of Tannaitic origin since it is usually unthinkable for the Amoraim to dispute a Tannaitic tradition.[118] For Gulak's assertion to be correct, one would have to maintain that there was another Tannaitic opinion that supported R. Johanan's view that the two types of error are alike. There are, however, no grounds for maintaining this.

Assuming, then, that the maxim is of Amoraic origin, *toeh bidevar mishnah* is a judge who hands down a decision in ignorance of a legal principle stated in the Mishnah of R. Judah Hanasi which has a bear-

---

112 bSanh.6a; 33a; bKet.84b; 100a; bBekh.28b; ySanh.1:1 (18, 1); yKet.9:2 (33, 1).
113 Gulak, *Yesodei Hamishpat Haivri* (Berlin, 1922) vol. 4, p. 180.
114 See W. Bacher, *Die Exegetische Terminologie der Judischen Traditionsliteratur* (Leipzig, 1899-1905) vol. 1, s.v. Mishnah; J. Epstein, *Mavo Lenusach Hamishnah* (Jerusalem, 1948) p. 804 and the sources listed there.
115 Epstein, *ibid*.
116 yKet.9:2 (33, 1). See discussion commencing in text at note 131 below.
117 R. Assi was a disciple of R. Johanan; see bShab.45b; bHag.13a. On R. Assi, see Zuri, "Hatafkidim bevaad R. Ammi ve R. Assi" 6 *Sinai* (1940) 26-35; 193-201.
118 See bErub.50b; Elon, *Jewish Law: Its History, Sources, Principles* (Jerusalem, 1973) p. 232.

OPPOSITION TO EXTRA-LEGAL CONSIDERATIONS 135

ing on the issue under consideration. As was pointed out, while Mishnah in Amoraic terminology originally referred to the corpus of R. Judah Hanasi, it was later extended to the pronouncements of the Elders,[119] thereby encompassing statements that were not incorporated into the Mishnah of R. Judah Hanasi.[120] In the last generation of the Amoraim in Babylonia the notion of Mishnah (in the context of the maxim) was further expanded to include the teachings of the Amoraim as well as the Tannaim.[121] The constant expansion of the term mishnah may also reflect a tendency to increase the scope of legal principles, the ignorance of which would render a decision void.[122]

Toeh beshikul ha'da't is a more complicated and controversial notion. The Talmud provides the following explanation:

70 Said R. Papa: If for example two Tannaim or Amoraim are in opposition and it has not been explicitly settled with whom the law rests, but he [the judge] happened to rule according to the opinion of one of them, whilst the general practice[123] follows the other, then this is a case of [an error] in the weighing of [conflicting] views.[124]

Gulak, followed by Cohn,[125] argues that *ta'ut beshikul ha'da't* originally referred to any error on the part of the judge in the course of his exercise of judicial discretion. On this view, R. Papa's remark illustrates the principle but does not exhaust it.[126] Gulak argues that

---

119 yKet. *loc. cit.*
120 This, however, may well have already been included in the original meaning of *mishnah*; see Epstein *op. cit.* p. 805.
121 bSanh.6a; 33a. It is already implied by R. Papa's remark, *ibid.*
122 This is also true of post-Talmudic literature. See Rosh on bSanh.33b (§6).
123 The current edition of the Talmud reads here "And the trend of the Talmudic discussion follows, etc." The reading adopted in the text agrees with Ms. M, Rif, Rosh, and Rashi. See *Dik.Sof. ad loc.*
124 bSanh.33a.
125 Gulak, *op. cit.*; Cohn, *Encyclopedia Judaica*, vol. 13, pp. 957-8.
126 Gulak finds support for his view in ySanh.1:1 (18,1), but the passage is obscure; see Alon, *op. cit.* vol. 2, pp. 31-2. Gulak also finds support in bSahn.29b, but no mention is made there of *ta'ut beshikul ha'da't*. The opening words of R. Papa's remark, "if for example," however, do constitute evidence for his position.

it was only in post-Talmudic literature that R. Papa's remark came to be considered the only possible example of the principle.[127] If this argument is accepted, it follows that originally decisions based on extra-legal considerations may have fallen into this category, since an unhappy litigant could claim that the judge who based his ruling on extra-legal considerations erred in exercising his discretion. It seems, however, that there are good reasons to reject Gulak's claim, and to consider R. Papa's view as the only correct interpretation of *ta'ut beshikul ha'da't.*

The sources quoted above speak of "judicial errors" without stipulating how, by whom, where, or when these errors are discovered. This is not an accidental omission. I think it is safe to assent to H. Mantel's claim that "no appellate court system in the modern sense existed in Palestine either before or after the Destruction."[128] Although instances are recorded in which legal decisions were overruled by judges who did not deliver the original ruling,[129] these "appellate" judges did not do so on the basis of any legal warrant but because they were more socially influential and more respected than the judges[130] who presided at the original hearing.

It seems to me that the lack of any institutionalized organs to supervise the decisions of inferior courts on the one hand, and the reference to judicial errors on the other hand, make it probable that the errors referred to are those that can easily be detected by the injured party without deliberation, and, once pointed out, are not subject to further dispute. *Ta'ut bidevar mishnah* is precisely such an error, since it can easily be identified by citing the relevant Mishnah alleged to have been overlooked by the judge.

---

127 Gulak *op. cit.*; cf. Rif ad bSanh.33a.
128 H. Mantel, *Studies in the History of the Sanhedrin* (Cambridge, Mass. 1961) p. 222. This view contests that of Zuri, *Shilton Hannessiot Vehawad*, (Paris, 1931) vol. 1, pp. 62-5. See also L. Finkelstein, *Jewish Self-Government in the Middle Ages* (New York, 1964) p. 379, and A. Mechlowitch, "Finality of Judgments in Jewish Law," 1 *Dine Israel* (1969) p. 7. See also A. Weiss, *Court Procedure* (Hebrew) (New York, 1957) pp. 152-3. For a different interpretation, see R. Shrira Gaon's Responsum in *Sharei Zedek* 4:7:35.
129 yKet.9:1 (32, 4); 9:2 (33, 1); yB.B.8:5 (16, 2); bJev.60b; bKet.50b; 54b; 84b; bB.K.12a; 117a; bB.M.66a; bB.B.111a; bHul.132b.
130 yKet.9:2 (33, 1). See also bKet. 84b and 100a.

On the other hand, to claim that a judge made a mistake in the exercise of his judicial discretion would necessitate a full-scale re-examination of the decision, and considerable jurisprudential qualifications would be expected of anyone who presumed to discover such alleged errors. Given the lack of institutions within which this process could be carried out and whose decisions would be binding, it would be pointless to hold a judge responsible for compensating the injured party, or, indeed, to consider this type of error at all since there would be no mechanism for discovering the alleged error. If the sources do refer to *ta'ut beshikul ha'da't*, then it must be a mistake that can be discerned relatively easily by the concerned party, and *ta'ut beshikul ha'da't*, as understood by R. Papa, satisfies these conditions. No doubt, the task of determining the general practice of judges requires legal skill and is more complicated than discovering an allegedly overlooked Mishnah. However, if an unhappy litigant criticizes a judicial decision at all, it would certainly be on this ground rather than on the ground of mistaken exercise of judicial discretion.

There is a passage in the Yerushalmi which appears to support this explanation of the notion of *ta'ut beshikul ha'da't* and, in general, sheds further light on the subject. Earlier in this chapter, reference was made to the dispute between R. Johanan and Resh Lakish on whether *ta'ut bidevar mishnah* is the same as *ta'ut beshikul ha'da't*.[131] R. Johanan maintained that the categories are the same in the sense that in both cases the decision cannot be reversed. By contrast, Resh Lakish maintained that *ta'ut bidevar mishnah* differs from *ta'ut beshikul ha'da't* but is the same as *ta'ut bidevar torah*. That is to say, in the case of *ta'ut bidevar mishnah*, the decision is reversed.

---

131 yKet. *loc. cit.*; *cf.* bKet.84b. I do not go into the significance of this dispute. Does it echo a controversy about the recognition and the binding power of the Mishnah of R. Judah Hanasi soon after its compilation? See D. Weiss-Halivni, "The Reception Accorded to Rabbi Judah's Mishnah," *Jewish and Christian Self-Definition* (ed. E.P. Sanders), vol. 2 (1984) p. 204. Note also that R. Assi, a disciple of R. Johanan (*cf.* note 118 above), adopts the view of Resh Lakish here.

We can thus distinguish three categories of judicial errors:
1. a judicial decision ignoring a rule explicitly stated in the Torah;[132]
2. a judicial decision ignoring a rule explicitly stated in the Mishnah;[133]
3. a judicial decision ignoring a rule usually followed by the majority of judges but not stated explicitly in the Torah or in the Mishnah.

Thus presented, the categories enumerate three possible sources of legal material listed in descending order of authority. Resh Lakish grants the Mishnah the same authoritative power as the Torah; a decision ignoring a rule stated in either of them is void. R. Johanan is more conservative. According to him, the Mishnah lacks the power to render void a decision that ignores its rules. Both, however, agree that *ta'ut beshikul ha'da't* does not affect the validity of the decision. It would appear that the occurrence of *ta'ut beshikul ha'da't* along with *ta'ut bidevar mishnah* and *ta'ut bidevar torah*, and the fact that the three form a hierarchy of legal sources, support the conclusion that all three forms of judicial errors contemplated by the Talmud result from ignorance: a specific rule escaped the mind of the judge. The criterion for whether a judicial error (in the Talmudic sense) has occurred is a positive answer to the question: Would the judge have ruled differently had additional legal material been known to him?[134] By contrast, in the case of a judicial decision based on extra-legal considerations, the inconsistency between the decision reached and the requirements of the law results from a deliberate judicial deviation from the law and not from mere ignorance of the law.

Having established that the Rabbinic sources discussed above deal solely with the ignorant judge, we can turn to the question of whether there is a sound jurisprudential basis for distinguishing between an inconsistency which results from a lack of knowledge of legal material and one which results from a deliberate deviation from the law. It is

---

132 The notion of *devar Torah* is sometimes referred to as "a matter in which the Sadducees accept authority." See bSanh.33b; bHor.4b; and *ET*, vol. 7, pp. 2-4.
133 See discussion in text commencing at note 113 above.
134 See Rif and Rosh on Sanhedrin 33a.

not being asserted that deliberate deviation is permitted or justified, rather that the nullification of decisions involving the former does not imply nullification of decisions involving the latter. That is to say, the nullification of a decision due to inconsistency resulting from ignorance of legal material might be justified on the basis of an argument that is not applicable to cases of deliberate deviation from the law.[135]

To ensure that justice will be done, a litigant has a right to expect that all legal material relevant to his case will be considered and weighed by the court before a decision is made. Failure to do so deprives the litigant of his basic right and should render the decision void. This right, which may be termed the right to total exposition of the law, is designed to ensure thorough deliberation and to prevent impetuous decisions. A decision which ignores relevant legal material is one in which the judge did not consider the case with sufficient thoroughness.

Different legal systems vary as to the scope of this right. In English law it is not recognized as far as early precedents are concerned. While precedents are binding in theory, the duty to inform the judge of its existence is counsel's; the more tenacious the counsel is, the more likely he is to find supporting precedents.[136]

In Talmudic Law the right is fully recognized as far as *devar torah* and *devar mishnah* are concerned. Ignorance of these sources means that the judge is not qualified to decide the case.[137] Deliberate deviation from the law, on the other hand, does not imply carelessness or lack of knowledge on the part of the judge, for he may have reached his decision after a careful examination of the case and of the legal positions of the parties concerned.

---

135 This distinction is also made by the Rosh, *ibid.*
136 See, for example, Allen, *Law in the Making* (7th ed.) (Oxford, 1964) p. 315.
137 bHor.4b. A similar problem is discussed in the Responsa literature in the context of the *kim li* plea. To what extent does the judge have to search for halakhic opinions supporting the defendant in order to meet the demands of the doctrine of *kim li*? See H. Ben Menahem, "Towards a Jurisprudential Analysis of the *kim li* Argument," *Shenaton Ha-Mishpat Ha-Ivri*, volume vi-viii, (1979-80) p. 45, at p. 52.

If it is true that judges are always bound to follow the law, this claim cannot be derived from the case of the ignorant judge. It therefore follows that the provisions regulating the case of the errant judge have no bearing on the problem of extra-legal considerations.

Having thus far established that the Babylonian Talmud does not prohibit judicial deviation, although in certain circumstances it does criticize and even object to it, we must now turn to an opposite task. We must inquire whether or not the cases of judicial deviation recorded in the Talmud are warranted by some general rules or principles which authorize departure from the generally accepted practice. This task is undertaken in the next chapter.

CHAPTER 6

POWER-CONFERRING RULES ALLOWING JUDGES TO DEPART FROM THE GENERALLY ACCEPTED RULES

6.1 General Considerations

The prior analysis of judicial decisions decided on the basis of extra-legal considerations focused on the reasons for the decisions, either as presented by the judges themselves or as ascribed to them by later authorities. No speculation about whether these decisions could have been justified on legal grounds was entertained, on the premise that if the judge explicitly admits to having deviated from the law (or if such a claim is ascribed to him) it becomes irrelevant whether the same solution could have been reached through legal means.

However, this reasoning may be objectionable. Suppose that Talmudic law contains a norm or a set of norms allowing judges to depart from the general rules in given cases and under certain circumstances. The effect of such norms would be that if a judge deviates from the general rules he does not necessarily rule beyond the limits of the law. It is conceivable that the judge has supplied only a partial reasoning with the missing part being implied or assumed. It follows that, even if the judge explicitly recognizes that the general rule was not followed, this is not the sole criterion for determining that the judge has deviated from the law. Such a conclusion can be reached only after ruling out the possibility that norms allowing departure from the law were applied.

Accordingly, we will now examine whether the Talmud contains any norms which may be invoked to justify departures from generally accepted rules and to determine the jurisprudential limits of their applicability. The term "norm allowing departure" refers to norms which exist independently of the judicial decisions based on them.

Since no legal norm is self-generating, a power-conferring rule that can be derived from a given decision cannot be the legal ground for that decision. At most, the derived rule can serve as a legal ground for subsequent decisions, if it is introduced into the system by custom, precedent or the like. Once again, it is important to reiterate the methodological presupposition of this book. Namely, the Talmudic material here discussed is conceived of as representing a complete description of a legal system. We do not assume the existence of any hidden, unspoken or unarticulated legal norms.

6.2 The Rule of Rabbi Eliezer b. Jacob: Beth Din May Pronounce Sentences Even Where Not Warranted by Law

The rule of R. Eliezer b. Jacob concerning the power of the Beth Din to pronounce sentences even where not warranted by law, constitutes one of the most direct references in Talmudic law to the problem of judicial deviation. It therefore requires special examination. As will be seen, when properly analyzed the scope of this principle is far more limited than is generally assumed.

The maxim is recorded in three different versions[1] which seem to reflect a gradual expansion of its scope. The original, or at least the oldest, form of the maxim occurs in the Yerushalmi:

71 We learned: R. Eliezer b. Jacob said: I heard that they punish not according to the halakhah *and they punish not according to the Torah [italics supplied] (veonshin shelo katorah).*[2]

A close examination will reveal that the words *veonshin shelo katorah* (and they inflict punishments even where not warranted by the Torah), which are traditionally read as an integral part of the

---

1 yHag.2:2 (78, 1); bJev.90b (bSanh.46a; Midrash Tanhuma Mishpatim 6); Megilat Ta'anit, H. Lichtenstein, "Die Fasternrolle," 8-9 *HUCA* (1931-32) p. 257 at p. 336.
2 yHag. *ibid.* See *Ahavat Zion Veyerushalayim ad loc.* Since there are two Tannaim of the same name, one who lived during the period of the Destruction, and the other a pupil of R. Akiba, it is difficult to determine which of the two was the author of certain halakhot including the present one. See *Judaica*, vol. 6, p. 624 and the literature cited there.

maxim,³ are in fact the beginning of the subsequent Talmudic query. That is, immediately following the maxim, the Yerushalmi reports a dispute between two Palestinian Amoraim about the scope of the maxim. It is suggested that the words *veonshin shelo katorah* are introductory and should be read with a question mark.⁴ The other two sources which record the maxim (bSanh.46a and Megilat Ta'anit) omit both these words and the accompanying Palestinian dispute. Accordingly, the translation of the Yerushalmi report should be:

> R. Eliezer b. Jacob said: I heard that they punish not according to the halakhah. And they punish not according to the Torah? How far?

It is interesting to note that the Yerushalmi speaks only of *onshin*, unlike bSanh.46a which has *makin* and *onshin* and Megilat Ta'anit which has *horgin, malkin* and *onshin*. In some cases, *onshin* refers exclusively to monetary punishments, i.e., fines,⁵ but the usage is not consistent. It seems that in the present context *onshin* originally excluded both capital and corporal punishment.⁶ bSanh.46a, an improved and more detailed version of the maxim, makes little sense if *onshin* itself refers to capital punishment. The Babylonian Talmud version thus reads:

72   R. Eliezer b. Jacob said: I heard that courts mete out lashes and punishments not according to the law.⁷

---

3   See, for example, Elon, *Jewish Law*, vol. 2, pp. 422, n. 94; W. Greene, "Extra-legal Juridical Prerogatives," 7 *JSJ* (1976) p. 152 at p. 160.
4   The Yersuhalmi often repeats a challenged proposition as a question; for example, see ySanh.9:7 (27, 2); yPea1:1 (15, 4); yTan.2:8 (65, 4). If the reading suggested here is correct it removes the difficulty raised by Elon *op. cit. ibid.*
5   See mKet.3:2; mNed.2:5; Sifre ad Deut. (ed. Finkelstein) 181; bKet.46a; bSanh.17b (see Dik. Sof. *ad loc.*); but compare yKid.4:12 (66, 2), and see also Alon, *Mehquarim Betoldoth Yisrael*, (Tel Aviv, 1958) vol. 2, p. 21.
6   As against the view of Elon, *op. cit.* and Greene, *op. cit.* This restricted view of the Yerushalmi squares with its overall tendency to reduce the discretion of the courts. See Chapter 4 above and, in particular, the text accompanying note 95.
7   bJev.90b (bSanh.46a). In some manuscripts and Rishonim the maxim is attributed to R. Eleazer; see Gilat, "A Rabbinical Court May Decree the Abrogation of a Law of the Torah" (Hebrew) in 7-8 *Bar Ilan Annual*

In fact, the Bavli in bSanh.46a, goes a step further than the Yerushalmi by including corporal punishment as well as fines.

Megilat Ta'anit is even more extreme. It reports a dispute between two sages which is not mentioned elsewhere. According to one of them, the maxim allows capital as well as corporal punishment, whereas according to the latter the maxim authorizes only monetary and corporal punishment.

> 73 R. Eliezer b. Jacob said: I heard that courts flog and execute not according to the law. Of the house of Levi, R. Shimon said: I heard that courts punish with fines and mete out lashes not according to the law.[8]

Megilat Ta'anit differs from the earlier sources in that it refers explicitly to capital punishment and reports a dispute on that very point. This also indicates that the earlier sources do not authorize the execution of an offender without a legal sanction.

The rule in all of the versions is followed by two judicial cases which illustrate its applicability, one of which reports the stoning of a person who, according to the law, did not deserve capital punishment.

> It once happened that a man rode a horse on the Sabbath in the Greek period and he was brought before the court and stoned, not because he deserved this penalty, but because the times so required. Again it happened that a man had intercourse with his wife under a fig tree. He was brought before the court and flogged, not because he deserved it but because the times so required.[9]

Since in neither of its Talmudic versions does the rule authorize capital punishment, it follows that the stoning verdict cannot illustrate the applicability of the maxim. By presenting an additional extreme view according to which capital punishment is also warranted, Megilat Ta'anit reconciles the stoning verdict with the maxim.[10] That the

---

(1970) p. 117. See also Epstein, *Mavo Lenussach Hamishnah*, (Jerusalem, 1948) vol. 2, pp. 1180-82.

8   Megilat Ta'anit *loc. cit.*

9   bJev. *loc. cit.*; bSanh. *loc. cit.*; yHag. *loc. cit.*; Megilat Ta'anit *loc. cit.*

10 The tradition of Rabbi Eliezer ben Jacob is recorded in the scholium to

extreme view is indeed secondary is also indicated by its reference to *malkin* instead of the usual *makin*.[11]

The discrepancy noted here between the stoning verdict and the maxim apparently escapes Alon. He argues that the maxim was constructed in order to cover early recorded cases which, due to changes in the halakhah, were no longer in accordance with the prevailing law.[12] In fact, if we wish to go along with Alon, we can only argue that the maxim was invoked (but not constructed) to justify early recorded cases.

Yerushalmi Hag.2:2 differs from bSanh.46a and Megilat Ta'anit in another respect as well. In the Yerushalmi version there is no direct reference to Beth Din. This omission might be significant. It might indicate that the maxim contemplates punitive measures inflicted on the offender outside the framework of the court, such as the alleged execution of the eighty witches by R. Simeon b. Shetah.[13] However, one is on much safer ground in assuming that the term Beth Din should be read into the Yerushalmi version and that this apparent difference is of no consequence.[14]

Megilat Ta'anit. The text in Megilat Ta'anit itself, to which the tradition is appended, speaks of "killing the apostates." This constitutes an additional reason to modify the tradition of Rabbi Eliezer ben Jacob so that it will be relevant in the context of Megilat Ta'anit.

11 *Makin* is a more appropriate term in the context of the maxim of Rabbi Eliezer ben Jacob. *Malkin* appears to be a term reserved for the Biblical 40 lashes which were inflicted in well-defined circumstances. See mMak.3:10; yNaz.3:4 (53, 1-2). *Makin*, on the other hand, seems to denote disciplinary flogging (*makot mardut*). See yNaz.3:4 (53, 2) and bKet.86b; but see tMak.4:17. See also Aruch, s v *malkot*; B. Jacob, "Gott und Pharo," 68 *MGWJ* (1924) 276-281. It should be noted that Megilat Ta'anit has both *malkin* and *makin*; but whereas *makin* appears in the conservative view which does not permit the infliction of capital punishment, *malkin* appears in the extreme view, which allows the court to execute without legal warrant to do so. It should also be noted that Megilit Ta'anit reverses the order of the cases to correspond with the rule itself.

12 Alon, *op. cit.*, vol. 1, p. 104, n.64.

13 Alon, *ibid.*, pp. 103-4, notes further examples in which offenders were executed on the spot without trial.

14 See mSanh.9:5; yMK.3:1 (81, 4) for other examples where this type of ellipsis is used.

This brings us to a crucial dilemma. In Tannaitic sources, the term Beth Din refers to both the judicial and the legislative functions of the court.[15] Its precise meaning, in a given passage, must be determined contextually. And it is clear that if Beth Din in the maxim under consideration refers to the legislative power of the court, then the maxim represents a legislative principle and has no direct bearing on the issue of judicial deviation.

Elon, following traditional commentators, cites the maxim as a legislative principle but does not justify his opinion in any way.[16] *Prima facie*, it seems that there are two possible arguments supporting such a view. First, bSanh.46a adds a qualification to the maxim: "yet not with the intention of disregarding the Torah but in order to make a fence (*seyag*) around it." This qualification does not modify or add anything to the meaning of the maxim; it merely explicates the maxim. The term it employs, however, is significant. The concept of *seyag* always refers to legislative activity,[17] and this would suggest that the maxim constitutes a legislative principle. However, Elon regards the qualification "yet not with the intention of disregarding the Torah, etc." as a late Amoraic insertion; hence, no reference can be made to it in interpreting the original meaning of the maxim.[18]

Second, bJev.89b discusses whether the court may legislate new rules that conflict with Biblical law. In an attempt to resolve this question reference is made to the maxim of R. Eliezer b. Jacob. One could argue that as the query relates to the legislative function of the court, so also must the principles referred to by the Talmud in response to the query. However, this argument also indicates only the meaning ascribed to the maxim and not its original significance. Moreover, the assumption made here is questionable. bJev.89b refers *inter alia* to the incident in which Elijah, on Mount Carmel, transgressed Biblical law in order to demonstrate the supremacy of God. This can hardly

---

15 For examples of the judicial function, see mKet.11:5; bJev.67b (and parallels); bKet.48a; bB.M.55a; bSanh.17b; bSanh.81b. For the legislative function, see bJev.89b; bGit.55b; bB.K.81b; bA.Z.36a (and parallels).
16 Elon *op. cit.* p. 421; see Greene *op. cit.* p. 159, who also regards the maxim as a legislative principle.
17 See mAvot 1:1; 3:13; Mekhilta (ed. Horovitz) p. 19; Sifre ad Deut. (ed. Finkelstein) p. 25; bBer.4b; bNid.3b. See also Aruch, vol. 6, p. 14.
18 Elon *op. cit.* p. 422.

be regarded as a legislative activity. It follows that bJev.89b does not maintain a clear conceptual distinction, and hence the assumption underlying the above argument is false.

On the other hand, there are good reasons for regarding the maxim as a judicial principle. First, the terms *makin, onshin,* and *horgin* have punitive denotations suggesting judicial activity. Second, as noted above, the applicability of the maxim is illustrated by two judicial cases and not by reference to any *takkanah* or *gezera,* which, had the maxim constituted a legislative principle, would have been more appropriate. Finally, the very wording of the rule itself indicates that it is referring to the Beth Din as a judicial institution. All versions of the rule of R. Eliezer b. Jacob preserve the literary form of "I heard that." The expression "I heard" preceding a statement indicates that its content was not generally known, but was transmitted orally from teacher to pupil in a more or less private manner. Furthermore, this opening appears to be a technical term denoting a tradition which is either obscure,[19] not vindicated by any other source[20] or disputed;[21] in short, it denotes a tradition that is deficient in some way.

The qualifying nature of the "I heard" tradition can be further supported by examination of another term used in introducing traditions. Tractate Eduyoth of the Mishnah records testimonies of various sages regarding numerous traditions. The most common introduction is "R. testified." Regarding this term, B. De Vries comments: "The term testified had a particular meaning. It is from the vocabulary of courts and means that the halakhah was heard by an official or official body such as a council, a Beth Din or the president of the Beth Din."[22] Like "testified," "I heard" is also taken from court terminology, but signifies that the statement it introduces is deficient in some way and cannot be used as testimony. Now, the legislative power of the Beth Din

---

19　mPes. 9:6; mJev.8:4; tZev.1:8; yJev.8:2 (9, 1); bShab.52b; bZev.13a; bZev.37b.

20　mEr. 2:6; mJev.16:7

21　mShebi.6:5-6; mOr.1:7; mEd.8:6; mShek.4:7. On *shama'ti* see W. Bacher, *Tradition und Tradenten in dem Schulen Palestinas und Babyloniens* (Leipzig, 1914), p. 9; B. Gerhardsson, *Memory and Manuscript* (Uppsala, 1961) p. 133. Gerhardsson considers the possibility that traditions prefaced by *shama'ti* were parts of *megilot starim.* See also Zuri, *Shilton Hanessiut Vehavad* (Paris, 1931) pp. 56-57.

22　B. DeVries, *Mehkarim Besifrut Hatalmud* (Jerusalem, 1968) p. 223.

to enact new rules contrary to Biblical law was a well established principle, at least until the Amoraic period.[23] It is therefore inconceivable that a statement introduced by the "I heard" formula reports such a commonplace tradition. On the other hand, the judicial power of the Beth Din to punish in a manner at variance with the law, without proper legislation, is not mentioned by any of the sources preceding R. Eliezer b. Jacob, and his statement undoubtedly had its opponents.

A. *Limits of the Maxim*

In focusing on the jurisprudential limits of the maxim, it is clear that the maxim refers only to the domain of penal law, thus excluding civil cases (*dine mamonoth*) from its scope. This can be shown not only from the terms employed by the maxim itself which reflect court-inflicted punitive measures, but also from the cases illustrating it which are limited to acts of a criminal nature.

Moreover, even within the domain of penal law the maxim has limited application. The rule covers only judicial conduct which evidences a harsher attitude toward the offender than that prescribed by law. Thus, it permits the infliction of a punishment not stipulated by law.[24] However, the maxim does not authorize judges to mitigate the law, to be less severe with offenders than required by law.[25]

---

23   Gilat, *supra* note 7.
24   *Midrash Ruth Hanelam* (Zohar Haddash, ed. Margalioth, Jerusalem, 1953) p. 154 interprets the maxim as a duty-imposing rule, requiring the judge when dealing with "villains" to be more severe than required by law; cited by Beth Yoseph on Tur Hoshen Mishpat, Chapter 2.
25   This point needs special emphasis in view of a recent article by W. Greene claiming the very opposite. Discussing the qualification of the maxim presented in the Babylonian Talmud ("Yet not with the intention of disregarding the Torah but in order to make a fence around it"), Greene says:
>   This declaration is paradoxical. However, there is significance in the fact that the Talmud goes out of its way to state that a Beit Din will not intentionally violate the Torah. It must mean that a Court may not be more stringent than the Torah. It cannot prohibit what is Biblically permitted. This stricture would apply in all cases. However, leniency in the place of Pentateuchal strictness is allowed as evidenced from Elijah at Mt. Carmel. (Greene, *supra*

POWER-CONFERRING RULES

The application of the maxim may be restricted to an even greater extent. The common denominator of the two illustrative cases is that in both situations the departure from the general rule was justified on grounds of the needs of the time. This may indicate that the maxim permits only social, as opposed to individual, considerations[26] as the grounds upon which departure from the law can be justified.[27]

In addition to these limitations referred to in the maxim itself, the Yerushalmi, as discussed above,[28] substantially restricted the application of the maxim by confining it to matters of procedure.[29]

---

note 3, p. 172).
As authority for his view, Greene cites Rabbi Kook. To be sure, R. Kook comments on a view expressed by the seventeenth-century commentator, the Taz, a view which he himself finds difficult to comprehend. A.I. Kook, *Mishpat Kohain* (Jerusalem, rep. 1973) section 143, p. 317. (The reference in Greene's paper to Kook's *Mishpat Kohain* is mistaken). However, Greene misrepresents the view. The Taz refers only to actions explicitly permitted by the Torah. See Taz on Yoreh Deah, section 117. It is only in this case, the Taz argues, that the Beth Din may not prohibit what has been explicitly permitted. In any event, Greene's sweeping statement is refuted by the evidence provided by the two illustrations that follow the maxim, in which the court dealt severely with the offenders.

26 On the distinction between social and individual considerations, see Chapter 1, section 1.5, above.
27 This limitation is explicitly stated in a passage attributed to the Geonim; see *Otzar Hageonim on Sanhedrin* (Jerusalem, 1966) *ad loc.* and R. Meir of Lublin, Responsa, No. 138. But compare yHag. *loc. cit.*, from which it appears that the maxim can also be applied in a case of individual censurable behavior. See J. Ginzberg, *Mishpatim Leisrael* (Jerusalem, 1956) pp. 53ff, and see also *ET*, vol. 8, p. 523. See also N. Rakover, "Remuneration for Committing Offence in Jewish Law," (Hebrew) *Mishpatim*, vol. 2 (1970), p. 481 at p. 484.
28 See Chapter 4 at section 4.3.
29 A further substantial limitation is found in post-Talmudic literature. In his commentary on Deuteronomy 17:8 Abravanel cites the maxim of Rabbi Eliezer ben Jacob as follows: "Rabbi Eliezer ben Jacob said: I have heard that the Great Beth Din in Eretz Yisrael used to inflict punishment, etc." This reading, which significantly limits the applicability of the maxim by regarding it as a special prerogative of the High Court in Jerusalem and thus suggesting that its importance is only historical, is also found in a censored edition of the Talmud. See *Hesronoth*

6.3 *Shuda Dedaynee*

Shuda dedaynee[30] is a Talmudic term denoting judicial discretion. The Talmud stipulates that, in some cases and under certain circumstances which involve a factual doubt which cannot be resolved, judges must exercise discretion. The cases in which *shuda dedaynee* is applied are limited,[31] but it is nevertheless appropriate to explore the precise scope and nature of the discretion granted to Talmudic judges.

Originally, *shuda dedaynee* was applied only to cases involving doubt about the identity of the beneficiary of a gift, and the judicial discretion authorized by *shuda dedaynee* was confined to ascertaining the donor's true intention. It will be seen that at a later stage the scope of *shuda dedaynee* was expanded to encompass doubts arising in other transactions as well and that the nature of the discretion was widened.

The Talmudic sources dealing with *shuda dedaynee* can be divided into two groups: (a) those sources which indicate or describe the factual situation in which *shuda dedaynee* is applied; (b) those sources which refer to *shuda dedaynee* but do not specify the factual situation involved.[32]

Group (a) consists of 6 cases:

1. One Deed Too Many

74   If two deeds bearing the same date [are presented in court] Rav ruled [the property in question] should be divided [between the two claimants]

Hashass (Koenigsberg, 1860) on bSanh.46a p. 44. The view that the applicability of the maxim is restricted to the High Court alone is explicitly stated by Abravanel (*ibid.* 16:18) and is consistent with his overall political philosophy. See B. Netanyahu, *Don Isaac Abravanel* (Philadelphia, 3rd. ed. 1972) p. 163. Similar interpretations are found in other commentators as well, notably Ran. See Ran on bSanh.27a and 46a, and, in particular, the detailed discussion in his *Derashoth*, ed. L.A. Feldman (Jerusalem, 1973) p. 192ff.

30   On *shuda dedaynee*, see Chapter 4, section 4.2 above.
31   See text at note 53 below.
32   bKid.74a; bShebu.30a-b (Tanhuma Mishpatim 6).

and Samuel ruled *shuda dedaynee* [the case is to be decided at the discretion of the court].³³

2. Two Tobiahs

75 A man once said to those around him: Let my estate be given to Tobiah and then he died. If two Tobiahs appear [to claim the estate] one of whom was a neighbor and the other a scholar, the scholar is to be given precedence. If one is a relative and the other a scholar the scholar is given precedence. ... If both are relatives or both are neighbors or both are scholars, *shuda dedaynee*.³⁴

3. The Undecided Mother

76 The mother of Rami b. Hama gave her property in writing to Rami b. Hama in the morning, but in the evening she gave it in writing to Mar Ukba b. Hama. Rami b. Hama came before R. Shesheth who confirmed him in possession of the property. Mar Ukba b. Hama appeared before R. Nahman who similarly confirmed him in possession of the property. R. Shesheth thereupon came to R. Nahman and said to him: What is the reason that the Master has acted this way? And what is the reason [the other retorted] that the Master has acted in this way? Because [the former replied] Rami b. Hama's deed was written first. Are we then [the other retorted] living in Jerusalem where the hours are inserted in the deeds? Then why [the former asked] did the Master act in this way? I treated it [the other retorted] as a case of *shuda dedaynee*. I too [the first said] treated it as *shuda dedaynee*. In the first place [the other retorted] I am a judge and the Master is not a judge, and further you did not initially come with this argument.³⁵

4. The Doubt of the Agent

77 If a man said to another, take a *maneh* to so and so, and he went and looked for him and did not find him [alive], he must return the money

---

33 bKet.94a; yKet.10:4 (33, 4).
34 bKet.85b. *Cf.* tSanh.7:7 (last three lines).
35 bKet.94b.

to the sender. If in the meantime the sender has also died, R. Nathan and R. Jacob say that he should return it to the heirs of the sender or as some say to the heirs of the person to whom the money was sent. R. Judah Hanasi said in the name of R. Jacob who said it in the name of R. Meir, that it is a religious duty to carry out the wishes of the deceased. The Sages say that the money should be divided, while here [in Babylon] they say that the bearer should do whatever he wished.[36]

5. Two Claimants

78 If there are two claimants to a property and one says: It belonged to my father, while the other says to my father [without either of them bringing any evidence], R. Nahman says that whoever is stronger can take possession. Why [it may be asked] should the ruling be different here from the case in which two deeds relating to the same property and bearing the same date are presented in court, in which case Rav rules that the property should be divided [between the two claimants] and Samuel says *shuda dedaynee*? In that case there is no chance that further evidence should come to light, here there is a chance that further evidence may come to light.[37]

6. Doubtful Ruling

There are two versions of a certain ruling ascribed to Rava pertaining to land law. Thus the Talmud rules:

79 According to one version the rule is one way, and according to the other version the rule is the other way (so we leave the judges to use their own discretion) *shuda dedaynee*.[38]

The last situation deals with discretion given to judges in the case of a legal uncertainty, where the exact law governing the issue under consideration is not clear due to contradictory accounts of a certain ruling by Rava. (6) thus differs from the other cases listed above, all of which deal with factual doubt. The Nimukey Yoseph reports a tradition claiming that the ruling of *shuda dedaynee* in (6) is an insertion of R. Yehudai Gaon, who inserted the ruling on the basis of a tradi-

---

36 bGit.14b-15a.
37 bB.B.34b-35a.
38 bB.B.62b.

tion passed down by the Savoraim.[39] It follows that Talmudic law proper did not grant discretion to judges in this case, and that the Talmudic concept of *shuda dedaynee* was confined only to cases involving a factual doubt.

The Talmud at bKet.94b cites (4) as the Tannaitic authority for Samuel's rule in case (1). As seen above, (4) deals with an agent who was authorized to deliver a sum of money as a gift, but who received no instructions concerning disposition of the money in the event that the donee dies before receiving the gift. If the donor also dies before the money is returned to him, then the agent is confronted with a dilemma as to whom the money should be given: to the heirs of the donor or to the heirs of the donee? The factual situation contemplated here is one in which incomplete instructions of a donor render execution of his actual intent impossible. According to the Babylonian Sages, the agent is permitted to step into the shoes of his former principal and is authorized to act at his own discretion.

A similar situation is contemplated in (2), where a donor's vague instruction to give his estate to an unspecified "Tobiah" creates difficulties if two equally qualified claimants named Tobiah appear to claim the estate after the donor has died. In direct opposition to tB.B.11:13, the ruling here is that the court should exercise its discretion and assign the estate in full to one of the two claimants.[40]

The case of the undecided mother (3) is the only recorded judicial decision employing *shuda dedaynee*.[41] There a certain property was

---

39 Nimukey Yoseph *ad loc*. Many of the Savoraic insertions are commonly attributed to R. Yehudai Gaon. See B. Lewin, "Rabanan Savorai Vetalmudam" *Azquara Larav Kook* (Jerusalem, 1938) part 4, p. 145.
bShebu.48b. deals with a certain point of procedure which is not agreed upon and the Talmud rules as follows: R. Hama said: "Now since the law has not been stated either in accordance with the view of R. Elazar, if a judge decides like Rav and Samuel it is legal, if he decides like R. Elazar it is also legal." Though the term *shuda dedaynee* is not referred to in this passage, the ruling of R. Hama was regarded by the Geonim as based on it. See the statement of R. Nahshon Gaon in *Otzar Hageonim* on bKet.94a.
40 See Yaron, *Gifts in Contemplation of Death in Jewish and Roman Law*, (Oxford, 1960) p. 183ff.
41 For similar cases, see bB.B.58a; bB.B.151a; yPea 3:6 (17, 4).

delivered twice, to two different people, as a gift. In that case the doubt over who owns the property in question originates in two contradictory documents of transfer being made by the donor.[42]

These three cases deal explicitly with gifts; the factual situation contemplated in (1) is less clear. Nevertheless, the fact that the Talmud bases (1) on (4), and the implied reference to (1) in (3), strongly suggests that (1) also refers to a case in which the same property is given twice.

This analysis suggests that the application of *shuda dedaynee* was originally limited to cases of obscure, incomplete or contradictory expressions of a donor's will. Although the Talmud nowhere articulates such a limitation on the concept of *shuda dedaynee*, this may be due to an expansion of the concept which already had taken place in Talmudic times, to which we now turn.

Case (5) expands the application of the concept of *shuda dedaynee* by attempting to relate it to a factual doubt of a different nature. In (5) the doubt stems from lack of decisive evidence about the actual facts, and not from an obscure expression of the donor's wishes. Two claims are presented with regard to a certain property, in each of which the claimant maintains that the property in question belonged to his father and that he inherited it. The Talmud rules that "whoever is stronger can take possession" and refuses to refer the matter to the judges' discretion. The explanation given is that *shuda dedaynee* is applicable only in cases of factual doubt which cannot be resolved (e.g., an obscure expression on the part of a deceased donor). In (5), the Talmud argues, there is a chance that further decisive evidence might be obtained; hence the concept of *shuda dedaynee* is not applicable.[43] The fact that the Talmud makes no reference in case (5) to the distinction between doubts pertaining to gifts and doubts pertaining to other transactions, a distinction which would serve equally well

---

42 A deed is effective from the moment it is delivered to the donee. See bGit.9b and parallels. In this case, two deeds bearing the same date were issued with regard to the same property. Since there was no decisive evidence as to which was delivered first, both were equally valid.

43 Whether this qualification reflects the original meaning of *shuda dedaynee* or is a later development is hard to determine. It is not clear whether all cases in which *shuda dedaynee* was applied meet this criterion.

to exclude the application of *shuda dedaynee* in (5), indicates that the Talmud no longer holds the view that *shuda dedaynee* is confined to cases falling into the former category.[44]

In addition, the view that case (5) indeed represents an expansion of the concept of *shuda dedaynee* also follows from the following argument. In a manner similar to the above reasoning, it reveals the exceptional character of (5). Analysis of the Tosefta, a late Tannaitic-early Amoraic source, reveals that the nature of the discretion granted by *shuda dedaynee* was originally limited to the interpretation of the true intent of a donor, and hence *shuda dedaynee* could not originally be applied to case (5).

The concept of discretion in the judicial context has been analyzed by Ronald Dworkin. He distinguishes between three different meanings in which discretion can be used:

> Sometimes we use "discretion" in a weak sense, simply to say that for some reason the standards an official must apply cannot be applied mechanically but demand the use of judgment. . . . Sometimes we use the term in a different weak sense, to say only that some official has final authority to make a decision and cannot be reviewed and reversed by any other official. . .
>
> I call both of these senses weak to distinguish them from a stronger sense. We use "discretion" sometimes not merely to say that an official must use judgment in applying the standards set him by authority, or that no one will review that exercise of judgment, but to say that on some issue he is simply not bound by standards set by the authority in question.[45]

If judges have discretion only in the two weak senses, they are not thereby entitled to introduce extra-legal considerations into their reasoning. Only discretion in the third, strong sense entitles judges to rely on discretion when basing their decisions on extra-legal considerations.

Raz surveys three different sources of judicial discretion in the strong sense, of which the third is laws of discretion. "Most legal sys-

---

44 *Cf.* Rif *ad loc.*
45 R. Dworkin, *Taking Rights Seriously* (Harvard University Press, 1977) pp. 31-32. For further analysis of the term, see Kadish & Kadish, *Discretion to Disobey* (Stanford, 1973), and, in particular, p. 42ff.

tems," says Raz, "contain laws granting courts discretion not only as to the weight of legally binding considerations, but also to act on considerations which are not legally binding."[46]

Returning to the nature of the discretion granted by *shuda dedaynee*, we must consider whether *shuda dedaynee* is a law of discretion, or whether it merely authorizes discretion in the weak sense. Opinions differ on this.

The main representative of the latter view is Rashi. He holds that *shuda dedaynee* is discretion guided by binding legal standards. In his commentary on case (2), Rashi says: "The judges have to decide according to what they estimate the deceased would have preferred, or, alternatively, the estate must be given to the one whose conduct is better so that we may assume that the deceased would have preferred him."[47]

R. Tam is of the opposite opinion. He holds that *shuda dedaynee*, when applicable, grants judges discretion to act on whatever considerations they deem appropriate, and that in such cases judges are not guided by any legal standards.[48] It seems that both views are partially correct.

Shuda dedaynee, when it was applied only to gifts, was a type of discretion in the weak sense of the term (Rashi's view). However, as the scope of *shuda dedaynee* expanded, the nature of the discretion changed and *shuda dedaynee* came to represent discretion in the strong sense (R. Tam's view).

Tosefta B.B.11:13 sheds light on the original meaning of *shuda dedaynee*. The Tosefta contemplates the same problematic situation discussed in case (2), but the ruling here follows the view of Rav:

80 ... If someone says: "Give 200 denar to Joseph b. Simeon," and there were two Josephs b. Simeon, one does not interpret the words of a lay man [i.e., one does not attempt to estimate the intent of the donor] in the sense of "the one he loved and the other he did not love," but both

---

46 J. Raz, "Legal Principles and the Limits of Law," 81 *Yale L.J.* 823 at p. 846.
47 Rashi on bKet.85b. This view is shared by Maimonides, *Laws of Acquisition and Gifts*, 11:3; Meiri on bKet.85b; Rashbam on bB.B.35a.
48 Tosafoth on bKet.85b and on bKid.74a. Among others, this is also the view of Ritba and Ran on bKet.85b; Rashba on bB.B.35a.

take equal shares . . .[49]

The Tosefta not only rules that the money should be divided between the two claimants (Rav's ruling), but also explicitly precludes an alternative ruling: "One does not interpret the words of a layman." That the Tosefta refers to this alternative ruling in negative terms suggests that it was current in some circles and the view alluded to is easily recognized as that of Samuel. The Tosefta thus contains the two alternative rulings which in case (1) appear in the form of a dispute between Rav and Samuel. It is evident that the view rejected in the Tosefta maintains that the money should be given in full to the claimant considered by the court to be the donor's favorite. The discretion of the court is thus limited to interpreting the donor's true intent; all other considerations are excluded.

The only case in which such an interpretation of *shuda dedaynee* is impossible is case (5). It has been argued that reference to *shuda dedaynee* in case (5) indicates that the concept is that of discretion in the strong sense since (5) does not involve a donor whose will is in doubt, and hence the judges' discretion referred to in (5) cannot be a case of merely interpreting someone's intent.[50]

This argument thus shows that case (5) is unlike the other cases listed above, not only with regard to the scope of the discretionary power of the judges, but also with regard to the nature of the discretion. It appears that coupled with the expansion of the application of *shuda dedaynee* the nature of the discretion also changed, and *shuda dedaynee* came to represent discretion in the strong sense.

To summarize briefly, from the foregoing analysis of the Talmudic sources, the following emerges concerning the application of *shuda dedaynee*:

The most extreme restriction is that stated in case (5). Namely, the concept is applicable only in cases involving factual doubts that cannot be resolved. Furthermore, it follows from case (3) that: (a) only qualified judges are authorized to resort to *shuda dedaynee*;[51] and (b)

---

49   tB.B.11:13. See S. Lieberman, *Tosefot Rishonim ad loc.* On *dorshin leshon hediot*, see yKet.4:8 (28,4); bB.M.104a.
50   Tashbetz, Part 2, 272.
51   See H. Rajnes, *Massot Vemequharim Bemussar Uvemishpat Yisrael* (Jerusalem, New York, 1972) p. 89.

the concept must be applied in the course of the decision-making process. It cannot be employed as a *post factum* justification.[52]

Shuda dedaynee cannot, therefore, be regarded as an all-inclusive principle of universal applicability. Rather it is a limited device for deciding otherwise unsolvable cases of a particular nature under specific circumstances.[53]

6.4 Judges May Deviate from the Halakhah on the Basis of a Minority View

As a rule, the halakhah follows the opinion of the majority.[54] Although minority views are frequently recorded, their significance is debated in an apparently unedited collection of Mishnayoth, Ed. 1:4-6.[55] The material found there ranges from ethical implications (mEd.1:4), an issue which concerns us only marginally, to the pragmatic, jurisprudential implications of citing minority views, which are the subject of our inquiry (mEd.1:5).

> 81 And why do they record (*mazkirin*) the opinion of the individual against that of the majority, since the halakhah may only be according to the opinion of the majority? So that if a court approves of the opinion of the individual it may rely upon him, since a court cannot annul the opinion of another court unless it exceeds it both in wisdom and in number.

According to mEd.1:5, "If a court approves of the opinion of the individual it may rely upon him." That is, provided they can base their decision on it, a recorded minority view enables judges to deviate from the halakhah, and in turn it becomes the authority for their

---

52 See discussion in text commencing at note 65 below.
53 For post-Talmudic interpretation of *shuda dedaynee* see *Pahad Yitzhak* on *shuda dedaynee*.
54 mEd.1:5; bBer.9a and parallels; yKet.8:2 (32,1). See also C. Chernowitz, "Yahid Verabim," in *Festschrift zu Israel Lewy* (Breslau, 1911) pp. 1-11.
55 The unedited nature of these Mishnayoth might explain the repetition of the question in mEd.1:6 and the difference between mEd.1:4 and 1:5. On this Mishnah see Weiss, *Dor Dor Vedorshav* (Wein, 1876) vol. 2, p. 64; Halevi, *Doroth Rishonim* (Berlin, 1923) vol. 1, p. 291; Albeck, Commentary on the Mishnah, *ad loc.*

POWER-CONFERRING RULES

decision.[56] Although this rule does not specify the conditions which must obtain before judges may have recourse to this procedure, it has to be assumed that the statement is not unqualified, for otherwise the concept of a majority ruling would be meaningless.

Indeed, the general framework within which this rule operates is limited by the Tosefta to an emergency.[57] Namely, to cases where the judge believes that the application of the law is inappropriate due to a state of emergency declared by the judge in his own discretion. Failing such a declaration of emergency, the rule is inoperative.

Judges may resort to this procedure to obviate the difficulty posed by the principle that "an ordinary court cannot change the law or annul previously enacted *takkanoth*" (mEd.1:5). This rule, which empowers judges to deviate from the law without amending the law itself, was introduced to lessen inflexibility in the administration of justice. By requiring the judge to base the decision on a recorded minority view, the scope of his freedom to act is defined and institutionalized by the halakhah. At the same time, the prerequisite of a state of emergency ensures that the applicability of such a decision is restricted to the case in question without any precedent being set.

The Talmud reports several incidents in which Rabbis employed or referred to this technique and deviated from the halakhah on the basis of a minority view. This demonstrates that the quoted Mishnah in Ed.1:5 was not a purely theoretical qualification.[58]

A diffferent point of view, that of R. Judah, who opposes the position of the Sages, is presented in mEd.1:6:

82 R. Judah said: If so, why do they record the opinion of the individual against that of the majority when it does not prevail? That if one shall say, "I have received such a tradition," another may answer, "You have heard it only as the opinion of such-a-one."

---

56 For other interpretations of this Mishnah, see Ravad *ad loc.*; Chajes, *Mishpat Hora'a* (Jerusalem, 1958) ch. 7, p. 387; Albeck, *op. cit. ibid.*
57 tEd.1:4; Although the Mishnah is not unequivocal, it seems to be identical with the Tosefta in this respect. See Ravad *ibid.*; *Hasdei David* on Tosefta *ad loc.* But see S. Federbush, *Yahid Verabim*, in *Festschrift Herzog* (Jerusalem, 1962) p. 575 at 577.
58 bBer.9a; bShab.45a; bGit.19a; bNid.6a (*ibid.* 9b); bEru.46a; yNid.1:4 (49, 2-3). See also *Hasdei David ibid.*

According to R. Judah, a minority view is recorded in order to dismiss it from further consideration altogether. As a reported minority view, it is shown to have been considered and rejected, and any further reference to it in the course of determining the law is proscribed. R. Judah says that the judge is bound to apply the halakhah literally, regardless of any special considerations or extraordinary features the case might have. This conservative attitude of R. Judah in administering the law, and his strict adherence to the halakhah under all circumstances, is attested to in a great number of Talmudic cases.[59]

The jurisprudential significance of the rule endorsed by the Sages has received little attention. Perhaps this is due to the fact that it is not formulated explicitly as a power-conferring rule, or, indeed, as a rule at all.[60] It is generally regarded as an academic exercise of no practical significance, in spite of exhaustive evidence to the contrary.

In any event, a number of questions regarding the nature of the minority views referred to in mEd.1:5 require further clarification, since it can hardly be assumed that such a significant rule covers all minority views. Historically speaking, the fact that R. Judah is reported to have commented on the rule endorsed by the Sages excludes the possibility that the rule originally referred to minority views recorded in the Mishnaic corpus of R. Judah Hanasi. It is highly probable that the latter compiled his corpus only after the death of R. Judah. The Tosefta and the Baraitoth have to be ruled out for the same reason. We must, then, identify the subject of the original debate and reconstruct its generalization into an independent legal principle.

The key word, of course, is record (*mazkirin*). Does this term refer to a deliberate act which facilitated the availability of dissenting views for use under certain circumstances, or does it merely describe an editorial idiosyncrasy, the recorded views having gained their status *post factum*? Were the individual views selected as second-best alternatives of an inherent normative status or did they acquire their status over

---

59   bShab.29b; bEru.91a; bSuk14b; bSuk31a-b. See also *Melechet Shelomo* on mEd.1:5.

60   For Rabbinic post-Talmudic analysis of the rule see *Pahad Yitzhak*, s.v. *Keday hu R. Ploni*.

time by their accidental survival? The second alternative is possible, though unlikely. Even if we assume that the rule referred to any minority view which scholarly circles deemed worthy of discussion and transmission and which, though rejected, was granted a limited normative status, nevertheless this criterion is applicable only retrospectively and does nothing to clarify the status of current minority views.

The following explanation seems more likely. Both R. Judah and the Sages refer to a specific official recording of opinions. This may well point to a solution to the question of the synchronic status of minority opinions. We know that R. Judah participated in the synod of Jabneh when the tractate of Eduyoth was compiled.[61] The term *mazkirin* must refer to any opinion recorded at that gathering, and the principle of mEd.1:5 becomes valid for Eduyoth and for Eduyoth only. From tEd.1:1 it appears that the main purpose of the Jabneh synod was to preserve the teachings of the Rabbis.[62] Therefore it seems that minority views were recorded in order to perpetuate them, and that the debate between the Sages and R. Judah about the limited normative status of minority views arose later. The Sages maintain that if a particular minority view was chosen to be recorded at the official gathering, then that opinion received a certain institutional recognition and gained a limited normative status. Hence, it could be relied upon. By analogy, we could extend the scope of the rule and apply it to minority views recorded in the Mishnah of R. Judah Hanasi and perhaps in the Tosefta as well, thereby considering them to have some kind of official recognition. We can thus state with some certainty that the rule is limited in its application, and refers only to those minority views which received institutional recognition by being included in an authoritative compilation. As noted above, the Talmud reports several cases in which the rule endorsed by the Sages was employed. The formula used in these cases is "So and So deserves

---

61 mEd.5:1; bShab.33b, and see Hyman, *Toledoth Tannaim Veamoraim* (London, 1910) p. 535.
62 On the question of whether this was the first attempt to compile a Tannaitic tractate and whether the present Eduyoth is identical with the original, see Epstein, *Mevot Lesifrut Hatannaim* (Jerusalem, 1957) p. 422, Albeck, *Introduction to the Mishnah* (Hebrew) (Tel Aviv, 1960) p. 63 and, in particular, p. 82.

to be relied upon." In all cases but one the authority is the Mishnah, with the exception being the Tosefta.[63]

One of these cases deserves particular attention. It is related that in a case brought before him pertaining to the laws of *nidah*, R. Judah Hanasi ruled according to R. Eliezer.[64] It is further reported that "after having realized, he declared: R. Eliezer deserves to be relied upon in a case of emergency."

The Talmud analyzes this rather obscure statement as follows:

83 What is the meaning of "after having realized." If it be explained "after having realized that the halakhah was not in accordance with R. Eliezer, but in accordance with the Sages," then the difficulty would arise: How could he act according to the former's ruling even in a case of emergency? Hence the statement means after he realized that it was not stated whether the law was in agreement with R. Eliezer or with the Sages, and having realized that it was not an individual that differed from R. Eliezer but that many differed from him [in which case he should have ruled according to the majority] he declared R. Eliezer deserves to be relied upon in a case of emergency.[65]

At first glance it appears that this passage imposes a further substantial limitation on the applicability of the rule: that it applies only in those cases where there is an individual opinion that goes against the majority opinion, but the halakhah has not yet been explicitly decided. Such a limitation, however, is not substantiated by any other Talmudic source.

Indeed, a closer examination reveals that this is not the only plausible conclusion. The Talmud would hardly introduce such a substantial limitation so casually, especially one contradicting every known similar case. Rather, the Talmud is concerned with a point of judicial procedure which seems to have been ignored in this particular case. This is the only case where the principle "So and So deserves to be

---

63 bGit.19a; bShab.45a; bNid.6a, on the individual views recorded in the Mishhah; bBer.9a, on the individual view recorded in the Tosefta. None of these cases used minority views recorded in Eduyot. In addition, note the common terminology of *samakh* in the formula and in mEd.1:5.
64 bNid.6a and parallels.
65 bNid. *ibid.* What constituted the emergency is debated by the commentators; see Rashi and Tosafoth *ad loc.*

relied upon" is invoked retrospectively without being introduced into the deliberations during the decision-making process, thus constituting a *post-factum* justification for the ruling.

Post-factual argumentation is regarded as inferior by the Talmud, as is shown in a case involving *shuda dedaynee*. In the case of Rami b. Hama, when opposed rulings were given by R. Nahman and R. Shesheth, the former argued that his decision should be validated since it was based on *shuda dedaynee*. When R. Shesheth claimed that his decision could also be based on that very principle, R. Nahman retorted, "In the first place I am a judge and you are not; furthermore you did not at first come with this argument."[66] R. Nahman rejected the retrospective argument of R. Shesheth, and this view is endorsed by the Talmud.

In this light, the distinction between a case in which the halakhah has been decided against the view of an individual and a case in which an individual opinion exists alongside that of the majority view but the halakhah has not been decided, applies only to the possibility of retrospective argumentation. In the former case it is rejected, in the latter, it is permitted. By contrast, where contemporaneous reasoning is involved the rule could indeed be used by a judge even though the halakhah had been decided against the minority opinion. However, in such a case, it cannot serve as a legal basis for his decision if there is no explicit rendering of the minority opinion.

A report of the controversy between the Sages and R. Judah is also found in tEd.1:4, but there it has been edited.

84 The halakhah is always according to the opinion of the majority. The opinion of the individual is recorded against that of the majority only to render it invalid. R. Judah says. The opinion of the individual is recorded against that of the majority only because the time may require it and they may rely on it. And the Sages say: The opinion of the individual is recorded against that of the majority only because one might say unclean and one might say clean; one might say unclean according to R. Eliezer. They may say to him according to R. Eliezer you have heard.

The Tosefta omits the saying which occurs in mEd.1:4, as it is not consistent with that found in mEd.1:5, and replaces it by a different

---

66   bKet.94b. See text at note 35 above.

saying which does not contradict it. It omits altogether the principle stated in the second part of mEd.1:5, as it is not a necessary element in the unit. The Tosefta also omits the repetition of the question in mEd.1:6, instead presenting the dispute between the Sages and R. Judah in the traditional form.[67] All of this indicates that the Tosefta is an improved version of the Mishnah. In light of this observation, the two other changes in the Tosefta's version are significant. First, the Tosefta reverses the positions: the view of the Sages is ascribed to R. Judah and that of R. Judah is ascribed to the Sages.[68] Second, the Tosefta differs from the Mishnah in explicitly ascribing the view of the Sages to the *hahamim*. In fact, in the Mishnah, the view which was previously attributed throughout to the Sages is quoted anonymously.

Taken together, these differences generate the impression that the Tosefta was anxious to eliminate the possibility that judges would have the power to base their rulings on a minority view. It thus ascribes the opinion which allows judges to do so to R. Judah (contrary to what is known of him) and juxtaposes it with the opinion of the *hahamim*, who now are reported to have proscribed any reliance upon minority views. According to the principle stated at the beginning of tEd.1:4, the view of R. Judah ought to be rejected, as it is opposed by the majority, the *hahamim*. This conclusion could not have been reached had the Tosefta reported the view of the Sages anonymously, as did the Mishnah, since in that case it might have been treated as just another individual opinion.

The legal conclusion which emerges from the Tosefta, that judicial decisions cannot be based on a minority view, was deliberately fabricated.[69] There are two possible ways to account for this difference in attitude between the Mishnah and the Tosefta.

Albeck believes that the Tosefta in its present form was not edited before the end of the fourth century C.E., and that it was composed in Eretz Yisrael, since the Baraitoth which it contains resemble those

---

67 The only peculiarity is that the opinion of the Sages is first reported at the beginning of tEd.1:4 anonymously.
68 A different version of the Tosefta is recorded in Ravad's commentary on mEd.1:5.
69 Cf. bGit.20a and see Chernowitz *op. cit.* p. 8 for further examples of tendentious attributions of halakhic views.

of the Yerushalmi more than those of the Babylonian Talmud.[70] According to this view, it could be argued that the Palestinian Amoraim who were responsible for editing the Tosefta presented the dispute between the Sages and R. Judah in such a way that the legal conclusion that could be derived from it would harmonize with their general disapproval of any deviation from the law. On the other hand, if we reject Albeck's view and conceive of the Tosefta, as Epstein did,[71] as a genuine Tannaitic collection, then the difference between the two sources should be regarded as reflecting a current debate over the power of judges to deviate from the law. In such a case, the difference between Palestinian and Babylonian Amoraim would have its origin in Tannaitic times. No attempt will be made here to draw any conclusions regarding the dating of the compilation of the Tosefta, since this complex issue is clearly beyond the scope of the present work. At most, we can only refer to two possible accounts of the differences between the Mishnah and the Tosefta.

6.5. Absolute Obligation to Obey the Law

The next limiting rule occurs in Sifre and in the Yerushalmi in two contradictory versions. Sifre interprets Deuteronomy 17:11 in the following way:

85 Right and left: even if they show it before your eyes that left is right and right is left, listen to them.[72]

One important difference between this rule and the preceding ones is immediately evident. The present rule does not stipulate that judges have the power to rule contrary to the law. Rather, the rule imposes an absolute obligation on the addressee of the rule to obey all deci-

---

70   Albeck, *Mehquarim Babratioth Uwatosefta* (Jerusalem, 1954), and, in particular, p. 137.
71   Epstein, *op. cit.*, pp. 245-51.
72   Sifre ad Deuteronomy (ed. Finkelstein) p. 207; Midrash Shir Hashirim 1(3), 2; Midrash Lekah Tov on Deut. 17:11; Yalkut Shimeoni on Deut.17:11. Midrash Hagadol on Deut. (ed. 3. Fish, Jerusalem, 1972) p. 392 derives this exegesis from Deut. 17:10. See also Midrash Tannaim (ed. D. Hoffman) pp. 102-3.

sions of the court, whether or not they are in accordance with the law. In jurisprudential terms the difference between the present rule and the preceding ones is that between a power-conferring rule and a duty-imposing rule.[73] It is true that by implication the rule grants judges a correlative absolute power to exercise their authority over the addressee, in circumstances yet to be defined. The formulation of the rule, however, indicates that its concern is not to define the conditions and limits under which the court can exercise its power but to create an absolute obligation on the part of the addressee to obey the court's decisions. But even if one conceives of the principle as a power-conferring rule, it does not follow that the rule justifies judicial deviation from the law. Its function is merely to validate incorrect rulings, not to authorize them.

Power to act in a certain way does not necessarily imply that the agent is legally justified in performing the act. A married man might have the power to marry a second wife, yet according to R. Gershon's ban he would be committing an offense in exercising this power.[74]

In his comments on Salmond's *On Jurisprudence*, Williams observes:

> A power is usually combined with a liberty to exercise it; that is to say, the exercise of it is not merely effectual but rightful. This, however, is not necessarily the case. It may be effectual and yet wrongful; as when, in breach of my agreement, I revoke a license given by me to enter upon my land. Such revocation is perfectly effectual, but it is a wrongful act ...[75]

The same point was made by Sartorious in a more relevant context: "That a supreme appellate court may have the power to ignore the decisional standards which it ought to apply by no means implies that it has the institutional authority to do so."[76] It is one thing to say that

---

73 I follow Hart's terminology. See *The Concept of Law* (Oxford, 1972) p. 26ff.
74 On the *takkanah* of R. Gershon see Z.Z. Havlin, "The Takkanot of Rabbenu Gershon Ma'or Hagola in Family Law in Spain and Provence," *Shenaton Ha-Mishpat Ha-Ivri* vol. 2 (Jerusalem, 1975) p. 200 and the literature cited there.
75 Salmond, *On Jurisprudence* (11th ed.) (London, 1975) p. 274, note (a).
76 R.E. Sartorius, *Individual Conduct and Social Norms* (Dickenson Publishing Company, California, 1975) p. 183.

the decision is valid and effectual, it is quite another to say that the decision is correct. We may thus distinguish between two types of power-conferring rules: authority-granting rules and validity-determining rules. A validity-determining rule does not stipulate that the act in question is permitted, but merely that it is legally valid. Authority-granting rules, however, imply that the act is both legally valid and permitted.

As an example of a validity-determining rule, we may cite the Talmudic maxim of *hefker Beth Din hefker*, that expropriation (of property) by Beth Din is a valid expropriation.[77] In Tannaitic and Amoraic literature, the maxim is related to the legislative function of the Beth Din (that is, to *takkanoth*)[78] and, as such, it has no bearing on the issue of judicial pronouncements.[79] However, even within the framework of legislative activity the maxim plays a limited role: its unqualified formulation signifies that the doctrine does not aim at guiding those engaged in legislation on how to proceed in their task, but at providing the Beth Din with a legal means through which it can realize its goals. Whether the goals set by the court are justified and their achievement is legitimate cannot be inferred from the maxim, the sole function of which is to validate the measures taken by the court.[80]

The notion of validity-determining rules is a prerequisite for any intelligible discussion of extra-legal considerations in judicial deci-

---

77   tShek.1:3; yPea 5:1 (18, 4) (see Ahavat Zion *ad loc.*); yShek.1:2 (46, 1); bJev.89b; bGit.36b. See also mPea 6:1 and tPea 2:5. See also *E.T.*, vol. 10, p. 95.
78   bM.K.16a ; yM.K.3:1 (81,4). This differs from the view of G. J. Blidstein, "Notes on Hefker Bet-Din in Talmudic and Medieval Law," *Dine Israel*, IV (1973) p. xxxv, at p. xl.
79   bJev.89b (bGit.36b) reports an Amoraic controversy about the source from which the maxim of *hefker Beth Din hefker* can be derived. According to R. Eliezer the doctrine is derived from Joshua 19.51, whereas according to R. Isaac the source is Ezra 10:8. H.H. Cohn suggests that the latter prefers Ezra 10:8 in order to indicate that the concept refers to the judicial power of the court, ("Courts as Expropriators" (Hebrew) in *Papers of Fourth World Congress of Jewish Studies*, vol. 1 (Jerusalem, 1967) p. 185). However, Ezra 10:8 can hardly be regarded as representing a judicial activity.
80   But see Elon's uncritical account of the maxim in *Jewish Law*, vol. 2, p. 415.

sions. If a legal system contains a norm which renders null and void any judicial decision not based on the strict law, then a decision based on extra-legal considerations altogether fails to be a judicial decision and is not binding. It follows that in attempting to provide a jurisprudential analysis of extra-legal considerations in judicial decisions the validity of decisions of this type must be assumed; it must be assumed that the legal system under examination contains, at least tacitly, a validity-determining rule which validates judicial decisions based on extra-legal considerations.[81]

It is not easy to specify when an act is not only effectual (legally valid) but also correct. Naturally, the power-conferring rule may be so formulated that it leaves no doubt as to its nature, as, for example, when it employs permissive terms. In other cases it may be possible to determine the nature of the act with the help of external information: the ban of R. Gershon renders the act of marrying a second wife illegal though it does not invalidate the marriage. The existence of effectual but wrongful acts should make one wary when dealing with power-conferring rules. In our case, however, the formulation of the rule is decisive. The rule (imposing an absolute obligation to obey the law) is formulated as a duty-imposing rule, and the correlative rule that can be deduced from it implies only the validity of incorrect rulings.

Elon, following post-Talmudic commentators, cites the rule uncritically when dealing with what he considered to be the extensive power of the Sages to interpret the Torah as manifested in the Talmud. According to Elon the rule was regarded in Talmudic times as a source which empowered the Sages to exert extensive authority at their own discretion.[82] Elon's account is both conceptually confused and historically inaccurate. Close analysis reveals the scope of the rule was originally far more limited than later interpreters claim. In his commen-

---

81 Hart bases the justification for such an assumption on the interests of public order. "It is obviously in the interests of public order that a court's decision should have legal authority until a superior court certifies its invalidity, even if it is one which the court should not legally have given." The *Concept of Law* (Oxford, 1972) p. 30. See also B.N. Cardozo, *The Nature of the Judicial Process* (New Haven, 1921) p. 129.

82 Elon, *Jewish Law*, vol. 1, p. 225.

tary on Deuteronomy 17:11, Abravanel limits the scope of the rule to decisions issued by the High Court in Jerusalem. Under this view the duty to obey decisions contrary to the law refers only to decisions of the High Court. Abravanel explicitly states that decisions of other courts are not binding if they are contrary to the law; hence, if a judge in a local court has erred, there is no duty to obey him.[83]

Abravanel's view is certainly not groundless. The passage in Deuteronomy 17 of which verse 11 is a part deals with legal issues that are transferred from the local court to the central one because of their complexity. It follows that the absolute obligation to obey all decisions which is derived from an exegesis based on verse 11 must refer exclusively to decisions of the central court.

Moreover, the passage in Sifre refers to two specific courts, the High Court in Jerusalem and that in Jabneh. The latter came into prominence only after the Destruction and was viewed as taking the place of the former.[84] Sifre, confronted with the destruction of Jerusalem and its institutions, provided that complicated legal issues would henceforth be transferred to Jabneh.[85] The court in Jabneh is thus granted a status similar to that of the High Court in Jerusalem.[86]

The explicit reference to these two distinguished courts clearly indicates that Sifre was anxious to exclude all local courts from the scope of the passage. This suggests that the maxim refers only to pronouncements issued by the central court in its capacity as a legislative body. This suggestion is supported by the following consideration. As interpreted by Sifre, an addressee of the rule is a judge who has transferred a legal issue to the central court for clarification.[87] He is duty-bound to accept and follow the ruling of the central court regardless of its legal correctness. The case of an individual who is faced with an erroneous ruling, however, is different. The reason for the distinction between an officiating judge and individuals who are not judicial

---

83 See also note 29 above.
84 G. Alon, *op. cit.* vol. 1, p. 291ff.
85 Sifre ad Deuteronomy (ed. Finkelstein) p. 206, and n.10.
86 With the exception that capital punishment could only be inflicted for disobedience of a ruling issued by the High Court in Jerusalem. See Sifre ad Deuteronomy (ed. Finkelstein) p. 207 and n.4.
87 Hoffman, in his commentary on Deuteronomy *ad loc.*, argues that this is also the case according to Scripture itself.

officials originates in Sifre. The severe attitude towards such a "rebellious elder" is reflected in the following:

86 R. Josiah said: Three things did Ze'ira tell me as emanating from the men of Jerusalem: a *sotah*, if her husband wished to pardon her he may do so; a stubborn and rebellious son, if his father and mother wished to pardon him they may do so; a rebellious elder, if his colleagues wished to pardon him they may do so.

When, however, I came and put these rules before R. Judah b. Betera, he agreed with me in respect of two but did not agree with me in respect of one. In respect to a *sotah* and a stubborn and rebellious son he agreed with me, but in respect to a rebellious elder he did not agree with me because a rebellious elder introduces disputes in Israel.[88]

Thus, the desire to eliminate legal controversies dictated a rigid and uncompromising attitude toward the rebellious elder. The capital punishment, which according to the law is to be meted out to him, cannot be mitigated. This desire to eliminate schism is one manifestation of the ongoing attempt to unify the halakhah. The main threat to the unity of the halakhah is a situation where contradictory rulings are issued by different organs within the system. Awareness of this danger led to the creation of an absolute obligation on the part of subordinate organs to obey all rulings of the supreme court. By contrast, individuals who do not partake in the decision-making process, and who are not responsible for the enforcement of the law, do not constitute a threat to halakhic unity. Consequently, they are not under the same absolute obligation as are judges. Accordingly, the *sugya* in bHor.2b implies that there is no duty, indeed no right, on the part of individuals to obey erroneous pronouncements of the central court.

We can now turn to the Yerushalmi's version of the maxim, which is diametrically opposed to that of the Sifre. The Yerushalmi reads as follows:

87 It was taught: One might think that even if they tell you that right is left and left is right that you should listen to them; [therefore] Scripture says "to go right and left," that they will tell you that right is right and left is left.[89]

---

88   Sifre ad Deut. (ed. Finkelstein) p. 251 and parallels.
89   yHor.1:1 (45, 4).

From this Baraita it appears that the duty to obey the court is restricted to legally correct rulings. Traditional as well as modern scholars have attempted to reconcile the contradiction between these two sources.[90] Finkelstein, in a paper containing much speculation and unsupported presuppositions, has argued that the Yerushalmi records the earlier exegesis, dating back to the pre-Hasmonean period, when the Sages did not participate in the High Court in Jerusalem. Sifre, he contends, represents a modified version of the original exegesis which reflects the salient political change of the successful penetration of the Pharisees into the High Court. In other words, when the Sages were not part of the High Court they limited the duty to obey its decisions, but when they gained control of it they demanded absolute obedience to their rulings.[91]

This historical reconstruction is highly questionable. On the basis of form-analysis it can be shown that the Yerushalmi's Baraita was inspired by, and is based upon, the exegesis recorded in Sifre, which means that Sifre's interpretation preceded that of the Yerushalmi.

The exegesis in the Yerushalmi is introduced by the formula *ya'kol talmud lomar* (one might think that ... [therefore] Scripture says). This is a common formula in Tannaitic exegesis: the formula first presents an opinion and then rejects it on the basis of exegetical exposition of Scripture. The opinion which follows the *ya'kol* in this Baraita is precisely that which is adopted by Sifre.

Weiss has suggested that anonymous opinions introduced by the formula *ya'kol talmud lomar* are opinions that prevailed among the Sadducees and hence are opinions the Pharisees took great care to refute.[92] While some exegeses of the form were no doubt generated by Sadducee-Pharisee disputes,[93] it is unlikely that all of the many exegeses of that form reflect such disputes. It does, however, seem reasonable to assume that in most cases, this formula was used when a current opinion, not necessarily a Sadducean one, was rejected. This is even more likely when the rejected view is odd, is not a

---

90 For a summary of these attempts, see Hoffman, *Das Oberste Gerichtshof*, (Berlin, 1878) p. 9ff.
91 L. Finkelstein, "Baraita Debet Din," 32 *HUCA* (1961) 19. See also J. Lauterbach, *Rabbinic Essays* (New York, 1973) p. 34.
92 Weiss, *op. cit. supra* note 55, p. 118.
93 See the examples cited by Weiss *op. cit. ibid.*

straightforward inference, or is referred to in a separate and independent source. Accordingly, it appears that the exegesis in the Baraita in yHor. was elicited by a well-known current opinion, namely, the view endorsed by Sifre which was rejected. This conclusion also follows if we apply a technique similar to that of Neusner's "logical sequence." It makes little sense to object to an interpretation which has no proponents and which does not follow immediately from Scripture. Only if we assume the existence of Sifre's exegesis is that of the Yerushalmi intelligible. It seems safe to conclude, then, that the interpretation in the Yerushalmi is based on Sifre.

What remains to be considered is why the Yerushalmi reverses Sifre's interpretation. In answering this question, it is important to keep in mind the context of the Baraita in the Yerushalmi.

Unlike Sifre, yHor. makes no allusion to the rebellious elder. This suggests that yHor. is concerned only with the duty of individuals to obey erroneous pronouncements. The whole *sugya* in yHor. deals precisely with this issue. The Baraita in the Yerushalmi, anticipating the analogy between individuals and judges with regard to the duty to obey all decisions of the court, is anxious to emphasize that individuals are under no obligation to abide by incorrect decisions. The addressee of the Baraita, then, is any individual confronted with the problem of obeying or disobeying a fallacious ruling. The Yerushalmi differs from Sifre in that it does not expound verse 11 in the passage in Deuteronomy 17 as part of a single unit but as a separate part of it. Thus the Yerushalmi is able to interpret verse 11 out of its immediate Scriptural context.[94]

The contradiction between the two sources is thus resolved since two different issues are being discussed. It is interesting to note that

---

[94] Compare, however, Hoffman's suggestion (Hoffmann *op. cit. ibid.*) that yHor. interprets a different Biblical verse, Deuteronomy 28:14. This view is based on the Biblical quotation in yHor., *"laleket yamin usemol"*. The word *laleket* occurs in Deuteronomy 18:14 but not in Deuteronomy 17:11, though in the former it follows *yamin usemol* rather than precedes it. However, the present text of yHor. is greatly damaged (see S. Lieberman, "Yerushalmi Horajot," *Festschrift Albeck*, Jerusalem, 1963) and yHor. might possibly have an incorrect quotation of Deut. 17:11. See also Rabinowitz, *Sha'are Torat Eretz Yisrael* (Jerusalem, 1940) p. 577.

the Yerushalmi's concern with the conditions under which the decisions of the court are invalid, rather than the conditions under which the decisions of the court are valid, is in line with the overall attitude of the Yerushalmi that judges cannot rule beyond the limits of the law.

To conclude, the rule recorded in Sifre is formulated as a duty-imposing rule, but even the correlative rule that can be inferred from it is limited. The rule addresses itself to a judge, the "rebellious elder," and only he is subject to the absolute power of the central court. This rule, therefore, cannot account for, or serve as the legal justification for, the extensive judicial deviation from the law recorded in the Talmud.

6.6 *Horat Sha'a*

Unlike the principles discussed above, *horat sha'a* does not appear as an independent concept. Rather, it is always related to a particular case or incident. The Hebrew idiom *horat sha'a*, though very frequent in Talmudic and post-Talmudic literature, occurs in the Mishnah only once, in tractate Para, which is devoted to the laws of the Red Heifer and the water of lustration.[95] In the Mishnah, the idiom occurs in a recorded judicial decision concerning the preparation of the water of lustration. The water of lustration was prepared by drawing spring water and then scattering some of the ashes of the Red Heifer on it. The principle stated in the Mishnah specifies, *inter alia*, that any work not connected with the rite which is performed while drawing the water or thereafter (but before mixing the water with the ashes) "invalidates" the water by making it ritually unacceptable.[96]

Chapter 7 of mPara illustrates the applicability of the principle with some concrete examples, one of which was the subject of an actual court case.

> 88 He who carries in his hand a [borrowed] rope [to its owner]: if it is on his way [to scatter the ashes], [the water] remains valid; if it is not on his way, [the water] becomes invalid.[97]

---

95 mPara 7:6; 7:7
96 mPara 4:4; tPara 4:11; Sifre ad Num. (ed. Horovitz) p. 158; bHul.29b.
97 mPara 7:6.

A man borrowed a rope for the purpose of drawing water in order to prepare the water of lustration. After drawing the water, but before mixing it with the ashes, he wanted to return the rope to its owner.[98] If he did so on his way to mix the water with the ashes, without going out of his way, the water remains valid; otherwise, the water becomes invalid. The Mishnah further relates:

88   This question was sent to Jabneh on three festivals and on the third festival it was ruled that the mixture was valid, as a temporary measure.[99]

The Mishnah thus reports that the court in Jabneh once permitted the use of this water of lustration in spite of the fact that the Mishnaic law was violated in its method of preparation.[100]

The author of Tiferet Israel argues that mPara 7:6 does not report a case that was actually brought before the court, but rather an hypothetical question asked at the Academy in Jabneh. His argument is based on the fact that it took a full year for the Rabbis to reach a decision, and that it is inconceivable that the water would be kept for a full year without being damaged or that the ritual purity status of a person who used the controversial water would be suspended for a full year.[101] There are, however, good reasons to reject this interpretation and to regard the incident as the report of an actual case.

First, the incident recorded in mPara 7:6 is also reported in the Tosefta:

89   With regard to this law, the people of Assia made enquiry when they came up to Jabneh on each of the three festivals.[102] On the third festival the Rabbis declared it to be valid as a temporary measure.[103]

---

98   Cf. tPara 7:4.
99   mPara *loc. cit.*
100 But *cf.* Neusner, *History of the Mishnaic Law of Purities*, Part 9 (Leiden, 1976) pp. 129-130.
101 Tiferet Yisrael *ad loc.* See also Hassdei David on tPara. 7:4.
102 On the verb *ala* used in this passage, see J. Derenbourg, *Histoire de la Palestine* (Paris, 1867) p. 319, note 2; see also Alon, *Toledoth Yisrael* (Tel Aviv, 1952) vol. 1, p. 145.
103 tPara.7:4.

We know of two more questions that the people of Assia brought to the court in Jabneh. These two questions, one concerning the kashruth of an animal[104] and the other involving the validity of a *mikveh*,[105] are reported in exactly the same form as tPar.6:4 (with the exception that the idiom *horat sha'a* does not occur there). The former is also recorded in bHul. in a slightly different version:

90 This was an actual case about which the people of Assia made enquiry when they came up to Jabneh on each of the three festivals. On the third festival the Rabbis declared it to be permitted.[106]

According to this version the people of Assia came to Jabneh to obtain a judicial decision. It therefore seems reasonable to assume that the other two enquiries were also initiated in response to actual cases.

Second, we know of at least two other instances, though in a much later period, when a full year was required to reach a decision:

91 i) A certain idolator once said to an Israelite: "Cut some grass and throw it to my cattle on the Sabbath; if not I will kill you as I have killed So-and-so, that son of an Israelite to whom I said 'Cook me a dish on the Sabbath' and whom, as he did not cook for me, I killed." His wife heard this and came to Abaye. He kept her waiting for three festivals.[107]

92 ii) There once came to Abaye the case where the bone was broken and protruded outside, and a fragment thereof had broken off. He held the case over three festivals.[108]

In these instances it is clear that the Talmud reports actual cases, yet a full year was required to reach a decision. In particular, case (ii) should be noted, since it deals with the kashruth of an animal. It therefore seems that the fact that a period of one year had elapsed before a decision was reached does not indicate that the question was hypothetical.

---

104 *Ibid.*; tHul.3:10.
105 tMik.4:6.
106 bHul.48a.
107 bJev.121b; 122a. On *tlata rigle*, see M. Beer, *The Babylonian Exilarchate* (Tel Aviv, 1970) p. 133.
108 bHulin 77a. It should be noted that in both cases the hesitating judge was Abaye; *cf.* bGit.38a.

Third, according to the Talmud, *horat sha'a* is referred to only with regard to actual cases. The Mishnah in Jevamoth discusses the contingency of two betrothed women who, in entering the bridal chamber, were exchanged by mistake. The Mishnah rules that "if they were minors incapable of bearing children, then they may be restored at once."[109] On this ruling Rav comments: "This was *horat sha'a*."[110] The Talmud immediately raises the objection: "Does this imply that such a case actually occurred (since the Mishnah obviously speaks of a contingency and not of a fact)?"[111] Because of this objection, the Talmud modifies the tradition of Rav to read "this was like *horat sha'a*."

Finally, the third person plural past tense, which occurs both in the Mishnah and in the Tosefta, suggests that an actual case was at issue.[112]

It has been noted that the Mishnah and the Talmud employ various methods to reconcile the law with recorded early decisions incompatible with it.[113] One of these methods is to ascribe extra-legal reasoning to the early case, thereby removing the contradiction between the reported case and the law.[114] Some scholars maintain that the concept of *horat sha'a* is a typical example of such a step taken by the Amoraim to reconcile extra-judicial acts recorded in the Bible with the later development of the law.[115] However, it seems that in this particular case *horat sha'a* forms a part of the original tradition, and this view is supportable by the following analysis.

The report of the case follows a rule stated in the Mishnah without dissent. That the rule is stated without dissent means that there was

---

109 mJev.3:10.
110 bJev.35a.
111 *Ibid.*
112 Likewise, S. Klein (*Festschrift Jacob Freimann*, 1937, p. 122, n. 31) deduces from the words of R. Jossi in tPara 7:4, "They declare it valid in the past and invalid in the future," that an actual case was at issue. See also M. Poglmann, "Al Efer Para Aharei Hahurban," 54 *Sinai* (1963) p. 192.
113 See Alon, *Mehquarim Betoldot Yisrael*, (Tel Aviv, 1957) vol. 1, p. 104; Falk, *Introduction to Jewish Law* (Hebrew) (Tel Aviv, 1971) p. 34.
114 bJev.35a; bKet.15a; bSanh.78b; bSanh.80b.
115 See bA.Z.24b; bHor.6a; bZev.108b; bMen.50b; bTem.15b; bYoma 69b; bPes.82b.

no one interested in citing a conflicting case unless the case was originally reported to have been based on *horat sha'a*. If the cited case does include the element of *horat sha'a*, it proves by implication the correctness of the rule: On the grounds of *horat sha'a* the water, although not prepared in accordance with the rule, was permitted, otherwise it was forbidden. Since the case is cited not to oppose the rule but to support it, we must assume that it originally included the element of *horat sha'a*, otherwise it would have been left out.

In tPara R. Yossi records a tradition according to which the ruling in Jabneh on the ground of *horat sha'a* was related to a different issue:

> Said R. Yossi: Not [concerning] this did they give a decision, but concerning one who coils the rope at the end of the process. They declared that it is valid in the past and invalid in the future.[116]

It therefore seems that there clearly was an early tradition that the court in Jabneh ruled on the basis of *horat sha'a*, although the actual issue it involved was disputed. It stands to reason that not only was *horat sha'a* part of the original tradition, but also that the court explicitly stated that its decision was based on *horat sha'a*. This was done to ensure that the decision would not set a precedent. The significance of this point may be illuminated by examining the difference between *ad hoc* decisions and the English device known as distinguishing of precedents. This device is designed to enable judges to free themselves from the restrictions resulting from the doctrine of binding precedent. A direct result of employing this device is that a particular decision, if distinguished, can be isolated so that it will not be followed. Retrospectively, the decision might appear to be *ad hoc* in the sense that its *ratio* was operative only in a particular case. But, and this is the crucial point, the decision was not delivered as such. An English judge who delivers a decision which is later distinguished, feels that his judgment represents the law. The uniqueness of the decision is not declared by the judge, but is a consequence which emerges from subsequent cases.

Neither the Mishnah nor the Tosefta gives the reasons for the court's deviation. The reasons, however, are not difficult to find. The

---

116 tPara 7:4.

venue of the court, Jabneh, indicates that the case was brought after the destruction of the Temple.[117] Ashes of the Red Heifer which survived the Destruction were of great importance, since the ashes could be prepared only when the Temple was in existence. Apparently, the court decided to permit the use of the water of lustration even though it was not prepared according to the law, in order to save the ashes that had been used in its preparation.[118]

Thus presented, the court based its decision on a social consideration. However, it should be noted that the idiom *horat sha'a* as such does not indicate the kind of reasoning employed by the court. This last point deserves special emphasis in view of the way in which the idiom is used by modern scholars.

Modern scholars refer to *horat sha'a* as a term equivalent to the "needs of the time."[119] For example, the incident of Shimon b. Shetach and the eighty witches in Ashkelon is referred to as a case based on *horat sha'a*, even though the idiom does not appear in any of the sources relating the story.[120] That is, modern scholars understand the idiom as indicating the reasons which led to the decision in question, namely, the needs of the time.

However, if we confine ourselves to the way this idiom is used in Talmudic sources it appears that its precise meaning is slightly different. Rather than denoting the reasons for the decision, the term indicates that the ruling in question is intended to have an *ad hoc* effect, either because the time so required or for any other reason.[121] In this respect, the idiom *horat sha'a* should be considered in the light of its

---

117 Alon (*Mehquarim*) has convincingly established that there was no distinct court in Jabneh prior to the Destruction. See also S. Safrai, "Raban Johanan b Zakkai," *Festschrift fur G. Alon* (Tel Aviv, 1970) p. 203. But see also Derenbourg, *op. cit.* 288.
118 *Cf. ET* vol. 8, p. 527. For a similar reasoning, see tNid.1:9; bNid.9b. In passing, it should be noted that this Mishnah provides further proof that the ashes of the Red Heifer were used after the Destruction. See Gilat, *Mishnato Shel R. Eliezer* (Tel Aviv, 1968) p. 252.
119 Cohn in *Judaica* vol. 6, p. 1073; P. Dykan, *Criminal Law* (Hebrew) vol. 6, p. 1268; Elon, *Jewish Law* p. 425; Assaf, *Haonshin Aharei Tekufat Hatalmud* (Jerusalem, 1922) 12.
120 Sifre ad Deuteronomy (ed. Finkelstein) p. 253; mSanh.6:4; yHag.2:2 (78,1); ySanh.6:8 (23, 3).
121 See Rashi on bNid.9b; bJev.35a; bKet.15a.

opposite. Sifra Emor 19 contrasts *horat sha'a* with *minhag ledoroth*. *Ya'kol horat sha'a ... talmud lomar ... yehe minhag ledoroth*. This juxtaposition indicates that *horat sha'a* denotes a ruling whose application is limited to the case at issue, as opposed to *minhag ledoroth* which is universally applicable.[122] This meaning also emerges from tPara 7:4. R. Yossi refers to *horat sha'a* as referring to a ruling which is valid for the past and not for the future. This stresses the temporary nature of the decision and not the reasons which led to it.

It should be noted that the type of judicial decision at stake here, as in the other enquiries made by the people of Assia, is not the result of a dispute between two parties. Rather, it involves a decision on an issue concerning one party only, usually termed a declaratory judgment.[123] It is significant that the other judicial decisions described as being based on *horat sha'a* are also declaratory judgments.[124] Moreover, all these cases advise leniency rather than severity, mitigation instead of strict application of the law. It thus appears that *horat sha'a* denotes a permissive decision in a declaratory judgment.[125]

---

122 See also Gilat, "A Rabbinical Court May Decree the Abrogation of a Law of the Torah," 7-8 *Bar Ilan Annual* (1972) 117; Urbach, "Halakhah Venevua," 18 *Tarbiz* (1946) p. 5. And see also Hasdei David in tPara 7:4 and Sifre ad Deut. (ed. Finkelstein) 221.
123 See text accompanying note 3 in Chapter 2 above.
124 tPara 7:4; tNid.1:9.
125 See bKet.7a and *cf*. P.R. Weis, *Mishnah Horayoth: Its History and Exposition* (Manchester, 1952) p. 4.

CHAPTER 7

CONCLUSION

Western legal thinking demands total obedience to the letter of the law, making no allowance for extra-legal considerations. A very good reason underlies this approach. Man is an arbitrary and capricious creature and, therefore, cannot be trusted to rule other men. Justice and legal stability can be maintained only if society is governed by laws and not by men. This principle in its Latin form, *Non sub Homine sed sub Deo et Lege*, became one of the cornerstones of Western thought. Thus, the fear of tyranny and despotism drove Western jurisprudence to this extreme position and induced it to create an external governing entity, the law. The law is assumed to be impartial, beneficial and just, the best man could create. If it is obeyed, then all is well.

Unfortunately there is a flaw in this reasoning. The law must be understood before it can be obeyed. In order to be understood, it has to be interpreted by qualified persons who are, of course, human, with all of the shortcomings mentioned above. Thus, the problem remains unsolved, since the keys of the great fortress built to safeguard man against the arbitrary rulings of others are deposited into the hands of those not to be trusted, other human beings.

Talmudic law employs a different approach. It allows judges to deviate from the law if, in their opinion, such a course is justified. This is not due to an insensitivity about the importance of legal certainty and stability. Rather, while reasoning along the same lines as their Western counterparts, Jewish jurists arrived at a different conclusion: that good laws by themselves are not sufficient to protect people, and that imperfect laws do not necessarily lead to injustice. The only guarantees against arbitrariness are the judges' sense of responsibility, their esteem for their office, their fidelity to the spirit of the law, and their concern for society. No law by itself can prevent an unscrupulous judge from thwarting justice. Jewish law has come to terms with this problem by implicitly trusting its judges as the ultimate arbiters of justice. The law is regarded as a guiding instrument in their hands rather than as an external, independent entity.

In addition, it is arguable that an explicit judicial assertion that the law is being set aside in a particular case, with a ruling not warranted by the law being adopted, serves yet another purpose. By such occasional departures from the law, the court publicly indicates that when it feels that departure is appropriate it does not hesitate to do so, thereby reinforcing its authority and guaranteeing obedience in all other cases in which it enforces the halakhah proper.

In this book an attempt has been made to present a jurisprudential account of judicial deviation from the law as reflected in Talmudic sources. The central question of this study is not whether a given decision is legally correct. Rather, it focuses upon whether judges conceived of their role as requiring strict adherence to the law or whether judges occasionally exercised a degree of freedom to depart from legal rules and precedents in order to decide a particular case by resorting to extra-legal considerations. It has been demonstrated that an accurate exposition of the judicial process within the context of Talmudic law must take into account cases in which judges base their decisions upon extra-legal considerations without being expressly authorized to do so.

What our examination has shown is that Talmudic law does indeed contain norms which, taken together, introduce a certain degree of flexibility into the application of the law, and warrant occasional departure from the general rule. It is clearly wrong, however, to construe these norms as providing the legal justification for all recorded cases in which judges have deviated from the general rules. Analysis of recorded cases shows that the range of departure authorized by these norms is quite limited in comparison with the actual practice of Talmudic courts.

In addition, a variety of possible power-conferring rules that could be invoked to justify a departure from the generally accepted rule were examined. In so doing, it was demonstrated that the range of permissible departure that could be authorized by these power-conferring rules is rather limited in comparison with the degree of deviation practiced by Talmudic judges.

Moreover, it was seen that the two Talmudim fundamentally differ in their approach to the concept of judicial power. The Jerusalem Talmud holds that the power of judges is limited strictly to applying the halakhah proper. It does not consider extra-legal considerations as acceptable justifications for judicial decisions. On the other hand, the Babylonian Talmud is more flexible on this issue. It sometimes acquiesces in the power of judges to exceed the limits of the law. An attempt has been made to anchor this fundamental difference between the two Talmudim in the different cultural and social environments in which they were created.

To be sure, even in the Babylonian Talmud objections against particular rulings are occasionally voiced. However, the general concept of extra-legal considerations has not been rejected. Rather, a close watch is kept on the judicial process, and unjustified resort to extra-legal considerations is discouraged. In this way, Talmudic law is able to synthesize the rule of law and the role of its administrators without emasculating the former and without delegating undue power to the latter.

Diverse legal systems, such as, Roman law, Islamic law and English law, have at times adopted a dual system of law and equity courts. The phenomenon of a kind of equity court designated to do justice in cases where, for whatever reason, the law court is *incapable* of doing justice, repeats itself in these and other civilizations. Furthermore, as Martin Shapiro has demonstrated in his book *Courts*, appellate review is a nearly universal phenomenon: one of the salient purposes of courts of appeal is to ensure uniformity, to ensure that the law will not be one thing in one trial court and quite another in a different one. It should now be evident why Talmudic law is a notable exception. Uniformity of the law and supremacy of legal rules, principles, doctrines and concepts are not regarded as an ideal in Talmudic law. Futhermore, the role of the court, as perceived both by its officials and by the community, is such that it was never feared that judges would be incapable of doing justice. Thus in the case of Talmudic law, there was no pressure to establish courts of appeal or an alternative system of courts of equity.

Finally, it should be evident that a social structure in which judges enjoy such far-reaching powers can sustain justice only if those powers are controlled by an appropriate social mechanism operating to avoid abuse. And, indeed, in Talmudic society the typical judge draws his power not from his appointment but from his acceptance by the community which he serves. Accordingly, this social institution of acceptance (*kabalah*) is one which deserves further study.

APPENDIX OF HEBREW SOURCES

Chapter 2

1. משנה סנהדרין ג,ז
גמרו את הדבר היו מכניסין אותן הגדול שבדיינים אומר איש פלוני אתה זכאי איש פלוני אתה חיב.

2. תוספתא בבא מציעא א,יב
נאמן הדיין לומר לזה זיכיתי ולזה וייבתי אימתי בזמן שהדין לפניו אבל אם אין הדין לפניו הרי הוא כאחד מכל אדם.

3. ספרא קדושים פרשה ד,ה
לא תלך רכיל בעמך שלא תהיה רך דברים לזה וקשה לזה. דבר אחר שלא תהיה כרוכל שהוא מטעין דברים והולך.

4. בבלי סנהדרין לא, ב
איתמר נמי אמר רב ספרא (אמר רבי יוחנן) שנים שנתעצמו בדין אחד אומר נדון כאן ואחד אומר נלך למקום הוועד כופין אותו ודן בעירו ואם הוצרך דבר לשאול כותבין ושולחין.ואם אמר כתבו ותנו לי מאיזה טעם דנתוני כותבין ונותנין לו.

5. תוספתא יבמות ד,ז
חכם שדן את הדין טימא וטיהר אסר והיתיר וכן העדים שהעידו הרי אילו מותרין ליקח אבל אמרו חכמים רחק מן הכיעור ומן הדומה לכיעור.

6. בבלי בבא מציעא סט, א
הנהו תרי כותאי ד'עבוד עסקא בהדי הדדי אזיל חד מניהו פליג זוזי בלא דעתיה דחבריה אתו לקמיה דרב פפא אמר ליה מאי נפקא מינה הכי אמו' רב נחמן זוזי כמאן דפליגי דמו. לשנה זבון חמרא בהדי הדדי קם אידך פליג ליה בלא דעתיה דחבריה. אתו לקמיה דו'ב פפא. אמר ליה מאן פלג לך אמר ליה הא קא חזינא דבתר דידי קא אתי מר אמר רב פפא כהאי גונא ודאי צריך לאודועיה זוזי מי שקיל טבי ושביק חסרי (אמר ליה לא אמר ליה) חמרא כולי עלמא ידעי דאיכא דבסים ואיכא דלא בסים.

7. בבלי בבא מציעא לט, ב,

מרי בר איסק אתא ליה אחא מבי חוזאי אמר ליה פלוג לי אמר ליה לא ידענא לך אתא לקמיה דרב חסדא אמר ליה שפיר קאמר לך שנאמר ויכר יוסף את אחיו והם לא הכירוהו מלמד שיצא בלא חתימת זקן ובא בחתימת זקן אמר ליה זיל איתי סהדי דאחוה את. אמר ליה אית לי סהדי ודחלי מיניה דגברא אלימא הוא אמר ליה לדידיה זיל אנת אייתי סהדי דלאו אחוך הוא אמר ליה דינא הכי המוציא מחברו עליו הראיה. אמר ליה הכי דיינינא לך ולכל אלימי דחברך.

8. בבלי בבא קמא קיז, ב,

ההוא גברא דהוה מפקיד ליה כסא דכספא סליקו גנבי עילויה שקלה יהבה להו אתא לקמיה דרבה פטריה.

9. בבלי בבא קמא מח, א,

ההיא איתתא דעלתה למיפא בההוא ביתא אתא ברחא דמרי דביתא אכלה ללישא חביל ומית חייבה רבא לשלומי דמי ברחא.

10. בבלי בבא מציעא ה,א,

ההוא רעיא דהוו מסרי ליה כל יומא חיותא בסהדי יומא חד מסרו ליה בלא סהדי לסוף אמר לא היו דברים מעולם. אתו סהדי אסהידו ביה דאכל תרתי מינייהו.
אמר ר' זירא אם איתא לדר' חייא קמייתא משתבע אשארא.

11. בבלי בבא קמא סב, א,

ההוא גברא דבטש בכספתא דחבריה שדייה בנהרא אתא מריה ואמר הכי והכי הוה לי בגוה. יתיב רב אשי וקא מעיין ביה כי האי גוונא מאי אמר ליה רבינא לרב אחא בריה דרבא ואמרי ליה רב אחא בריה דרבא לרב אשי לאו היינו מתניתין דתנן ומודים חכמים לרבי יהודה במדליק את הבירה שמשלם כל מה שבתוכו שכן דרך בני אדם להניח בבתים. אמר ליה אי דקא טעין זוזי הכא נמי הכא (במאי עסקינן) דקא טעין מרגניתא מאי מי מנחי אינשי מרגניתא בכספתא או לא תיקו.

12. בבלי בבא מציעא צז, א,

ההוא גברא דשאיל שונרא מחבריה חבור עליה עכברי וקטלוהו יתיב רב אשי וקמיבעיא ליה כי האי גוונא מאי כי מתה מחמת מלאכה דמי או לא. אמר ליה

רב מרדכי לרב אשי הכי אמר אבימי מהגרוניא משמיה דרבא גברא דנשי קטלוהו לא דינא ולא דיינא. איכא דאמרי אכיל עכברי טובא וחביל ומית יתיב רב אשי וקא מעיין ביה כהאי גוונא מאי אמר ליה רב מרדכי לרב אשי הכי אמר אבימי מהגרוניא גברא דנשי קטלוהו לא דינא ולא דיינא.

13. בבלי בבא בתרא קמג, ב,

ההוא דאמר להו נכסיי לבניי. הוה ליה ברא וברתא מי קרו אינשי לברא בניי (ולסילוקי לברתא מעישור קאתי) או דלמא לא קרו אינשי לברא בניי ולמושכה לברתא במתנה קאתי. אמר אביי תא שמע ובני דן חושים.

14. בבלי בבא בתרא קמג, ב,

ההוא דאמר להו נכסאי לבנאי. הוה ליה ברא ובר ברא.קרו אינשי לבר ברא ברא או לא רב חביבא אמר קרו אינשי לבר ברא בר בר אשי אמר לא קרו איושי לבר ברא ברא.

Chapter 3

15. בבלי יבמות קי, א,

ההיא עובדא דהוה בנרש ואיקדישה כשהיא קטנה וגדלה ואותביה אבי כורסייא ואתא אחרינא וחטפה מיניה ורב ברונא ורב חננאל תלמידי דרב הוו התם ולא הצריכוה גיטא מבתרא אמר רב פפא בנרש מינסב נסיבי והדר מותבי אבי כורסייא רב אשי אמר הוא עשה שלא כהוגן לפיכך עשו בו שלא כהוגן ואפקעינהו רבנן לקידושיה מיניה. אמר ליה רבינא לרב אשי תינח דקדיש בכספא קדיש בביאה מאי שויוה רבנן לבעילתו בעילת זנות.

16. בבלי כתובות ג, א,

ומי איכא מידי דמדאורייתא לא להוי גט ומשום צנועות ומשום פרוצות שרינן אשת איש לעלמא אין כל דמקדש אדעתא דרבנן מקדש ואפקעינהו רבנן לקידושי מיניה.

17. בבלי גיטין מ, א־ב,

ההוא עבדא דבי תרי קם חד מינייהו ושחרריי לפלגיי אמר חשתא שמעי בי רבנן ומפסדו ליה מינאי אזל אקנייה לבנו קטן. שלחה רב יוסף בריה דרבא לקמיה דרב פפא שלח ליה כאשר עשה כן יעשה לו גמולו ישיב לו בראשו אנן קים לן בינוקא דמקרבא דעתיה לגבי זוזי מוקמינן ליה אפוטרופוס ומקרקיש ליה זוזי וכתב ליה גיטא דחירותא על שמיה.

Chapter 4

18. משנה יבמות יג, א

בית שמאי אומרים אין ממאנין אלא ארוסות ובית הלל אומרים ארוסות ונשואות. בית שמאי אומרים בבעל ולא ביבם ובית הלל אומרים בבעל וביבם. בית שמאי אומרים בפניו ובית הלל אומרים בפניו ושלא בפניו. בית שמאי אומרים בבית דין ובית הלל אומרים בבית דין ושלא בבית דין. אמרו להם בית הלל לבית שמאי ממאנת והיא קטנה אפילו ד׳ וה׳ פעמים. אמרו להם בית שמאי אין בנות ישראל הפקר אלא ממאנת וממתנת עד שתגדיל ותמאן ותנשא.

19. בבלי יבמות קז, ב

תניא אמרו להן בית הלל לבית שמאי והלא פישון הגמל מיאנה אשתו שלא בפניו אמרו להן בית שמאי לבית הלל פישון הגמל במדה כפושה מדד לפיכך מדדו לו במדה כפושה.

20. ירושלמי יבמות יג, א (יג,ג)

אמרו בית הלל לבית שמאי מעשה באשתו של פישון הגמל שמיאנו לה חכמים שלא בפניה אמרו להן בית שמאי משם ראיה לפי שמדד בכפישה לפיכך מדדן לו חכמים בכפישה. וקשיא אילו העושה דבר שלא כשורה שמא מתירין ערוה שלו אמר רב חסדא הדא אמרה עברה ומיאנה מן הנשואין על דבית שמאי מיאוניה מיאונין.

21. משנה בבא בתרא ח, ז

הכותב נכסיו לבניו צריך שיכתוב מהיום ולאחר מיתה דברי רבי יהודה. רבי יוסי אומר אינו צריך.

22. בבלי כתובות מט, ב

אמר רבי אילעא אמר ריש לקיש באושא התקינו הכותב כל נכסיו לבניו הוא ואשתו נזונים מהם.

23. בבלי כתובות מט, ב

איבעיא להו הלכתא כוותיה או לית הלכתא כוותיה תא שמע דרבי חנינא ורבי יונתן הוו קיימי אתא ההוא גברא גחין ונשקיה לרבי יונתן אכרעיה אמר ליה רבי חנינא מאי האי אמר ליה כותב נכסיו לבניו הוא ועשיתינהו לזניה. אי

APPENDIX OF HEBREW SOURCES 187

אמרת בשלמא לאו דינא משום הכי עשייניהו אלא אי אמרת דינא עשייניהו בעי.

24. בבלי ראש השנה ו,א,
תנו רבנן מוצא שפתיך - זו מצות עשה, תשמור - זו מצות לא תעשה, ועשית—אזהרה לבית דין שיעשוך.
פסיקתא רבתי לג,
השופט דן את הדין והשוטר מעשה את הדין.
מכילתא (הוצאת האראוויטץ) עמוד 246,
גט המעושה בישראל כשר ובגוים פסול.
בבלי כתובות עז, א,
אמר רב יהודה אמר רב אסי אין מעשין אלא לפסולות.

25. ירושלמי פאה א, א, (טו, ד)
רבי יונתן ורבי ינאי הוו יתיבין אתא חד בר נש ונשק ריגלוי דרבי יונתן אמר ליה רבי ייני מה טיבו הוה שלים לך מן יומוי אמר ליה חד זמן אתא קבל לי על בריה דיזוניניה ואמרית ליה איזיל צור כנישתא עלוי ובזיתיה. אמר ליה ולמה לא כפיתיניה אמר ליה וכופין ליה אמר ליה ואדיין את לזו חזר ביה רבי יונתן וקבעה שמועה מן שמיה.

26. משנה בבא בתרא ט, ז,
המחלק נכסיו על פיו רבי אליעזר אומר אחד בריא ואחד מסכן נכסים שיש להן אחריות נקנין בכסף ובשטר ובחזקה ושאין להן אחריות אינן נקנין אלא במשיכה. אמרו לו מעשה באמן שלבני רוכל שהיתה חולה ואמרה תנו כבינתי לבתי והיא בשנים עשר מנה ומתה וקימו את דבריה. אמר להן בני רוכל תקברם אמם.

27. בבלי בבא בתרא קנו,ב,
מאי טעמא קא לייט להו אמר רב יהודה אמר שמואל מקיימי קוצים בכרם היו ורבי אליעזר לטעמיה דתנן המקיים קוצים בכרם רבי אליעזר אומר קדש וחכמים אומרים לא קדש אלא דבר שכמוהו מקיימין.

28. ירושלמי בבא בתרא ט, ז, (יז,ב)
אמר ר' יוסי בי רבי בון עולא היה רוצה לקללן שהן זורעין כורכמין בכרם.

29. בבלי כתובות נ, ב,

רבי אלעזר סבר למיזן ממטלטלין אמר לפניו רבי שמעון בן אליקים רבי יודע אני בך שאין מדת הדין אתה עושה אלא מדת רחמנות אלא שמא יראו התלמידים ויקבעו הלכה לדורות.

30. ירושלמי כתובות ו, ו, (ל, ד)

ר׳ יסא איתפקד גביה מדל דיתמין והוה תמן יתמין בעיין מפרנסא אעיל עובדא קומי רבי אלעזר וקומי רבי שמעון בר יקים אמר רבי שמעון בר יקים לא מוטב שיתפרנסו משל אביהן ולא מן הצדקה אמר ליה רבי אלעזר דבר שאילו יבוא לפני רבותינו ואין רבותינו נוגעין ואנו עושין אותו מעשה.

31. ירושלמי בבא מציעא ו, ז, (יא, א)

תני רבי נחמיה קדר מסר קדרוי לבר נש תברין אריס גולתיה אתא גבי רבי יוסי בר חנינה אמר ליה איזיל אמור ליה למען תלך בדרך טובים אזל ואמר ליה ויהב גולתיה. אמר ליה יהב לך אגרך אמר ליה לא אמר ליה זיל ואמור ליה וארחות צדיקים תשמור אזל ואמר ליה ויהב ליה אגרייה.

32. בבלי בבא מציעא פג, א,

רבה בר בר חנן תברו ליה הנהו שקולאי חביתא דחמרא שקל לגלימייהו אתו אמרו לרב אמר ליה הב להו גלימייהו אמר ליה דינא הכי אמר ליה אין למען תלך בדרך טובים יהיב להו גלימייהו אמרו ליה עניי אנן וטרחינן כולה יומא וכפינן ולית לן מידי אמר ליה זיל הב אגרייהו אמר ליה דינא הכי אמר ליה אין וארחות צדיקים תשמור.

33. בבלי כתובות צד, ב,

תניא וחכמים אומרים יחלוקו וכאן אמרו מה שירצה השליש יעשה.

34. ירושלמי כתובות י, ד, (לג, ד)

שמואל אמר שוחדא דדייני לשני שטרות שיצאו על שדה אחת אי זה מהן שירצו בית דין להחליט מחליטין.

35. ירושלמי חגיגה ב, ב, (עח, א)

תני אמר רבי אליעזר בן יעקב שמעתי שעונשין שלא כהלכה ועונשין שלא כתורה עד איכן ר׳ לעזר ב׳ רבי יוסי אמר עד כדי זימזום רבי יוסה אומר בעדים אבל לא בהתרייה מעשה באחד שיצא לדרך רכוב על סוסו בשבת והביאוהו לבית דין וסקלוהו והלא שבות הוית אלא שהיתה השעה צריכה לכך שוב מעשה

באחד שיצא לדרך ואשתו עמו ופנה לאחורי הגדר ועשה צרכיו עמה והביאוהו לבית דין והלקוהו והלא אשתו היית אלא שנהג עצמו בבזיון.

36. ירושלמי הוריות א, א, (מה, ד)
תני יכול אם יאמרו לך על ימין שהוא שמאל ועל שמאל שהוא ימין תשמע להם תלמוד לומר ללכת ימין ושמאל שיאמרו לך על ימין שהוא ימין ועל שמאל שהוא שמאל.

37. בבלי ראש השנה כה, א
...אמר לו הרי הוא אומר אתם אתם אתם ג' פעמים אתם אפילו שוגגים אתם אפילו מזידין אתם אפילו מוטעין.

38. בבלי שבת קל, א
תנו רבנן במקומו של רבי אליעזר היו כורתין עצים לעשות פחמין לעשות ברזל בשבת במקומו של רבי יוסי הגלילי היו אוכלין בשר עוף בחלב... אמר ר' יצחק עיר אחת היתה בארץ ישראל שהיו עושין כר"א והיו מתים בזמנן ולא עד אלא שפעם אחת גזרה מלכות הרשעה גזרה על ישראל על המילה ועל אותה העיר לא גזרה.

39. ירושלמי ברכות א, א, (ג, א)
ורבן גמליאל פליג על רבנין ועבד עובדיה כוותיה והא רבי מאיר פליג על רבנין ולא עבד עובדא כוותיה והא רבי עקיבא פליג על רבנין ולא עבד עובדא כוותיה ...והן אשכחן דרבי שמעון פליג על רבנין ולא עבד עובדא כוותיה כיי דתנינן תמן רבי שמעון אומר כל הספחין מותרין חוץ מספחי כרוב שאין כיוצא בהן בירקות השדה וחכמים אומרים כל הספחין אסורין רבי שמעון בן יוחאי עבד עובדא בשמיטתא חמא חד מלקט ספיחי שביעית אמר ליה ולית אסור ולאו ספיחי אינון אמר ליה ולאו את הוא שאת שמתיר אמר ליה ואין חברי חולקין עלי וקרי עלוי ופורץ גדר ישכנו נחש וכן הות ליה.

40. בבלי פסחים נא, א"ב
אמר רבה בר בר חנה סח לי רבי יוחנן בן אלעזר פעם אחת נכנסתי אחר רבי שמעון בן רבי יוסי בן לקוניא לגינה ונטל ספיחי כרוב ואכל ונתן לי ואמר לי בני בפני אכול שלא בפני לא תאכל אני שראיתי את רבי שמעון בן יוחי שאכל כדי הוא רבי שמון בן יוחי לסמוך עליו בפניו ושלא בפניו אתה בפני אכול שלא בפני לא תאכל.

41. ירושלמי שבת ה, ד, (ז, ג)

גניבה אמר הלכה היא הוה מלמד ובא כדא דתנן שלא ברצון חכמים תני רבי יודה בר פזי רב דלייה אמרו לו או עמוד מבינותינו או העבר רצועה מבין קרניה אמר רבי יוסי ב׳ רבי בון שהיה מתריס כנגדן אמר רבי חנניה פעם אחת יצאת והשחירו שיניו מן הצומות אמר רב אידי דחוטריה אשתו הית.

42. ירושלמי יבמות י, ד, (יא, א)

רבי יוסי שאיל לר׳פנחס היך סבר רבי אמר ליה כרבי ירמיה אמר ליה חזור בך דלא כן אני כותב עליך זקן ממרא.

43. בבלי נידה ז, ב,

תניא אמר לו רבי אליעזר לרבי יהושע אתה לא שמעת אני שמעתי אתה לא שמעת אלא אחת ואני שמעתי הרכה אין אומרים למי שלא ראה את החדש יבא ויעיד אלא למי שראהו. כל ימיו של רבי אליעזר היו עושין כרבי יהושע לאחר פטירתו של רבי אליעזר החזיר רבי יהושע את הדבר ליושנו כרבי אליעזר בחייו מאי טעמא לא משום דרבי אליעזר שמותי הוא וסבר אי עבדינן כוותיה בחדא עבדינן כוותיה באחרניתא ומשום כבודו דרבי אליעזר לא מצינן מחינן בהו לאחר פטירתו של רבי אליעזר דמצינו מחינן בהו החזיר את הדבר ליושנו.

44. ירושלמי נידה א, ב, (מט, א)

כל ימים שהיה ר׳ליעזר קיים היתה הלכה כר׳ יהושע משמת רבי ליעזר הנהיג רבי יהושע הלכה כרבי ליעזר מה נן קיימין אם בששמע רבי ליעזר מפי אחד ורבי יהושע מפי שנים בין בחיים בין לאחר מיתה תהא הלכה כרבי יהושע ואם בששמע מפי אחד ור׳ ליעזר מפי שנים בין בחיים בין לאחר מיתה תהא הלכה כר׳ ליעזר ...בחייו לא ראה דעתו לאחר מיתתו ראה דעתו.

45. ירושלמי סנהדרין ט, יא, (כז, ב)

מה ראה את המעשה ונזכר להלכה הבועל ארמית הקנאים פוגעין בו. תני שלא ברצון חכמים ופינחס שלא ברצון חכמים אמר רבי יודה בר פזי ביקשו לנדותו אילולי שקפצה עליו רוח הקודש ואמרה והיתה לו ולזרעו אחריו ברית כהונת עולם וגו׳.

46. בבלי יבמות יד, א,

אמר אביי כי אמרינן לא תתגודדו כגון שתי בתי דינים בעיר אחת הללו מורים כדברי בית שמאי והללו מורים כדברי בית הלל אבל שתי בתי דינים בשתי עיירות לית לן בה ...אלא אמר רבא כי אמרינן לא תתגודדו כגון בית דין בעיר

APPENDIX OF HEBREW SOURCES 189

באחד שיצא לדרך ואשתו עמו ופנה לאחורי הגדר ועשה צרכיו עמה והביאוהו לבית דין והלקוהו והלא אשתו היית אלא שנהג עצמו בבזיון.

36. ירושלמי הוריות א, א, (מה, ד)

תני יכול אם יאמרו לך על ימין שהוא שמאל ועל שמאל שהוא ימין תשמע להם תלמוד לומר ללכת ימין ושמאל שיאמרו לך על ימין שהוא ימין ועל שמאל שהוא שמאל.

37. בבלי ראש השנה כה, א,

...אמר לו הרי הוא אומר אתם אתם אתם ג' פעמים אתם אפילו שוגגים אתם אפילו מזידין אתם אפילו מוטעין.

38. בבלי שבת קל, א,

תנו רבנן במקומו של רבי אליעזר היו כורתין עצים לעשות פחמין לעשות ברזל בשבת במקומו של רבי יוסי הגלילי היו אוכלין בשר עוף בחלב ...אמר ר' יצחק עיר אחת היתה בארץ ישראל שהיו עושין כר"א והיו מתים בזמנן ולא עד אלא שפעם אחת גזרה מלכות הרשעה גזרה על ישראל על המילה ועל אותה העיר לא גזרה.

39. ירושלמי ברכות א, א, (ג, א)

ורבן גמליאל פליג על רבנין ועבד עובדא כוותיה והא רבי מאיר פליג על רבנין ולא עבד עובדא כוותיה והא רבי עקיבא פליג על רבנין ולא עבד עובדא כוותיה ...והן אשכחן דרבי שמעון פליג על רבנין ולא עבד עובדא כוותיה כיי דתנינן תמן רבי שמעון אומר כל הספחין מותרין חוץ מספחי כרוב שאין כיוצא בהן בירקות השדה וחכמים אומרים כל הספחין אסורין רבי שמעון בן יוחאי עבד עובדא בשמיטתא חמא חד מלקט ספיחי שביעית אמר ליה ולית אסור ולאו ספיחי אינון אמר ליה ולאו את הוא שאת שמתיר אמר ליה ואין חברי חולקין עלי וקרי עלוי ופורץ גדר ישכנו נחש וכן חות ליה.

40. בבלי פסחים נא, א־ב,

אמר רבה בר בר חנה סח לי רבי יוחנן בן אלעזר פעם אחת נכנסתי אחר רבי שמעון בן רבי יוסי בן לקוניא לגינה ונטל ספיחי כרוב ואכל ונתן לי ואמר לי בני בפני אכול שלא בפני לא תאכל אני שראיתי את רבי שמעון בן יוחי שאכל כדי הוא רבי שמון בן יוחי לסמוך עליו בפניו ושלא בפניו אתה בפני אכול שלא בפני לא תאכל.

41. ירושלמי שבת ה, ד, (ז, ג)

גניבה אמר הלכה היא הוה מלמד ובא כדא דתנן שלא ברצון חכמים תני רבי יודה בר פזי רב דלייה אמרו לו או עמוד מבינותינו או העבר רצועה מבין קרניה אמר רבי יוסי ב׳ רבי בון שהיה מתריס כנגדן אמר רבי חנניה פעם אחת יצאת והשחירו שיניו מן הצומות אמר רב אידי דחוטריה אשתו הית.

42. ירושלמי יבמות י, ד, (יא, א)

רבי יוסי שאיל לרפנחס היך סבר רבי אמר ליה כרבי ירמיה אמר ליה חזור בך דלא כן אני כותב עליך זקן ממרא.

43. בבלי נידה ז, ב

תניא אמר לו רבי אליעזר לרבי יהושע אתה לא שמעת אני שמעתי אתה לא שמעת אלא אחת ואני שמעתי הרכה אין אומרים למי שלא ראה את החדש יבא ויעיד אלא למי שראהו. כל ימיו של רבי אליעזר היו עושין כרבי יהושע לאחר פטירתו של רבי אליעזר החזיר רבי יהושע את הדבר ליושנו כרבי אליעזר בחייו מאי טעמא לא משום דרבי אליעזר שמותי הוא וסבר אי עבדינן כוותיה בחדא עבדינן כוותיה באחרנייתא ומשום כבודו דרבי אליעזר לא מצינן מחינן בהו לאחר פטירתו של רבי אליעזר דמצינו מחינן בהו החזיר את הדבר ליושנו.

44. ירושלמי נידה א, ב, (מט, א)

כל ימים שהיה ר׳ליעזר קיים היתה הלכה כר׳ יהושע משמת רבי ליעזר הנהיג רבי יהושע הלכה כרבי ליעזר מה נן קיימין אם בששמע רבי ליעזר מפי אחד ורבי יהושע מפי שנים בין בחיים בין לאחר מיתה תהא הלכה כרבי יהושע ואם בששמע מפי אחד ור׳ ליעזר מפי שנים בין בחיים בין לאחר מיתה תהא הלכה כר׳ ליעזר ...בחייו לא ראה דעתו לאחר מיתתו ראה דעתו.

45. ירושלמי סנהדרין ט, יא, (כז, ב)

מה ראה את המעשה ונזכר להלכה הבועל ארמית הקנאים פוגעין בו. תני שלא ברצון חכמים ופינחס שלא ברצון חכמים אמר רבי יודה בר פזי ביקשו לנדותו אילולי שקפצה עליו רוח הקודש ואמרה והיתה לו ולזרעו אחריו ברית כהונת עולם וגו׳.

46. בבלי יבמות יד, א

אמר אביי כי אמרינן לא תתגודדו כגון שתי בתי דינים בעיר אחת הללו מורים כדברי בית שמאי והללו מורים כדברי בית הלל אבל שתי בתי דינים בשתי עיירות לית לן בה ...אלא אמר רבא כי אמרינן לא תתגודדו כגון בית דין בעיר

אחת פלג מורין כדברי בית שמאי ופלג מורין כדברי בית הלל אבל שתי בתי דינין בעיר אחת לית לן בה.

Chapter 5

47. תוספתא סנהדרין ו, ו

אמר רבי יהודה בן טבאי אראה בנחמה אם לא הרגתי עד זומם בשביל לעקור מליבן של ביתוסין שהיו אומרים עד שיהרג הנידון אמר לו שמעון בן שטח אראה בנחמה אם לא שפכתה דם נקי שהרי אמרה תורה על פי שנים או על פי שלשה עדים יומת המת מה עדים שנים אף זוממין שנים באותה שעה קיבל עליו יהודה בן טבאי שלא יהא מורה הלכה אלא על פי שמעון בן שטח.

48. מכילתא הוצאת הוראוויטץ עמוד 327

כבר הרג שמעון בן שטח עד זומם אמר לו יהודה בן טבאי אראה בנחמה אם לא שפרח דם נקי ואמרה תורה הרוג על פי עדים הרוג על פי זוממים מה עדים שנים אף זוממים שנים.

49. בבלי נידה ז, ב

כל ימיו של רבי אליעזר היו עושין כרבי יהושע לאחר פטירתו של רבי אליעזר החזיר רבי יהושע את הדבר ליושנו כרבי אליעזר בחייו מאי טעמא לא משום דרבי אליעזר שמותי הוא וסבר אי עבדינן כוותיה בחדא עבדינן כוותיה באחרניתא ומשום כבודו דרבי אליעזר לא מצינן מחינן בהו לאחר פטירתו של רבי אליעזר דמצינו מחינו בהו החזיר את הדבר ליושנו.

50. ירושלמי סנהדרין ו, ג, (כג, ב)

אמר רבי יהודה בן טבאי אראה בנחמה אם לא הרגתי עד זומם שהיו אומרים עד שייהרג שנאמר נפש תחת נפש אמר לו שמעון בן שטח אראה בנחמה אם לא מעלים עליך כאילו שפכת דם נקי באותה שעה קיבל עליו שלא יורה אלא מפי שמעון בן שטח.

51. בבלי כתובות סג, ב

כלתיה דרב זביד אימרדא הוה תפיסא חד שירא יתיב אמימר ומר זוטרא ורב אשי ויתיב רב גמדא גבייהו יתבי וקאמרי מרדה הפסידה בלאותיה קיימין אמר להו רב גמדא משום דרב זביד גברא רבה מחניפיתו ליה והאמר רב כהנא מיבעיא בעי רבא ולא פשיט. איכא דאמרי יתבי וקאמרי מרדה לא הפסידה

בלאותיה קיימין אמר להו רב גמדא משום דרב זביד גברא רבה אפיכתו ליה
לדינא עילויה האמר רב כהנא מיבעיא בעי לה רבא ולא פשיט.

52. בבלי בבא קמא צו, ב,
ההוא גברא דגזל פדנא דתורי מחבריה אזל כרב בהו כרבא זרע בהו זרעא לסוף
אהדרינהו למריה אתא לקמיה דרב נחמן אמר להו זילו שומו שבחא דאשבח
אמר ליה רבא תורי אשבח ארעא לא אשבח אמר מי קאמינא נשיימו כוליה
פלגא קאמינא אמר ליה סוף סוף גזילה היא וקא הדרה בעינא דתנן כל הגזלנין
משלמין כשעת הגזלה אמר ליה לא אמינא לך כי יתיבנא בדינא לא תימא לי
מידי דאמר הונא חברין עלאי אנא ושבור מלכא אחי בדינא האי איניש גזלנא
עתיקא הוא ובעינא דאיקנסיה.

53. בבלי בבא קמא קיז, ב,
ההוא גברא דאחוי אכריא דחטי דבי ריש גלותא אתא לקמיה דרב נחמן חייביה
רב נחמן לשלומי יתיב רב יוסף אחוריה דרב הונא בר חייא ויתיב רב הונא בר
חייא קמיה דרב נחמן אמר ליה רב הונא בר חייא לרב נחמן דינא או קנסא
אמר ליה מתניתין היא דתנן אם מחמת הגזלן חייב להעמיד לו שדה ואוקימנא
דאחווי אחוויי בתר דנפק אמר ליה רב יוסף לרב הונא בר חייא מאי נפקא לך
מינה אי דינא אי קנסא אמר אמר ליה אי דינא גמרינן מיניה אי קנסא לא גמרינן
מיניה ומנא תימרא דמקנסא לא גמרינן דתניא בראשונה היו אומרים המטמא
והמנסך חזרו לומר אף המדמע חזרו אין לא חזרו לא מאי טעמא לאו משום
דקנסא הוא וקנסא לא גמרינן מיניה.

54. מכילתא משפטים, הוצאת האראוויטץ עמוד 323,
ודל לא תהדר בריבו למה נאמר לפי שהוא אומר לא תשא פני דל וגומר אין לי
אלא אלו חלופיהן מנין תלמוד לומר ודל לא תהדר בריבו.

55. מכילתא משפטים , הוצאת האראוויטץ עמוד 326,
לא תטה משפט אביונך בריבו למה נאמר לפי שהוא אומר ודל לא תהדר בריבו
אין לי דל דל עני תאב מנין תלמוד לומר לא תטה משפט אביונך בריבו. רשע וכשר
עומדין לפניך בדין שלא תאמר הואיל ורשע הוא אטה עליו את הדין לכך נאמר
לא תטה משפט אביונך בריבו אביון הוא במצות.

56. מכילתא דרבי שמעון בן יוחאי הוצאת מלמד עמוד 214
ודל לא תהדר יכול לא יהדרנו בממון תלמוד לומר בריבו שלא יהדרנו בדין שלא

תאמר עני זה בן טובים הוא אזכנו בדין ונמצא מתפרנס בנקיות תלמוד לומר ודל לא תהדר בריבו ולהלן הוא אומר לא תשא פני דל.

57. מכילתא דרבי שמעון בן יוחאי הוצאת מלמד עמוד 215

לא תטה משפט אבינך מה אני צריך והלא כבר נאמר לא תטה משפט אחד עני ואחד עשיר מה תלמוד לומר לא תטה משפט אבינך זה אביון במצות שלא תאמר רשע הוא חזקתו שהוא משקר וחזקת זה שאינו משקר אעבר עליו את הדין תלמוד לומר לא תטה משפט אבינך.

58. ספרא הוצאת וייס פרשת קדושים עמוד 89,א

לא תשא פני דל שלא תאמר עני הוא זה הואיל ואני והעשיר הזה חייבים לפרנסו אזכנו ונמצא מתפרנס בנקיות לכך נאמר לא תשא פני דל.

59. ספרא הוצאת וייס פרשת קדושים עמוד 89,א

ולא תהדר פני גדול שלא תאמר עשיר הוא זה בן גדולים הוא זה לא אביישנו ואראה בבושתו (על אחת) (עד) כמה שאני מביישו לכך נאמר לא תהדר פני גדול.

60. ספרי על במדבר הוצאת האראוויטץ עמוד 222,

ולא תחניפו את הארץ הרי זו אזהרה לחנפים.

61. ספרי על דברים הוצאת פינקלשטין עמוד 28,

כקטן כגדל תשמעון שמא תאמר הואיל ועני זה עשיר זה מצוה לפרנסו אזכנו ונמצא מתפרנס בנקיות תלמוד לומר כקטן כגדל תשמעון.

62. ספרי על דברים הוצאת פינקלשטין עמוד 28,

דבר אחר כקטן כגדל תשמעון שמא תאמר היאך אני פוגם כבודו של עשיר זה בשביל דינר אזכנו ולכשיצא לחוץ אני אומר לו תן לו שאתה חייב תלמוד לומר כקטן כגדל תשמעון

63. ספרי על דברים הוצאת פינקלשטין עמוד 198,

לא תטה משפט שלא תאמר איש פלוני נאה איש פלוני קרובי לא תכיר פנים שלא תאמר איש פלוני עני איש פלוני עשיר.

64. תוספתא סנהדרין א, ב,

רבי אלעזר בנו של רבי יוסי הגלילי אומר כל המבצע הרי זה חוטא והמברך את

המבצע הרי זה מנאץ לפני המקום על זה נאמר ובוצע ברך נאץ ה' אלא יקוב הדין את ההר שכן משה היה אומר יקוב הדין את ההר אבל אהרן היה עושה שלום בין אדם לחבירו שנאמר בשלום ובמישור הלך וכולי.

65. משנה כתובות ט, ב,

מי שמת והניח אשה ובעל חוב ויורשין והיה לו פקדון או מלוה ביד אחרים רבי טרפון אומר ינתנו לכושל שבהן רבי עקיבא אומר אין מרחמין בדין אלא ינתנו ליורשין שכלן צריכין שבועה ואין היורשין צריכין שבועה.

66. ירושלמי כתובות ט, ב, (לג, א)

רבי יוסי בר חנינא אמר לכושל שבראיותיו כגון מלוה בעדים ומלוה בשטר יינתנו למלוה בעדים כגון לכושל רבי יוחנן אמר לכושל בגופו הגע עצמך הוה עתיר כגון אילין דבר אנדראי אמר רבי אחא לכושל בגופו ועני כהדא קריביתיה דרבי שמואל בא אבא יהבו ליה משום כושל...הכל מודין שאם טינו בשיקול הדעת שאין מחזירין מדברי תורה מחזירין מה פליגין בטעות משנה שרבי יוחנן אמר בטעות משנה שקול הדעת רבי שמעון בן לקיש אמר טעות דבר תורה היא טעות משנה היא טעות זקנים.

67. משנה סנהדרין ד, א,

דיני ממונות מחזירין בין לזכות בין לחובה דיני נפשות מחזירין לזכות ואין מחזירין לחובה.

68. משנה בכורות ד, ד,

דן את הדין זכה את החיב וחיב את הזכאי טמא את הטהור וטהר את הטמא מה שעשה עשוי וישלם מביתו ואם היה ממחה לבית דין פטור מלשלם.

69. בבלי סנהדרין לג, א,

רב ששת אמר כאן שטעה בדבר משנה כאן שטעה בשיקול הדעת דאמר רב ששת אמר רב אסי טעה בדבר משנה חוזר טעה בשיקול הדעת אינו חוזר.

70. בבלי סנהדרין לג, א,

היכי דמי שיקול הדעת אמר רב פפא כגון תרי תנאי או תרי אמוראי דפליגי אהדדי ולא איתמר הלכתא לא כמר ולא כמר ואיקרי ועבד כחד מינייהו וסוגיא דשמעתא אזלי כאידך היינו שיקול הדעת.

Chapter 6

71. ירושלמי חגיגה ב, ב, (עח, א)
תני אמר רבי אליעזר בון יעקב שמעתי שעונשין שלא כהלכה ועונשין שלא כתורה עד איכן רבי ליעזר ב׳ רבי יוסי אמר עד כדי זימזום רבי יוסה אומר בעדים אבל לא בהתרייה.

72. בבלי סנהדרין מו, א
תניא רבי אליעזר בן יעקב אומר שמעתי שבית דין מכין ועונשין שלא מן התורה ולא לעבור על דברי תורה אלא כדי לעשות סייג לתורה ומעשה באחד שרכב על סוס בשבת בימי יונים והביאוהו לבית דין וסקלוהו לא מפני שראוי לכך אלא שהשעה צריכה לכך שוב מעשה באדם אחד שהטיח את אשתו תחת התאנה והביאוהו לבית דין והלקוהו לא מפני שראוי לכך אלא שהשעה צריכה לכך.

73. מגילת תענית הוצאת ליכטנשטיין עמוד 336,
בעשרין ותרין תבו לקטלא משמדיא...אמר רבי אליעזר בן יעקב שמעתי שבית דין מלקין והורגין שלא מן התורה אמר רבי שמעון שמעתי שבית דין עונשין ממון ומכים שלא מן התורה לא מפני שכתוב בתורה אלא משום שנאמר ובערת הרע מקרבך.

74. בבלי כתובות צד, א,
אתמר ב׳ שטרות היוצאים ביום אחד רב אמר חולקין ושמואל אמר שודא דדייני.

75. בבלי כתובות פה, ב,
שניהם קרובים ושניהם שכנים ושניהם חכמים שודא דדייני.

76. בבלי כתובות צד, ב,
אמיה דרמי בר חמא כתבתינהו לנכסה לרמי בר חמא בצפרא לאורתא כתבתינהו למר עוקבא בר חמא אתא רמי בר חמא לקמיה דרב ששת אוקמיה בנכסא אתא מר עוקבא לקמיה דרב נחמן אוקמיה בנכסא אתא רב ששת לקמיה דרב נחמן אמר ליה מאי טעמא עבד מר הכי אמר ליה ומאי טעמא עבד מר הכי אמר ליה דקדים אמר ליה אטו בירושלים יתבינן דכתבינן שעות אלא מאי טעמא עבד הכי אמר ליה שודא דדייני אמר ליה אנא נמי שודא דדייני

אמר ליה חדא דאנא דיינא ומר לאו דיינא ועוד דמעיקרא לאו בתורת הכי אתית לה.

77. בבלי גיטין יד, ב,

תניא הולך מנה לפלוני והלך ובקשו ולא מצאו יחזרו למשלח מת משלח רבי נתן ורבי יעקב אמרו יחזרו ליורשי משלח ויש אומרים ליורשי מי שנשתלחו לו רבי יהודה הנשיא אמר משום רבי יעקב שאמר משום רבי מאיר מצוה לקיים דברי המת וחכמים אומרים יחלוקו וכאן אמרו כל מה שירצה שליח יעשה.

78. בבלי בבא בתרא לד, ב – לה, א,

זה אומר של אבותי וזה אומר של אבותי אמר רב נחמן כל דאלים גבר ומאי שנא משני שטרות היוצאין ביום אחד דרב אמר יחלוקו ושמואל אמר שודא דדייני התם ליכא למיקם עלה דמילתא הכא איכא למיקם עלה דמילתא.

79. בבלי בבא בתרא סב, ב,

אתמר לה להאי גיסא ואתמר לה להאי גיסא שודא דדייני.

80. תוספתא בבא בתרא יא, יג,

האומר תנו מאתים דינר ליוסף בן שמעון והיו שם שני יוסף בן שמעון אין דורשין לשון הדיוט לומר לזה היה אוהב ולא לזה היה אוהב אלא שניהם חולקין בשוה.

81. משנה עדויות א, ה,

ולמה מזכירין דברי היחיד בין המרבין הואיל ואין הלכה אלא כדברי המרבין שאם יראה בית דין את דברי היחיד ויסמך עליו שאין בית דין יכול לבטל דברי בית דין חברו עד שיהיה גדול ממנו בחכמה ובמנין היה גדול ממנו בחכמה אבל לא במנין במנין אבל לא בחכמה אינו יכול לבטל דבריו עד שיהיה גדול ממנו בחכמה ובמנין.

82. משנה עדויות א, ו,

אמר רבי יהודה אם כן למה מזכירין דברי היחיד בין המרבין לבטלה שאם יאמר האדם כך אני מקבל יאמר לו כדברי איש פלוני שמעת.

83. בבלי נידה ו, א-ב,

מעשה ועשה רבי כרבי אליעזר לאחר שנזכר אמר כדי הוא רבי אליעזר לסמוך עליו בשעת הדחק והוינן בה מאי לאחר שנזכר אילימא לאחר שנזכר דאין הלכה

כרבי אליעזר אלא כרבנן בשעת הדחק היכי עביד כוותיה אלא (לאו) דלא איתמר הלכתא לא כמר ולא כמר וכיון שנזכר דלאו יחיד פליג עליה אלא רבים פליגי עליה אמר כדי הוא רבי אליעזר לסמוך עליו בשעת הדחק.

84. תוספתא עדויות א, ד,

לעולם הלכה כדברי המרובין לא הוזכרו דברי היחיד בין המרובין אלא לבטלן רבי יהודה אומר לא הוזכרו דברי יחיד בין המרובין אלא שמא תיצרך להן שעה ויסמכו עליהן וחכמים אומרים לא הוזכרו דברי יחיד בין המרובים אלא מתוך שזה אומר טמא וזה אומר טהור זה אומר טמא כדברי רבי אליעזר אמרו לו כדברי רבי אליעזר שמעתה.

85. ספרי על דברים הוצאת פינקלשטין עמוד 207,

לא תסור מן התורה אשר יגידו לך מצות לא תעשה ימין ושמאל אפילו מראים בעיניך על ימין שהוא שמאל ועל שמאל שהוא ימין שמע להם.

86. ספרי על דברים הוצאת פינקלשטין עמוד 251,

אמר רבי יאשיה שלשה דברים סח לי זעירא משום אנשי ירושלם סוטה אם רצה בעלה למחול לה מוחל בן סורר ומורה אם רצו אביו ואמו למחול לו מוחלים זקן ממרא על פי בית דין אם רצו חביריו למחול לו מוחלים וכשבאתי והרציתי הדברים לפני רבי יהודה בן בתירה על שנים הודה לי ועל אחד לא הודה לי על סוטה ועל בן סורר ומורה הודה לי ועל זקן ממרא על פי בית דין לא הודה לי מפני שהיה מעמיד מחלוקת בישראל.

87. ירושלמי הוריות א, א, (מה, ד)

תני יכול אם יאמרו לך על ימין שהיא שמאל ועל שמאל שהיא ימין תשמע להם תלמוד לומר ללכת ימין ושמאל שיאמרו לך על ימין שהוא ימין ועל שמאל שהוא שמאל.

88. משנה פרה ז, ו-ז,

המוליך את החבל בידו לדרכו כשר ושלא לדרכו פסול זה הלך ליבנה שלשה מועדות ובמועד שלישי הכשירו לו הוראת שעה. המכנן את החבל על יד על כשר ואם כננו באחרונה פסול אמר רבי יוסי לזה הכשירו הוראת שעה.

89. תוספתא פרה ז, ד,

המוליך את החבל לבעלים כדרכו כשר ושלא כדרכו פסול הלכה זו עלו עליה בני אסייה שלשה רגלים ליבנה ברגל השלישי הכשירו להן הוראות שעה. אמר רבי

יוסי לא לזה הורו אלא למעלה את החבל וחזר ובנאו באחרונה הורו לו שהוא כשר לשעבר ופסול לעתיד לבוא.

90. בבלי חולין מח, א,
זה היה מעשה ועלו עליה בני עסיא ג רגלים ליבנה לרגל שלישי היתרוה להם.

91. בבלי יבמות קכא, ב - קכב, א,
ההוא עובד כוכבים דהוה קאמר ליה לישראל קטול אספסתא ושדי לחיואי בשבתא ואי לא קטילנא לך כדקטילנא לפלוני בר ישראל דאמרי ליה בשיל לי קדירה בשבת ולא בשיל לי וקטילתיה שמעה דביתהו ואתאי לקמיה דאביי שהייתא תלתא ריגלי אמר לה רב אדא בר אהבה זיל לקמיה דרב יוסף דחריף סכינא אזלה קמיה... .

92. בבלי חולין עז, א,
ההוא נשבר העצם ויצא לחוץ דאישתקיל קורטיתא מיניה אתא לקמיה דאביי שהייה תלתא ריגלי אמר ליה רב אדא בר מתנא זיל קמיה דרבא בריה דרב יוסף בר חמא דחריפא סכיניה... .

INDEX OF SOURCES

BIBLE
Genesis
42:8.................................... 35
46:23...................................39

Exodus
18:21....................................78
23:3............................118, 119
23:6............................118, 119
32:1-7.................................125
37:27.................................. 125

Leviticus
19:15..........................118, 119
9:16.................................... 25
23:2..............................85, 86
23:4.....................80, 85, 86
23:37............................ 85, 86

Numbers
32:22..................................28
35:30..................................83
35:33................................ 119

Deuteronomy
1:17...................................120
14:1.................................... 94
16:19................................. 120
17:6............................ 83, 101
17:11................... 85, 169, 172
18:14................................ 172
19:15...................................83
19:18................................ 103
28:14................................ 172

Joshua
19:51............................... 167

Judges
21:21...................................42

I Kings
15:19...................................82

II Kings
16:8................................... 82

Obadia
1:15............................52, 78

Malachi
2:6.................................... 125

Psalms
10:3...................................125
105:37...............................129

Proverbs
2:20................................... 75
17:8................................... 82
21:14.................................. 82
21:30................................ 124

Job
4:4................................... 129
38:15...........................9, 78

Ezra
10:8................................. 167

MISHNAH
Pe'ah
6:1.................................... 167

INDEX

Kilayim
5:8.................... 69, 70

Shebi'it
6:5-6..................... 147
9:1....................... 89
9:9....................... 44

Halla
2:7....................... 44
4:11...................... 73

Orlah
1:7...................... 147

Shabbat
5:4....................... 89
19:1...................... 87

Erubin
2:6...................... 147
5:4...................... 125

Pesahim
9:6...................... 147

Shekalim
1:2....................... 68
3:2....................... 28
4:7...................... 147

Betza
2:8....................... 89

Rosh Hashanah
2:9....................... 85

Jevamot
2:10...................... 20
3:10..................... 176
8:4...................... 147
10:2..................... 132
13:7...................... 60
13:11............. 56, 57, 60
16:7..................... 147

Ketubot
3:2...................... 143
4:11...................... 71
9:2...................... 128
9:3...................... 128
11:5............... 132, 146

Nedarim
2:5...................... 143

Nazir
5:4....................... 32

Gittin
4:5.................. 51, 52
5:4................ 105, 115
9:8....................... 64

Kiddushin
3:1....................... 44

Baba Kamma
4:3....................... 31
6:4....................... 11

Baba Metzia
6:8....................... 76
8:8....................... 21

Baba Bathra
8:5............... 45, 46, 68
9:7........... 47, 51, 66, 121
9:9....................... 32

Sanhedrin
1:1...................... 133
3:7.................. 21, 24
3:8...................... 133
4:1............... 132, 133
6:4...................... 178
7:2................ 32, 102
9:5................ 83, 145
11:2...................... 90

Makkot

1:10	131
3:10	145

Eduyot

1:4	158, 163
1:5	158, 160-164
1:6	159
3:12	89
5:6	91
6:1	60
8:6	147

Avodah Zarah

1:4	21

Avot

1:1	146
1:8	79
1:9	24
1:11	73
1:12	126
3:13	146

Horayot

1:3-5	132

Hullin

8:4	87

Bekhorot

2:8	129
4:4	20, 132, 133

Para

3:3	104
4:4	173
7:6	173, 174
7:7	173

Nidah

1:3	104

TOSEFTA

Pea

2:5	167
4:15	28

Terumah

3:6	44
4:10	44

Shabbat

12:12	88

Erubin

6:13	125

Pesahim

8:10	73

Shekalim

1:3	167

Yoma

2:5-6	28

Betza

4:4	44

Rosh Hashanah

1:15	105
3:1	86

Hagigah

2:9	27

Jevamot

4:4	45
12:6	87
12:13	64

Ketubot
4:9 42
5:10 101
10:2 51

Kiddushin
3:7-8 76

Baba Kamma
4:2 31
6:16-17 11
7:19 44
8:15 46

Baba Metzia
1:9 22
1:12 22

Baba Bathra
8:14 53
10:6 67
11:13 157

Sanhedrin
1:2-3 .... 124, 125
1:4-5 132
5:4 19
6:3 21
6:4 133
6:6 .... 23, 100, 103
7:1 27
7:7 .... 34, 151
8:3 101
9:11 32

Makkot
4:17 145

Eduyot
1:1 161
1:4 .... 159, 163, 164
1:5 20

Avodah Zarah
3:7 21

Zevahim
1:8 147

Hullin
2:24 28
3:10 175

Bekhorot
2:7-8 129
3:9 28
3:19 28

Kellim
1:1 67

Ohalot
4:2 88

Para
4:11 173
7:4 .... 174, 176, 177, 179

Nidah
1:5 91
1:9 .... 178, 179

Mikva'ot
4:6 175

MIDRESHEI HALAKHAH

Mekhilta (ed. Horovitz)
Page 19 146
Page 171 101
Page 198 78
Page 246 .... 31, 64
Page 323 118
Page 326 .... 68, 118, 130
Pages 327-8 .... 101, 133
Page 336 87

Mekhilta D'Rabbi Simeon (ed. Melamed)
Page 214 119
Page 215 119

INDEX

Sifra

Hova Parashata 13:13............... 112
Kedoshim 4.............21, 24, 25, 119
Emor 9:9........................... 86

Sifre ad Num. (ed. Horovitz)

Page 102.............................26
Page 158............................ 173
Page 115............................44
Page 222..................... 111, 119

Sifre ad Deut. (ed. Finkelstein)

Page 25.............................146
Pages 26-27.................31, 108
Page 28............................120
Page 63..............................73
Page 158............................94
Page 163............................87
Page 165........................... 128
Page 181........................... 143
Page 198........................... 120
Page 205............................90
Page 206....................90, 169
Page 207............85, 90, 165, 169
Page 221........................... 179
Page 251........................... 170
Page 253........................... 178
Page 326............................46

Midrash Tannaim (ed. Hoffman)

Pages 102-3......................... 165
Page 117........................... 100
Page 134............................28

Avot de Rabbi Natan

Chapter 2...........................28

PALESTINIAN TALMUD

Berakhot

1:1 (3, 1)...........................88
1:3 (3, 2)...........................73
2:3 (4, 3)...........................90
8:1 (11, 1)......................... 87

Pea

1:1 (15, 4)................... 64, 143

1:1 (16, 1).......................... 25
1:1 (16, 2).......................... 72
2:4 (17, 1).......................... 34
3:6 (17, 4).........................153
4:8 (18, 3).........................123
5:1 (18, 4).........................167

Demai

3:3 (23, 3).......................... 89

Shebi'it

9:4 (39, 1).......................... 89

Terumah

10:2 (47, 2).........................91

Halla

4:5 (60, 2)......................... 73

Shabbat

1:4 (3, 4)........................... 91
5:4 (7, 3)...........................90
19:1 (16, 4).........................20

Erubin

1:4 (19, 1)......................... 87
10:1 (26, 1).........................90

Pesahim

7:2 (34, 2).......................... 89
10:1 (37, 2).........................73

Shekalim

1:2 (46,1)..........................167
3:2 (47,3)..........................28

Betza

2:1 (61,2).......................... 34
2:8 (61,4).......................... 90
4:3 (62,3).....................88, 89

Rosh Hashanah

2:7 (58,2).......................... 86
3:1 (58, 3)......................... 86

Ta'anit

2:8 (65, 4).............................143
2:14 (66,1).............................74

Moed Katan

3:1 (81,4)..................91, 145, 167
3:5 (82, 4).............................34

Hagigah

1:1......................................84
2:2 (78, 1)............17, 83, 142-3, 178

Jevamot

1:2 (3, 1)..............................74
1:6 (3, 2)..............................94
2:11 (4, 2).............................67
8:2 (9, 1)............................147
10:4 (11,1)............................90
13:1 (13, 3)..................45, 59, 68
15:3 (14, 4)............................42

Ketubot

4:8 (28, 4)..............42, 61, 65, 157
4:10 (29, 1)............................79
6:6 (30, 4).............................71
8:2 (32,1)............................158
9:1 (32,4)............................136
9:2 (33, 1)..............9, 129, 134-137
10:4 (33,4)......................81, 151
10:5 (34, 1)............................81
13:1 (35, 4)............................39

Nedarim

6:8 (40, 1).............................86

Nazir

3:4 (53, 1-2).........................145

Gittin

5:3 (46, 4)........................71, 74
5:5 (47, 1)...........................114
8:6 (49, 3).............................90
9:8 (50, 3).............................22
9:9 (50, 4).............................66

Kiddushin

1:1 (58,4)..............................74
1:7 (61,1)...........................62-64
3:12 (64, 4).............................9
4:12 (66, 2)..........................143

Nidah

1:3 (49, 1)........................74, 91
1:4 (49, 2-3)........................159
2:7 (50, 2)............................34

Baba Kamma

4:3 (4,2)..............................31
8:4 (6, 3).............................72
10:6 (7,3)........................114-117

Baba Metzia

6:8 (11,1).............................75

Baba Bathra

8:5 (16, 2)...........................135
9:4 (17, 1).......................24, 79
9:7 (17, 2).............................70

Sanhedrin

1:1 (18, 1)...............128, 134, 135
1:1 (18, 2)...........................124
3:2 (21, 1).............................27
3:8 (21, 3).............................79
3:9 (21, 3).............................19
3:10 (21, 4).......................21, 34
4:9 (22, 2)...........................123
6:3 (23, 2)......................100, 106
6:8 (23, 3)...........................178
9:7 (27, 2)...........................143
9:10 (27, 2)...........................84

Shebuot

4:1 (35, 2).............................19
9:4 (39, 1).............................89
10:4 (39,4).......................78, 79

Avodah Zarah

2:8 (41,4).............................91
3:10 (43,2)............................89

INDEX

Horayot
1:1 (45,4).................85, 170, 172

BABYLONIAN TALMUD

Berakhot
4b...146
9a................................. 158, 159
11a...................................58, 73
19a............................... 91, 110
19b..124
23a...90
27a..123
53b...
56a...37

Shabbat
12b..11
15a..58
29b.................................. 58, 160
33b..161
45a.................................159, 162
52b..147
54b..90
116b..82
119a............................... 110, 111
121b......................................110
130a............................87, 88, 89
139b.......................................110
153b..24

Erubin
7a..11
41a..23
46a..159
50b..134
58a..125
91a..160
96a..90

Pesahim
13a..28
51a..89
52a...............................110, 111
53b..110
54b..101
56a..97

69a..67
82b..176
100a..73

Yoma
38a..28
53a..104
69b..176

Sukkah
14b..160
31a-b.....................................160

Betza
16a..127
28b..11

Rosh Hashanah
6a..64
17b..72
22b..105
25a..................................85, 91

Ta'anit
4a..46
11a..101

Megilah
20a..32
25b..83

Mo'ed Katan
11b..110
16a.................................26, 167
17a.................................110-112

Hagigah
13a..134
16b................................100, 101

Jevamot
14a..94
15a..23
35a.................................176, 178
60b..136

63b	82
67b	82, 146
77a	34
87b	58
89b	146, 167
90b	17, 48, 83, 142-144
92a	124
92b	44
99b	87
107b	32, 45, 57-59, 68
109a	60
109b	41
110a	10, 32, 42, 43, 47, 49, 59
112b	41
118b	114
121a	9, 110
121b	175
122a	175

Ketubot

3a	48
7a	179
11a	44
15a	176, 178
19a	35
20a-b	110
27b	36
28b	87
36b	44
46a	143
48a	71, 146
49a	10
49b	35, 61
50b	10, 35, 70, 71, 74, 136
51a	71
52a	19, 71 79
53a	63, 64
54b	19, 136
63a-b	107, 122
63b-64a	30
68a	71
68b	71
77a	64
84a	19, 129, 130
84b	19, 30, 112, 130-31, 134, 136-7
85b	19, 32, 80, 151, 156
86a	10, 11, 43, 45, 53, 79, 145
92a	129
94a-b	80, 81, 151, 153
94b	151, 152, 163
100a	82, 134, 136
105a	35, 82, 123
105b	19, 82, 123

Nedarim

23a	37, 42
28a	93
50b	30
62a-b	110

Nazir

21a	26
32a	58
57b	67
59a	110

Sotah

12b	42
15a	44
41b	111

Gittin

9b	154
10b	93
14a	32
14b-15a	80, 81, 152
19a	9, 159, 162
20a	164
25b	44
27b	81
28b	82
33a	26, 48
35a	23, 30
36b	82, 167
37a	19
38a	175
38b	53
40a	51, 78
40b	51-54, 78
44a	114
52a	53
53a	114, 116-7
55b	146
56a	127
63b	37
73a	48
88b	64

INDEX

Kiddushin

12b.	35
14a.	23
26b.	67
32a.	64, 66
45b.	37, 42
49b.	111
54b.	123
58b.	44
59a.	45
70b.	112
74a.	22, 81, 150, 156
80a.	83
81a.	35, 83

Baba Kamma

11a.	39, 58, 75
12a.	136
19a.	44
20b.	58
27b.	35, 114
30b.	11
36b.	26
38a.	31
39a.	124
46a.	108
48a.	36
53a.	124
55b-55a.	11
59b.	34, 35, 110
62a.	38
68a-69b.	21
80a.	67
81b.	146
83a.	122
84a.	39
93a.	39
94a.	116
96b.	10, 39, 100, 112, 114-15
99b.	108
102a.	123
113a.	31, 93
113b.	93
116b-117a.	73, 100, 114, 136
117b.	36

Baba Metzia

5a.	37
9b.	110
17a.	21
31b.	29
34a.	81
37.	58
39b.	15, 36
42a-b.	39
44b.	19
55a.	146
58a.	76
59b.	91
66a.	136
68b.	110
69a.	27-29
72a.	51
75b.	62
77b.	38
82b.	76
83a.	10, 75, 78
88a.	128
90a-b.	51, 52, 75
97a.	38
101b.	52, 78
102b.	108
104a.	42, 157
117b.	124

Baba Bathra

5a.	19
6b-7a.	37
13b.	35
16a.	62
22a.	10, 13, 110, 111
29b.	32
32b.	108
33b-34a.	39
35a.	81, 152, 156
35b.	81
48b.	43, 48, 49
51a.	35
54b.	93
55a.	93
58a.	153

62b.	81, 108, 152
88a.	32, 34
94a.	114
111a.	136
121b.	67
130b.	22, 34
133b.	68
136a.	61
143b.	39
144a.	32, 110
151a.	153
153a.	22, 87
156a.	47, 52
156b.	68, 70
168a.	110
173b.	32
174a.	9, 11
174b.	110

Sanhedrin

6a.	124, 132, 134
6b.	35, 123, 124, 126
7a.	125
7b.	25
17b.	143, 146
21b.	24
26b.	83
27a.	150
27b.	62
29b.	135
30a.	22, 24
31b.	27
33a.	132-135, 138
33b.	138
34b.	123
36a.	123
36b.	123
45b.	134
46a.	83, 106, 142-144, 146, 150
52b.	32, 102
58b.	9, 78
68a.	67
78b-79a.	19, 176
80b.	176
81b.	146
82a-b.	93
81b.	83
97b.	124

Makkot

5b.	100, 103

Shebuot

30a.	112, 123, 150
30b.	74, 81, 110, 112, 150
31a.	25
32b.	39
41a.	111
47a.	39
48b.	153

Avodah Zarah

2b.	44
4b.	97
7a.	123
24b.	176
35a.	25
36a.	91, 146
40a.	87
49b.	67
55a.	46

Horayot

2b.	85, 170
4b.	138, 139
6a.	176

Zevahim

13a.	147
37b.	147
108b.	176

Menahot

6a.	44
50b.	176
58b.	117

Hullin

18b.	87
29b.	173
44b.	20, 28
48a.	175
57a.	87
57b.	105

INDEX

77a................................175
95a................................46
98a................................74
111b...............................91
127a...............................42
132b......................... 114, 136

Bekhorot
26a...............................123
28b...............................134
95b................................35
113a...............................35

Arakhin
22a............................11, 31
23b................................26

Temurah
4b.................................44
15b...............................176

Keritot
20a................................32
28b................................84

Nidah
3b................................146
4b.................................44
6a.........................159, 162
7a....................... 34, 91, 105
9b................................178
13b.................................9
20b................................20
52b................................58

MIDRASH RABBA
Bamidbar Rabba
11.................................52
11:3...............................20

Devarim Rabba
1..................................19

Kohelet Rabba
10.................................89

Shir Hashirim
1(3)..............................165

MIDRASH MISHLE
Proverbs
22:22.............................130

YALKUT SHIMONI
Ex. 20:12..........................64
Ex. 23:7..........................100
Deut. 17:11.......................165
Ps. 10:3..........................124

TANHUMA
Mishpatim 6................ 142, 150

Tanhuma (Buber)
Tazria 8...........................57

MIDRASH HAGADOL
Deut. 1:17.................124, 165

PESIKTA RABBATI
33.................................64

MIDRASH RUTH HANE'LAM
.................................148

MIDRASH LEKAH TOV
Deut. 17:11.......................165

INDEX OF AUTHORITIES

Abaye, 34, 39, 44, 94, 175
R. Abbahu, 108
Abimi of Hagronia, 38
R. Aha, 130
R. Aha the son of Raba, 38
R. Akiba, 85, 86, 128, 129, 130, 131, 142
Amemar, 107
R. Ashi, 33, 38, 43, 44-48, 50, 107, 109, 111
R. Assi, 133-134

R. Beruna, 42
R. Binyamin, 130

R. Elai, 61-62
R. Eleazar, 71, 72, 73, 145, 153, 167
R. Eleazar b. Azariah, 89, 90
R. Eliezer, 66-70, 87, 89, 91-92, 104-5, 124, 126, 162
R. Eliezer b. Jacob, 84, 142-149
R. Eliezer b. Rabbi Jose the Galilean, 125

R. Gamda, 107-9, 111
R. Gamliel, 85, 88-89

R. Habiba, 39
R. Hama, 37, 153
R. Hananel, 42
R. Hanina, 9, 62, 64
R. Hanina b. Papi, 108
Hillel, 46, 49
R. Hisda, 15, 35, 36, 59
R. Hiyya, 37
Honi, 110
R. Huna, 9, 12
R. Huna b. Hiyya, 73, 74, 100, 114-117

R. Isaac, 88, 167
R. Isaac Nappaha, 108

R. Johanan, 21, 27, 117, 127-130, 134, 137-8
R. Jonathan, 62-66
R. Jose, 61, 83, 84, 87
R. Jose bar Haninah, 130
R. Jose the Galilean, 87
R. Joseph, 34, 114-116
R. Joseph b. Raba, 51
R. Joshua, 85, 91, 92, 104, 105
R. Joshua b. Korhah, 126-7
R. Josiah, 170
R. Jossa, 71
R. Jossi, 90, 177
R. Jossi b. Hanina, 75, 79
R. Jossi b. R. Bun, 70
R. Judah, 38, 61, 87, 134-5, 152, 159-64
R. Judah b. Betera, 170
R. Judah b. Tabbai, 101-107

R. Kahana, 33-34, 107, 109

R. Lazar b. R. Jose, 83

Mar b. R. Ashi, 39, 111
Mar Ukba b. Hama, 151
Mar Zutra, 107
R. Mordecai, 38

R. Nahman, 29, 30, 73, 74, 100, 112-117, 151-2, 163
R. Nathan, 152
R. Nehemia, 75

R. Obadiah, 13

R. Papa, 29-31, 33, 43, 51, 52, 135-7
R. Pinchas, 90

Raba, 38
Rabba bar Bar Hanan, 75, 77
Rabina, 33, 38, 47, 48, 50

INDEX

Rami b. Hama, 151, 163
Rav, 41-43, 45, 75-78, 91, 150, 152, 157, 176
Rava, 13, 14, 34, 44, 94, 107, 109, 110-13, 152
Resh Lakish, 9, 21, 61, 109, 134, 137-138

R. Safra, 27
Samuel, 41, 68, 80, 81, 84, 91, 113, 151, 157
R. Shesheth, 151, 163
R. Shimeon b. Shetah, 101-106, 110, 145
R. Simeon, 89
R. Simeon b. Eliakim, 71, 72, 73
R. Simeon b Halafta, 105

R. Tarfon, 109, 128-131

R. Yanai, 64-66
R. Yemar, 111

R. Yoseph, see R. Joseph
R. Yossa, see R. Jossa
R. Yossi, see R. Jossi
R. Yossi b. Hanina, see R. Jossi b Hanina
R. Yossi b. R. Bun, see R. Jossi b. R. Bun

Ze'ira, 170
Zebid, 107-109
Zechariah b. Abkulas, 127
Zeiri, 9
R. Zera, 37

INDEX OF NAMES

Aberbach, M., 125
Abramski, Y., 103, 125
Abravanel, 150, 169
Albeck, H.,, 66-7, 104, 129, 159, 161, 164-5
Albeck, S., 19
Allen, C. K., 6, 139
Almadari, Y, 28
Alon, G., 29, 31, 101, 110, 131, 143-4, 169, 174, 176, 178
Assaf, S., 65, 178
Atlas, S., 49, 50
Austin, J., 6
Avi-Yonah, M., 96

Bacheer, W., 108, 134, 147
Bartenura, O., 67
Beer, M., 123, 175
Baer, Y., 97
Ben-Menahem, H., 49, 81, 93, 139
Ben-Jehudah, E., 127
Bentham, J., 6
Berkowitz, E., 114
Berggruen, N., 63
Berman, S., 78, 108
Blidstein, G., 61, 66, 167
Bodenheimer, E., 5
Bottomely, A. K., 121
Buckland, W. W., 6

Cardozo, B. N., 5, 168
Chajes, H. P., 33, 108
Chajes, Z. H., 103, 159
Chernowitz, C., 13, 40, 50, 101, 158, 164
Cohen, B., 7, 31, 42, 49, 77, 125, 130
Cohen, M. D., 24
Cohn, H.H., 135, 167, 178

Daiches, I., 70, 115, 117
De Vries, B., 33, 147
Dembitz, L. N., 125

Derenburg, J., 102, 174, 178
Dewey, J., 10
Dinari, Y., 19
Driver, G. R., 132
Dworkin, R., 6, 10, 155
Dykan, P., 178

Eliezer ben Nathan, 126
Elon, M., 13, 34, 40, 45, 48-9, 76, 83, 96, 134, 143, 146, 167-8, 178
England, I., 7
Epstein, J. N., 21, 22, 32, 38, 66, 80-2, 98, 122, 134-5, 144, 161, 165
Eschelbacher, N., 78
Estori ha-Perchi, 82
Evans, E., 97

Falk, Z., 21, 24, 42, 77, 101-2, 125, 176
Federbusch, S., 159
Feldblum, M. S., 51
Feldman, L. A., 150
Felix, J., 70
Finkelstein, L., 25, 27, 31, 65, 67, 101, 119, 124, 136, 171
Fishman, R., 58
Flick, G.A., 23
Frank, J., 23
Frankel, Z., 64, 74, 90
Freiman, A. H., 42, 45
Friedman, S., 132

Gafni, Y., 40
Geiger, A., 101
George, J. J., 21
Gerhardsson, B., 21, 147
Gershfield, E. M., 21
Gershom ben Judah, 67, 166
Gilat, Y. D., 26, 48, 91, 143, 148, 178-9
Ginzberg, J., 9, 106, 113, 149
Ginzberg., L., 26, 77, 88

INDEX

Goldberg, A., 26
Goldschmidt, L., 82
Goodblatt, D. M., 107
Green, E., 121
Greene, W., 5, 42, 50, 143,146,148
Grossman, A., 65
Gulak, A., 54, 108, 134-6
Guttman, Y. M., 33,38,39
Guttman, M., 92

Halevy, I., 74, 91, 158
Hart, H. L. A., 6, 11, 14, 166, 168,
Hatam Sofer, 15
Havlin, Z. Z., 166
Hecht, N., 19, 106
Heilperin, Y., 43
Heinemann, J., 96
Hershberg, A. S., 42
Heschel, A. J., 96
Herzog, I., 24,93
Hoenig, S. B., 35
Hoffman, D., 28, 169, 171, 172
Hyman, A., 31, 75, 161

Irsai, O., 96

Jackson, B. S., 7,31,83,93,112,121,123
Jacob ben Meir (Tam), 53, 156
Jacob, B., 145
Jacobs, L., 109
Jastrow, M., 63
Joseph Habiba, 26, 27, 152, 153
Judolowitz, M. D., 32, 42, 113

Kadish, M. R., 13, 155
Kadish, S. H., 13, 155
Kaminka, A., 33
Kaplan, J., 21, 48, 109
Kasowski, C. J., 117
Kelly, J. M., 133
Kister, M., 97
Klein, S., 176
Kook, A. I., 15, 16, 97, 98, 113, 124,
   131, 149

Lampronti, I., 160
Lane, E., 82
Lauterbach, J., 171
Levi, E. H., 5
Lewin, B., 131,153

Levine, L. I., 79
Levy, J., 70,81,101
Lichtenstein, H., 142
Lieberman, S., 19, 25, 29, 35, 42, 64,
   70, 71, 74, 75, 82, 83, 86, 88, 91,
   157, 172
Lifshitz, B., 102

Maharik, 53
Mann, J., 132
Mantel, H., 20,62,136
Margalioth, R., 58
Mechlowitch, A., 136
Medini, H., 26
Meir of Lublin, 149
Meiri, Menahem Ben Solomon, 26, 27,
   30, 52, 53, 56, 57, 67, 156
Melamed, E. Z., 33,73
Miles, J. C., 132
Mormelschtein, B., 108

Nachmanides, 31
Nahshon Gaon, 153
Netanyahu, B., 150
Neusner, J., 31, 33, 34, 37, 40, 52, 57,
   97, 101, 108, 113, 127

Ovadiah, E., 82

Pardo, D., 159, 174, 179
Parkes, J., 97
Patterson, D., 65
Poglman, M., 176

Quint, E., 19, 106

Rabinowitz, Y. M., 32, 75
Rabinovitz, Z. W., 172
Rajnes, H., 81,157
Rakover, N., 149
Ramban, 30, 56, 115, 156
Ran, 26, 30, 44, 54, 61, 107, 150, 156
Rashal, 27
Rashba, 27, 30, 59, 81, 115, 156
Rashbam, 54, 67, 156
Rashi, 26, 53, 63, 67,76, 78, 105, 107,
   113,125,130, 135, 156, 162, 178
Ratner, M., 64
Ravad, 159, 164
Raz, J., 67,155-6
Rema, 27, 67

INDEX

Rif, 62, 75, 76, 81, 135, 136, 138, 155
Ritba, 30, 43, 53, 156
Rokeah, D., 127
Rosental, E. S., 75
Rosh, 28, 56, 62, 75, 135, 138, 139
Rozenboim, S., 40

Safrai, S., 178
Salmond, J. W., 7, 166
Sanders, E. P., 137
Sartorius, R. E., 6, 166
Schacter, M., 66
Scherachewski, B., 71
Schwartz, D. R., 127
Shand, J., 23
Shapiro, M., 182
Shilo, S., 50, 77-78, 93, 113
Shochetman, E., 27, 44
Shrira Gaon, 136
Silberg, M., 75, 77, 78, 98
Smolar, L., 125
Stein, P., 23
Steinfeld, Z., 108
Stone, J., 5

Tashbetz, 53, 157
Taz, 149

Tertullian, 97

Urbach, E. E., 72, 78, 98, 110, 122, 179

Vermes, G., 36
Victor, D., 104

Warhaftig, S., 76
Wasserstrom, R. A., 5
Waxman, M., 21
Weingreen, J., 21
Weis, P. R., 179
Weiss, A., 21, 33, 43, 136, 171
Weiss, I. H., 74, 101, 103, 109, 158
Weiss Halivni, D., 49, 137
Weiszburg, Y., 33
Wiesner, J. A., 82

Yaron, R., 61, 63, 65, 67, 129, 153
Yehudai Gaon, 153

Zahavy, T., 89
Zeitlin, S., 50, 58, 101
Zucrow, Z., 5
Zuri, S., 33, 35, 45, 50, 53, 77, 79, 134

SUBJECT INDEX

Aaron, 126
Agent, 80, 151, 153
Aggadah, 96, 123
Analogy, 115
Anonymous exegesis, 122
Assignment of property, 61-66

Ban of R. Gershon, 166, 168
Banning of R. Eliezer, 91
Bar Kamza, 127
Beth Din, 145, 147
  great Beth Din, 149, 169
  judicial functions, 146
  legislative functions, 146, 167

Capital punishment, 102, 105, 106, 143, 144, 170
Case law system, 40
Case report, 35, 36, 37
Christianity, 96
Codification, 13
Compromise, 124, 125, 126
Concern of false deduction from observed behavior, 73
Conditions, 49
  implied clause, 49
Considerations
  economic, 14, 120
  ethical 14
  extra-legal, 14, 17, 19, 20, 41, 45, 55, 72, 74, 79, 83, 93, 99, 120, 124
  extra-legal, classification of, 17
  individual, 17, 19, 120, 121
  moral, 14
  negative considerations, 121
  political, 92, 105
  positive considerations, 121
  psychological, 14
  scientific, 14
  social, 17, 149

  sociological, 14
  their object, 17
Contradictory instructions of R. Joshua, 92, 105
Corporal punishment, 9, 143, 144
Courts of appeal, 23, 28, 136, 182
Courts of equity 182

David, 97
Decentralized legal system, 95
Dina demalkhuta dina, 93, 113
Discretion, 5, 6, 10, 80, 86, 129, 152, 168
Distorted account of a Tannaitic ruling, 91
Distraint, 77
Doubt, 150, 152, 153, 154, 157
Duress, 48

Eduyoth
  tractate, 161
Efficient legislator, 19
Elijah, 146
Employer-employee relations, 74-79
Evolutionary process of the law, 13
Experimental refutation of an halakhic opinion, 105

Fabricated traditions, 88, 164
False witness, 101
Fictitious transactions, 51
Formative years of Jewish Law, 8, 9

Garme, 114, 115
General jurisprudence, 6
Gentile litigation in Jewish court, 31
Get, 41, 48
Gezerah, 24, 49
Gift, 150
Gift in contemplation of death, 66
Gospels, 97

INDEX

Governed by men and not by rules, 54
Governed by rules and not by men, 54
Great man, 110, 111, 112, 118, 120

Halakhic disputation with the
    Pharisees, 97, 98
Hard cases, 5, 6
Hearsay, 83
Hefker Beth Din hefker, 167
Horat sha'a, 179
Hypothetical discussion, 34, 175

Illegal act
  validity of, 44, 168
Improper behavior of a litigant, 46,
    58, 68
Informer, 114
Islamic law, 182

Jabneh, 161, 169, 174, 175, 177, 178
Jesus, 96, 97
Judges
  accountability, 10
  controversy among judges, 21
  disrespect to, 29
  duties, 25, 28, 79, 123
  erroneous ruling, 102
  impartiality of, 30, 68, 108
  judges' conception, 10, 11
  judges' law, 12
  power of, 73, 74
  roles of, 10, 11, 54
Judicial cases, 19, 20, 33, 144, 147
  as opposed to declaratory
    judgments, 20
  as opposed to moral advice, 19, 78
Judicial decisions, 99, 131, 153, 164,
    168, 173, 175
  absolute obligation to obey, 85, 166,
    169, 171
  criticism of, 23, 26, 99
  discrepancy between the earlier rule
    and the later practice, 22
  erroneous decisions, 131
  factual errors, 132
  legal errors, 132
  oral versus written, 21
Judicial deviation, 5, 7, 9, 11, 45, 46,
    86, 95, 96, 173

Judicial power, 55, 56, 65, 83, 84, 86,
    91
Judicial process, 5, 6, 8, 10, 11, 12,
    13, 14, 19, 25, 47, 125
  elements of secrecy, 24
Judicial product, 12, 13
Justice should manifestly be seen to be
    done, 28, 29

Kabalah (acceptance), 182
Kamza, 127
Kilayim, 47, 68ff
Kim li, 139
Kissing as a form of gratitude, 62

Law of monopoly, 13, 111
Legal fiction, 50
Legal formalism, 47
Legal interpretation, 12, 13, 46
Legal pluralism, 86, 94, 95
  a master may not actually practice
    his individual concept of the law,
    88
  rebellious elder, 170
Legal positivisim, 7, 14
Legal principles, 12, 13, 54
Lehotzi melibam shel Zedokim, 104
Let the law cut through the mountain,
    124, 125, 127
Limits of law, 7
Litigants
  pious, 120, 130
  wicked, 120, 148
Lo titgodedu, 94
Logical sequence, 172
Luke, 97, 101

Mark, 97
Marriage, 42, 61, 71, 168
Matthew, 97
Measure for measure, 52
Megilat Ta'anit, 143, 144
Megilot starim, 147
Mercy, 72, 128, 130
Meun, 56
Mezonot, 71, 72
Mideorayta, 44
Miderabanan, 44
Midreshei Halakhah, 118, 120, 121,
    122, 123, 124

INDEX 219

Minor, 41, 45, 51, 56
Minority view, 158, 159, 160, 161, 164
Mishnah, 134, 135, 160
  binding power of, 137
Mistake of law, 32, 131
Moredet, 107
Moses, 125
Mosser, 114

Natural justice, 23
Needs of the time, 18, 106, 149, 178
Nemo iudex in re sua, 19
Nidah, 91, 104, 162

Pagan world, 96
Parnasah, 71, 72
Partnership, 30
Persian courts, 32
Pharisees, 97, 103, 171
Pinchas, 93
Pluralistic legal community, 9
Post-factum justification for the ruling, 163
Power of the Sages
  conferred upon them, 49
  intrinsic, 49
Precedent, 100, 115, 116
  distinguishing of, 177
Procedure, 149

R. Eleazar b. Azariah's cow, 89
Reasoning
  ascribed, 32, 43, 58, 68, 102, 176
  extra-legal, 32, 56, 60, 70
  legal, 11, 14
  original, 32, 102
Red Heifer, 173, 178
Reopening of a trial, 133
Right of refusal, 56
  informing minors about their rights, 60
Right to total exposition of the law, 139
Roman law, 182
Rules, 168
  authority-granting, 50, 167
  duty-imposing, 148, 166
  of recognition, 11, 18

power-conferring, 12, 55, 80, 93, 106, 141, 166
validity-determining, 50, 167

Sabbath, 84, 87, 89, 97
Sabbatical year, 89
Sadducees, 102, 171
Sanctify the Name, 31
Savoraim, 153
Self-help, 19
Sermon on the Mount, 96
Seyag, 146
Shuda dedaynee, 80, 150, 163
Shuhada, 81
Siege of Jericho, 97
Silence in Talmudic discourse, 58
Slave, 50, 52
Social pressure, 91
  public announcment in the Synagogue, 65
Soferim, 122
State of emergency, 159
Sud (Arabic), 82
Suppressed traditions, 92

Ta'ut beshikul ha'da't, 137, 138
Ta'ut bidevar mishnah, 136, 137, 138
Ta'ut bidevar torah, 137, 138
Takkanah, 45, 49, 71, 91, 114, 147, 159, 167
Talmud
  casuistic formulation, 33, 34, 121
  censored edition, 149
Talmudic maxims
  as he has done so it shall be done to him, 53
  Beth Din may pronounce sentences even where not warranted by the halakhah, 82-84, 142, 149
  ein danin dine kennassot bebavel, 113
  halakha that should not be practiced, 11
  hamozti mehavero alav hare'aya, 15, 36, 108
  hefker Beth Din hefker, 167
  hu asa shelo kahogen lefikakh asu imo shelo kahogen, 43, 45, 52
  kedai hu R. Ploni, 159

lehotzi melibam shel Zedokim, 104
let the law cut through the
  mountain, 124
lifnim mishurat hadin, 63, 78
may a Rabbinic scholar strip men of
  their cloaks?, 111
not culpable by the law of man but
  culpable by the law of heaven, 11
sinner should not profit from his
  sin, 44
Talmudic terms
  adam hashuv, 108
  ala, 174
  amar lefanav, 74
  amru hahamim, 21
  ase, 62, 63
  ata lekameh, 35, 36, 77
  davar aher, 25
  dilma, 35
  dina, 9, 114, 115, 116, 130
  dina haki, 75
  er'eh benekhama, 101
  gavra rabba, 108
  hahu gavra, 36, 37
  haver, 110
  horat sha'a, 173ff
  ika d'amri, 39, 109
  kayem, 67
  kenasa, 114, 115, 116
  kfysha, 57
  koshel, 129, 130
  ma'ase, 35, 74
  makin, 143, 144
  malkin, 143, 144
  mat'im, 25
  matin, 131
  mazkirin, 160

onshin, 143
rasha vekasher, 130
savar, 109
shama'ti, 147
sheilat haham, 20
shohad, 82
shuda dedaynee, 80, 150-158
shuhada dedaynee, 82
ta shma, 39
teyku, 38
tlata rigla, 175
ulbena dedaynee, 82
umena timra, 117
uveda, 35
ve'ka mibaye le, 38
ya'kol talmud lomar, 171
yativ, 107
zimzum, 83
zurba merabanan, 13, 108
Talmudim
  comparative analysis, 55ff
Tefilin, 90
Theft, 112
Theoretical discussion of the halakhah,
  47
Toeh beshikul ha'da't, 133, 135
Toeh bidevar mishnah, 133
Tosefta
  date of its compilation, 165
Tsedakah, 65, 66, 71

Usha regulations, 61, 62, 64, 65, 66

Written Law, 9

Zaken mamre, 90, 91, 170, 173